FREDERICK LEONG, PH.D.
THE OHIO STATE UNIVERSITY
DEPARTMENT OF PSYCHOLOGY
142 TOWNSHEND HALL
1885 NEIL AVENUE MALL
COLUMBUS OHIO 43210-1222

DEVELOPING
SOCIAL COMPETENCY
IN ADOLESCENCE

ADVANCES IN ADOLESCENT DEVELOPMENT

AN ANNUAL BOOK SERIES

Series Editors:

Thomas P. Gullotta, *Child and Family Agency, Connecticut*
Gerald R. Adams, *University of Guelph, Ontario, Canada*
Raymond Montemayor, *Ohio State University*

Advances in Adolescent Development is an annual book series designed to analyze, integrate, and critique an abundance of new research and literature in the field of adolescent development. Contributors are selected from numerous disciplines based on their creative, analytic, and influential scholarship in order to provide information pertinent to professionals as well as upper-division and graduate students. The Series Editors' goals are to evaluate the current empirical and theoretical knowledge about adolescence, and to encourage the formulation (or expansion) of new directions in research and theory development.

Volumes in This Series

Volume 1. **Biology of Adolescent Behavior and Development,** edited by Gerald R. Adams, Raymond Montemayor, and Thomas P. Gullotta

Volume 2. **From Childhood to Adolescence: A Transitional Period?** edited by Raymond Montemayor, Gerald R. Adams, and Thomas P. Gullotta

Volume 3. **Developing Social Competency in Adolescence,** edited by Thomas P. Gullotta, Gerald R. Adams, and Raymond Montemayor

GUEST REVIEWERS

Karen Anderson
Child and Family Agency, Connecticut

Colleen F. Selig, M.D.
Child and Family Agency, Connecticut

Gary Burgard
New London Public School System, Connecticut

DEVELOPING SOCIAL COMPETENCY IN ADOLESCENCE

Edited by
THOMAS P. GULLOTTA
GERALD R. ADAMS
RAYMOND MONTEMAYOR

ADVANCES IN ADOLESCENT DEVELOPMENT
An Annual Book Series Volume 3

SAGE PUBLICATIONS
The International Professional Publishers
Newbury Park London New Delhi

For information address:

SAGE Publications, Inc.
2111 West Hillcrest Drive
Newbury Park, California 91320

SAGE Publicatioins Ltd.
28 Banner Street
London EC1Y 8QE
England

SAGE Publications India Pvt. Ltd.
M-32 Market
Greater Kailash I
New Delhi 110 048 India

Printed in the United States of America

Library of Congress: 90-657291

ISBN 0-8039-3898-5
ISBN 0-8039-3899-3 (pbk.)

FIRST PRINTING, 1990

Sage Production Editor: Diane S. Foster

Contents

PART III: Concluding Remarks

Preface

Ten years ago Gerald Adams and I began our friendship and professional association. That relationship began with a textbook titled *Adolescent Life Experiences*. It was in the process of researching that work that I achieved one of those rare moments of insight that we all at some time in our lives experience. For me that insight involved understanding the meaning of how problem behaviors in young people develop.

Regardless of the difficulty—whether it was substance abuse, delinquency, suicide, truancy, and the list sadly goes on and on—a cluster of negative factors were ever present. The absence of a warm and caring family, faith in a God, caring school officials, and positive peer relationships were evident with troubled youth as were the presence of poor individual characteristics such as low self-esteem and self-concept, an external locus of control, and little or no interest in the welfare of the community.

This volume in the Advances in Adolescent Development series explores the relationship of these factors to the development of social competency in adolescence. As I worked with the fine authors contributing to this volume, I was again reminded of the diversity of opinion that exists on the meaning of the words *social competency*. In reviewing my colleagues' work I offer the following observations on the subject from a qualitative perspective.

It impresses me that socially competent people *belong*. That is, they are members of a society and have recognized roles and positions in that society. The great sociologist Émile Durkheim used the term *anomie* to describe the sense of aimless wandering that afflicts those who are not allowed to fit in. Like Dickens's character Jacob Marley, their bent and broken spirits roam society unable to matter.

Next I believe socially competent people are *valued*. It is not enough only to belong. It is not enough to possess a role and a position in society. Take the class clown, for example. Clearly, the class clown has a role and a position in the classroom. However, it is how this young person is perceived that in part will determine his or her sense of self. Should that young person be demeaned, it obviously will adversely affect his or her self. And should his or her position be frozen in the minds of future classmates and teachers, it will plague this young person like a regrettable film characterization forever plagues the actor. To be valued is to be seen as having worth, importance, and desirability.

Finally, belonging and having value are of no account if young people do not have the opportunity to *contribute.* There is no more frustrating experience or soul-damaging event as being unable to aid others in want, to help those who need it—in other words, to support the cause.

In my own experience I have come to believe that nearly all adults fall victim to the use of clichés such as "You're not old enough" or "You're too young to understand." How we squelch the fires of activism, creativity, and competency burning in the hearts of young people. To channel that fire into constructive outlets is *the* challenge for us all. If we can communicate by our actions and deeds that young people belong, are valued, and can contribute, and if young people understand our message, then the goodwill, good work, and good deeds that follow will ensure that our young people will grow into socially competent adults.

—Thomas P. Gullotta
Editor

PART I

FOUNDATIONS OF SOCIAL COMPETENCY

1. The Psychosocial Constructs of Social Competency

Martin Bloom
Rutgers University

This chapter presents an overview of psychosocial constructs of competency in adolescence. First, the literature on developmental tasks is reviewed. Second, a discussion of inhibitors and facilitators of this development will be presented. Finally, some of the implications for primary prevention in relationship to adolescent competency will be discussed.

It may be a good thing that most adolescents don't read the literature on adolescence or they might turn around and go back to childhood because the list of tasks assigned by theorists and practitioners to this developmental period is lengthy. Adapting Havighurst's (1972) laundry list of specific tasks and Erikson's (1950) panoramic poetry on psychosocial crises as well as some elements from other theorists (particularly Ausubel & Sullivan, 1970; Csikszentmihalyi & Larson, 1984), I will present a configural view (Bloom, 1984, in press) of adolescent development. The configuration of nested components includes the person, the relevant primary and secondary groups, and the sociocultural and physical environmental contexts in a given historical time frame.

Personal Factors

The Changing Physical Body

The developmental tasks related to a changing physical body include changes that are biological givens, such as those in bone structure and timing of puberty, as well as the changing meaning given to physical constants, such as the color of skin and one's biological gender. Other developmental tasks include the actions one can take with regard to one's body, such as nutritional habits, activities related to physical fitness, the augmentation of one's physique, and sleeping patterns to replenish energy.

The Developing Cognitive Structures

Overall, *cognitive structures* refers to intelligence in the broadest sense, including learning specific pieces of information (both knowledge in the academic sense and "street smarts" in the pragmatic sense) and the development of logical processing (Piaget) and problem-solving skills in general. It also includes the exercise of memory and one's inner imaginative life.

Whether or not it is appropriate to place the global Eriksonian concept of psychosocial identity under cognition is unclear. Erikson (1968, p. 40) defines this important concept as "the accrued confidence that the inner sameness and continuity gathered over the past years of development are matched by the sameness and continuity in one's meaning for others, as evidenced in the tangible promise of careers and life style." He goes on to further clarify matters by "detecting . . . an ideological seeking after an inner coherence and a durable set of values." Such confidences and inner coherences probably belong to more than the pure cognitive realm, but this is not clear.

Hirsch's (1987) concept of cultural literacy probably reflects the cognitive realm most completely, but in his usage such literacy is related to adult performance. In fact, the absorption of cultural literacy probably reaches its highest levels, for better or worse, during the adolescent years because of universal public education.

The Expanding Affective Structures

Adolescence is the time of legendary urgency in sexual feelings as relevant hormones become active at the same time social contexts provide opportunities for exploring one's own and others' bodies. In addition, affective structures include the expansion of feelings for others beyond the egocentrism of earlier childhood and adolescence (Elkind, 1976) to the potential altruism of later childhood and adolescence (Mussen & Eisenberg-Berg, 1977).

Important considerations concerning the development of moral judgments have been offered by Piaget and Kohlberg, and others, and there are others concerning legal reasoning (Tapp & Levine, 1977). Both moral and legal reasoning involve three stages (such as preconventional, conventional, and postconventional moral reasoning)—the third one of which usually develops during the adolescent years. Conceptual disputes continue concerning whether this third stage is the ultimate stage (see Gilligan, 1982).

In connection with cognitive abilities, feelings may be attached to abstract ideas in the political realm, as idealism, or in the religious area, as devotion of the true believer, both of which are susceptible to youthful overzealousness.

The Changing Behavioral Repertoire

Growing physical strength and agility, combined with new social opportunities and obligations, mean that adolescents may express themselves in less than well-coordinated ways that are new to themselves and possibly surprising to their significant others. Note, however, that many world-class athletes and musicians as well as mathematical protégés are still in their teenage years, so that grace and agility may be present even in adolescence. On the other hand, some new behaviors in the adolescent's repertoire may lead to decreases in competence—as when he or she learns both to drive and to drink at the same time. There is nothing that demands that developments related to competency are uniformly positive and progressive.

Interpersonal Factors

Changing Relationships Within the Family

Adolescence, as a transition period from childhood to adulthood, requires the change from child-parent relationships to young adult-parent relationships. This may not be an easy change for either youth or parents. This change has been conceptualized in many ways, such as in Ausubel's desatellitization/resatellitization, which emphasizes the systemic properties of relating—first belonging to the family system and then to a peer system, with all the requisite roles and rules. A more appropriate term would be *extrasatellitization,* referring to the fact that the adolescent does not so much lose one system as gain another.

Another important set of relationships are those that exist between siblings (see Goetting, 1986). For example, older siblings might model the use of drugs, smoking, and sexual activities for their younger siblings, intentionally or not.

The growth in importance of peer groups has been viewed as entailing a reduction of parental influence, but evidence suggests that long-term influence of the parents over major topics remains. Although not well recognized, adolescents must deal with the transitions their parents and grandparents may be going through at this same time, such as "midlife crises" and the issues of retirement, ill health, or death.

Changing Relationships with Peers

The general trend is toward the increasing importance of peer relationships, which provide vital intimate feedback to the adolescent in times of rapid personal and social change. This trend has several streams that should be distinguished. First, there is the change from same-sex groupings—which occurred initially in response to the differential rate of sexual maturity, by which girls are one to two years ahead of boys—to mixed-sex groupings. Then there may be a change in pairing off, from the same-sex chum to the opposite-sex friend and, ultimately, to opposite-sex intimates. The functions of the peer group (or peer groups, because individuals belong to multiple groups that may or may not all share the same values) differ by gender. For example, boys receive pressure for sexual activity from their male peers, and girls are more influenced by an immediate partner with regard to engaging in sex.

The development of homosexual relationships, which frequently first appear publicly in late adolescence, is unclear. Bell (1982) speculates that hormonal predispositions and life experiences for some youths may make exposure to opposite-sex people "finished business" (that is, they have had frequent contact with individuals of the opposite sex so they are less fascinating) in the general quest to find a love object who can "complete" oneself through intimate merger.

Social Relationships

Changing Relationships with Socially Significant Others in the Educational Arena

There are several types of significant others for adolescents. We can distinguish between primary group others, such as parents and peers, and people who are representative of secondary groups, such as high school teachers and bosses. An adolescent may form specialized relationships with multiple teachers in junior and senior high school, in contrast to the diffuse relationship with the grade school teacher, who may have a primary group relationship with the young child. For college-bound students, high school teachers become important as aids to adult career options through advanced college education. At the other end of the high school continuum, teachers become veritable jailers for high school students who want to drop out of school (Natriello, 1985).

Changing Relationships with Socially Significant Others in the Employment Arena

Perhaps the most significant new social relationship for the adolescent is that with the employer, an adult usually completely separate from family or friends, who employs the youth based on his or her competence in performing required services. Possibly of equal weight are the social relationships between the adolescent and coworkers, a new type of peer with frequency and proximity of interactions like friends at school but in a different type of relationship. The new employee is on the low end of the status hierarchy even though all similar workers are theoretically on the same level. The adolescent employee frequently needs to learn job skills, formal rules, and informal mores, which may be foreign to the teenager's previous experiences in getting along with peers, to produce profitable outcomes for the employer.

Changing Relationships with Socially Significant Others in the Civic Arena

Although adolescents have always been citizens and have probably been involved in relevant activities such as using the federal post office, obeying state laws, and the like, their activities become more noticed and their responsibilities grow significantly during the teenage years. For one, they may become taxpayers—or involved in the paperwork needed to apply for tax refunds—during this period of time. Or they may become involved with military services, voting, obtaining a driver's license or licenses for fire arms, and the like. All of these activities have correlate duties and privileges; all directly involve the individual and his or her state and community. Although juvenile criminal justice procedures and penalties may be less harsh than with adult offenders, they can be very significant in the lives of youths who come up against them. For example, there have been cases of youths put in jail for a first-time drinking and driving offense who commit suicide because they lack the maturity to effectively handle the stress. A criminal record does in fact impose some significant limitations on youths in terms of future job searching. In addition, youths are disproportionately represented as perpetrators in many types of crimes.

Intercultural Changes

The Changing Status of the Adolescent in His or Her Culture and Subculture

Even though cultures differ in how they handle the socialization of infants, children, and adolescents in terms of harshness or permissiveness—and in terms of the transitions between the stages—all cultures require their members to contribute to the continuity and development of the distinctive life-style pattern. The expectations, support, and sanctions delivered by representatives of one's culture may differ by sex as well as age, but everyone must learn the larger value patterns of that group and which activities are consonant with them.

Cultural rituals define when children become adults in the eyes of the culture, as with the bar or bat mitzvah or the weekly communion. This recognition confers a limited adult status to youths in contemporary society as compared with earlier times. Peer groups may also have entrance requirements, a youth-initiated rite of passage, serving roughly the same functions as the adult-initiated forms but with a less prosocial orientation.

In the larger sense, these rituals are devices to force adolescents to consider their place in the social order—what new roles they will take and what new rules they will follow. Religious and civic rituals connect the individual and the larger human group in time (history of our kind), place (our land, our turf), and existential concept (the meaning of life and one's place in it).

The Changing Use of Mass Media

Adolescents may be using mass media in ways not wholly intended by commercial developers or parents. Alan Bloom (1988), for example, hypothesizes that mass media music performs a quasi-sexual function for the mass of youth who gyrate to its rhythmic pulsations while sexual innuendos freely pass across censored boundaries that the youths themselves cannot easily traverse. Whether or not this particular thesis is accurate is less important than the fact that the modern mass media have enormous influences on all receivers, especially children and youth (see Eron, 1982). The influence is cognitive as well as affective: its meanings are social as well as personal. The media convey lies as well as truths, and the audiences have to sort out which is which to the best of their ability.

The Ecological Dimension: The Individual and His or Her Physical Environment and Time

The Changing Physical World of the Adolescent

A modern American youth lives in a world that is remarkably smaller than that of his or her immediate or distant ancestors. Not only has modern transportation enabled youths to move about more rapidly and to greater distances, but modern communication has changed the meaning of physical space itself. Moreover, changes in these technological innovations in our time occur so rapidly that some commentators raise questions about the effects of change itself on the adaptation capacities of human beings (Toffler, 1970). Teenagers bear the brunt of these changes as they face the brave new world without the benefit of their elders' wisdom.

INHIBITORS AND FACILITATORS OF
COMPETENCE IN ADOLESCENTS

Why is there all the fuss about adolescence, the so-called awkward age? In Shakespeare's words: "There is nothing but getting wenches with child, wronging the ancientry, stealing, fighting" (*The Winter's Tale*, 2:3). Can nature have planned to take an ungainly intermission in the peaceful development between childhood and adulthood? Is Anna Freud accurate in her challenging statement that effectively describes adolescents as crazy? She says: "The adolescent manifestations of growth come close to the symptom formation of the neurotic, psychotic, or dissocial order and merge almost imperceptibly into borderline states, or fully fledged forms of almost all the illnesses" (Freud, 1958).

Adolescence appears to be filled with pitfalls, but, in truth, there can be many sources of support during this developmental period as well. The last section of this chapter briefly summarizes some of the inhibitors and facilitators of competence in adolescents. For each type of developmental task, we may identify a wide range of factors that prevent or encourage competent growth and development. These factors will appear as aspects of the adolescents themselves as well as of their sociocultural and physical worlds.

Personal Factors

The body marches to its own drummer, despite whether the adolescent wishes it would speed up or slow down. Early-maturing adolescents have their own special burdens to carry, especially the expectations of elders that their social and intellectual deportment will be equal to their physical growth. The late-maturing adolescent suffers from similar problems of social and personal expectations, even though, by adulthood, the differences in height will have disappeared. However, the intellectual differences appear to remain into adulthood, for unknown reasons, as does the more subtle element of prestige. Tanner (1971, 1987) reports that early maturers in the United States are also more stable, more sociable, less neurotic, and more successful in society than their late-maturing peers.

However, no one ever died from developing breasts after one's girlfriends did or spurting up in height years after one's school buddies did. It only seems that way while the slow maturer waits as nature takes its own time. The recent scandals concerning muscle-enhancing drugs at the Olympic levels pose a new threat to the developing adolescent, because the destructive side effects are injurious to other organs and fertility, and youths in a hurry to become powerful adults may not assess the long view. This is a problem waiting to happen—and preventers should be aware of it (Fuller & LaFountain, 1987).

On the other hand, there are many opportunities to exploit other developmental assets in adolescence, as in exercising one's brain while waiting for one's muscles to grow. "Tell that to the late maturer," I hear my readers saying, which is a good idea. Let's, in fact, tell it to the late maturer to prevent the mental agony of being in the lowest decile of physical growth and the last to be chosen. There are constructive health patterns that can be entered into before and during adolescence from nutrition to exercise and fitness, for which lifetime skills are developed that can have immediate as well as long-range benefits. These are the messages that primary preventers have to communicate.

Cognitively, there are some important inhibitors of competence in adolescence. One is perceived invulnerability: the erroneous belief that it can't or won't happen to me (Hauser, Vieyra, Jacobson, & Wertlieb, 1985, Rutter, 1987). Perceived invulnerability has several classic dimensions: that I am not susceptible to the problem; that the condition isn't serious in any case; and that there is a cure for it, even if I do get it. This "Russian roulette" with public/private health matters gets very serious with regard to AIDS. For the other sexually transmitted diseases, such as the widely prevalent adolescent conditions of chlamydia and gonorrhea, youths frequently underestimate the risks or are ignorant of the complications (which can lead to sterility in some cases).

One of the central developments of adolescence is the growing sense of a self at the center of all these physical and psychological changes. *Self-concept,* jewel of the personality theorists, is a many-splendored thing, depending on the perspective from which the term is viewed. In this, the adolescent is just as eager an explorer as is the scientist and the therapist. Long hours spent talking, grooming, being alone, rushing to be part of a group—any group—all are part of the adolescent's search for a conception of self. This is part of the paradox of the connectedness and separateness of adolescence that Damon (1983) describes, or that of being conscious of being both observer and object observed, as William James described the "I" and the "me."

Other theorists recognize the lifelong transactions between the physical person and the continual flow of information back and forth among all significant others. Theorists of the self, such as Carl Rogers, provide innate starting materials, such as the drive for self-actualization, and extrinsic inhibitors, such as the conditions of worth imposed by parents and other of civilization's socializing agents. Freud distinguishes between the ego and ego ideals, and "self theorists" construct tests to map the changing distance between self and ideal self. The list of self theorists is lengthy.

However, cultural and societal norms tend to set the child's sense of self precociously in stereotypic terms, such as what girls are supposed to act like and be like. Their sense of self is truncated by cultural stereotypes, and problems that emerge from these restrictions are blamed on the victim, such as when talented and assertive women face humiliation from the male-dominated establishment. Young people passing through the stages of life into adulthood carry the stigma of oppression, whether based on gender, ethnicity, religion, handicap, or life-style. Self-concept is intrinsically sociocultural as well. The individual carries the self around, but society hangs weights or balloons on it, seemingly at its own discretion.

Another important aspect of the cognitive self is *intelligence* in the narrow sense of the term. Stable empirical differences between males and females show up during adolescence, when males display greater quantitative abilities and spatial abilities than females, and females, beginning at about puberty, show greater verbal ability as well as vocabulary, spelling, and writing skills (see Maccoby & Jacklin, 1974; but also see Ernest, 1976). Intelligence also has an interesting relationship to creativity. Reasonably high levels of intelligence appear to be a necessary but not sufficient condition for creativity (Getzels & Jackson, 1962). High levels of intellectual ability do not guarantee that a person will also be creative. During adolescence the individual has to learn the cumulated wisdom of humankind, and a great deal of time and energy is directed toward this goal. However, as the teenager becomes facile in using concepts and abstractions, he or she begins to combine ideas in new ways, which is one way to arrive at creative solutions. Thus a new generation of creative contributors begins (see Noble, 1987).

No one promises adolescents happiness, but there is a minimal expectation that a certain level of well-being will be provided for the socially immature who are not able or permitted to become independent economic units. As a nation we fail many of our children, especially minority children, in terms of providing for their well-being. Indicators like infant mortality rates (the United States ranks about 16th in the world), unwanted adolescent pregnancies (the United States is first among the industrial nations), and the number of children and youth living in families whose income is below the poverty line (about one child in six) tell the story. The social well-being of children and youth is an area of great concern for the primary prevention field.

The personal well-being of adolescents appears to be tied to their sense of self-esteem. Research by Rosenberg (1965) suggests that high self-esteem is associated with feelings of life satisfaction and a sense of control over one's life. Low self-esteem is correlated with lower reports of happiness and higher reports of feelings of anomie (not being in control of one's life).

Related to the study of self-esteem and well-being is research in attribution theory, including the reasons people give for their successes or failures. Males (especially white males) generally attribute their successes to themselves (internal factors) but failures are attributed to other events and circumstances (external factors). Females tend to attribute success to accidental factors (like studying hard for a test rather than being intelligent) but failures are thought to be due primarily to their own intrinsic characteristics. Blacks who accepted the oppressive majority stereotypes of minorities tend to view their own successes as luck and their failure as the result of external factors over which they lack control (Perlman & Cozby, 1983).

The concept of locus of control addresses these dimensions (see Rotter, 1966)—feeling that events in one's life are controlled by oneself (internal locus of control) or that events are controlled by others or fate. Evidence suggests that females are guided by an external locus of control while males operate with an internal locus of control, but, as with all research, new evidence is modifying these simplistic results. However, the preventive implications of a measure of one's control of one's life are endless, particularly if we can identify ways to strengthen internal sources of control. For example, assertiveness training has been shown to enhance self-esteem, and social skills training and problem-solving skills provide the actual tools for increased control of one's world. Evidence (summarized by Danish, Galambos, & Laquatra, 1983) suggests that skills training to enhance personal competence has been well documented, but Durlak (1983) offers a more mixed picture on the empirical results of problem-solving training. Note that these two terms, *social skills* and *problem-solving ability*, are seen as basic components of social competence.

Affective structures may be enhanced by an open awareness of these structures. For example, acceptance of one's sexuality is viewed by many as a protector against threats of indiscriminate and unplanned sexual activity (McAnarney & Schreider, 1984). However, the mask of silence, either from social taboos or from parental inadequacies (not knowing the facts, not being able to communicate the facts that are known, refusing to accept children as sexual beings, and so on) act as strong inhibitors of sexual competence. Our uptight society is not a good prospect for making major changes in these arrangements, which is all the more reason for the persistent efforts of leading organizations, like Planned Parenthood and the Guttmacher Foundation, to educate the nation about the costs—especially to teenagers—of ignoring the basic facts of life.

In terms of behavioral competencies, there are various inhibitors and facilitators. The adolescent period is one of rapid although irregular motion, both personally and in terms of the physical environment. For example, adolescents learn to drive—and to drink. There are drivers' education classes and various laws pertaining to driving. There are no drinking education classes per se—perhaps this content is covered in school in a health class—but adolescents must learn the limits of their drinking behavior on their own before the authorities enforce sanctions for the safety of the entire community. As personal behavioral competencies grow, adolescents are tempted to discover their limits—the limit of speed, endurance, whatever. Because of the unevenness of intellectual and social maturity, these behavioral competencies may be inadequately controlled by the adolescents and thus require social control. However, when social controls are enforced to stop or slow down the inevitable trend toward independence, there is a potential for conflict between the adolescent and the authority figure. Formal and informal social support systems act as buffers and interpreters for both parties, and life goes on.

Interpersonal Factors

It is readily apparent that every personal factor is set within a social and cultural context and that it is impossible to discuss a term, particularly in connection with preventive actions, without discussing both individual and environmental systems at the same time. The following section will consider the major social settings in which adolescents reside—families, peers, school, and work. For each of these, inhibitors and facilitators of competence will be examined briefly.

Family settings may magnify, diminish, or transform individual problems, depending on the degree of resilience the individual possesses (Garmezy, Masten, Nordstrom, & Ferrarese, 1979) and the structure of the family itself. This is especially poignant when the adolescent has a chronic illness, such as diabetes (see, for example, Hauser, Vieyra, Jacobsen, & Wertlieb, 1985). Research by Cheung and Lau (1985) suggests that Chinese family cohesion is positively correlated with adolescents' self-esteem, but family conflict has a negative correlation.

Because large numbers of children and adolescents live in families affected by divorce, it is worth considering its effects on innocent children. Berg-Cross and Shiller (1985) report how divorce affects children differentially at different stages of their development. For adolescents, divorce may overburden them as they are trying to deal with their own tasks of independence, so that the family dynamics may inhibit or speed up adolescents' development. However, with their more sophisticated defensive skills and coping mechanisms, adolescents generally handle divorce situations better than their younger siblings. Teenagers may be more nearly able to see the healthy side of a divorce for all parties concerned. Having a strong peer group alliance also helps the adolescent to distance him- or herself from the trauma of the divorce. Yet there may be more aggressive and antisocial behavior present, in part because adolescents are stronger and have greater mobility and imagination than younger children (Stolberg, 1987).

In school settings and among peers, adolescents face yet other inhibitors and facilitators of competence. In theory, the structured, sequential nature of public education should ensure academic competence, and opportunities to be with peers are thought to promote social skills. However, the realities of public education are filled with possible inhibitors, such as insensitive teaching, rigid structures, and harmful peer interactions. It is too easy to blame the victim, in the case of a poor fit between school and pupil. To look for patterns and epidemiological trends, preventers should consider change in the system as well as change in the individual. Both are intrinsically involved.

Adolescents have to deal with peer pressures, some of which have growth-enhancing potentials and others of which are destructive. A variety of skills are needed and can be taught (see LeCroy & Rose, 1986; Schinke & Gilchrist, 1984). For example, Perry and Murray (1982) describe a project to teach health behavior skills to adolescents and to provide environmental supports, because "health is for life—get ready for the 21st century," as their slogan read. Not only are destructive behaviors identified and skills provided to reject them but alternative (constructive) behaviors are represented as yielding more status for adolescents. Adolescence is a time of risk taking, but it is possible to show that rock climbing, dancing, traveling, and biking can be viewed as risk-taking activities that offer a better opportunity for independence than destructive teen behaviors.

Social and Cultural Factors

The social and cultural inhibitors and facilitators of adolescent competence are overwhelming, both in scope and in power. Society rewards competence and punishes incompetence, albeit half-heartedly. The overwhelming message in any culture is the model or models of acceptable paths to adulthood. These models project both behavioral and psychological attributes for success. For some in the United States, the paths toward success are clear, with well-stocked waystations; for others, there are barriers related to factors of race, gender, socioeconomic class, and religion, among other types of prejudice and oppression. Even when it would logically be in the best interests of the majority population to provide good education for minority youths, the society is doing poorly. It is likely that when these minority youths are adults they will not be able to command well-paying jobs and thus will not contribute their share to the social security fund. However, as minority people become a larger proportion of the population, fewer people with good earning potential will be supporting an increasingly large number of elderly. This will create new stresses on social security, among other things.

As never before the adolescent of today is personally affected by social conditions—national and international conditions reflecting the state of the world economy as well as national and local ones. Thus because unemployment for adolescents, particularly minority urban youth, is much higher than for adults, many will not become socialized as responsible world citizens. There are many more school dropouts among minorities, which limits them in becoming productive workers. If we pull the string to unravel the cloth of adolescent competence at one level, we find that we are tugging at strings at the individual, group, and societal levels at every turn. This is the configuration of forces with which we must deal in preventing problems and promoting the best interests of adolescents in development.

REFERENCES

Ausubel, D., & Sullivan, E. (1970). *Theory and problems of child development* (2nd ed.). New York: Grune & Stratton.

Bell, A. P. (1982). Sexual preference: A postscript. *Siecus, II*(2), 1-3.

Berg-Cross, L., & Shiller, V. (1985). Divorce and subsequent custody arrangements: Implications for child development and opportunities for preventive and interventive helping. In M. Bloom (Ed.), *Life span development* (2nd ed.). New York: Macmillan.

Bloom, A. (1988). *The closing of the American mind.* New York: Touchstone.

Bloom, M. (1984). *Configurations of human behavior: Life span development in social environments.* New York: Macmillan.

Bloom, M. (in press). *Introduction to the drama of social work.* Itasca, IL: Peacock.

Cheung, P. C., & Lau, S. (1985). Self-esteem: Its relationship to the family and school environment among Chinese adolescents. *Youth and Society, 14,* 373-387.

Csikszentmihalyi, M., & Larson, R. (1984). *Being adolescent: Conflict and growth in the teenage years.* New York: Basic Books.

Damon, W. (1983). *Social and personality development: Infancy through adolescence.* New York: Norton.

Danish, S. J., Galambos, N. L., & Laquatra, I. (1983). Life development intervention: Skill training for personal competence. In R. D. Felner et al. (Eds.), *Preventive psychology: Theory, research and practice.* New York: Pergamon.

Durlak, J. A. (1983). Social problem-solving as a primary prevention strategy. In R. D. Felner et al. (Eds.), *Preventive psychology: Theory, research and practice.* New York: Pergamon.

Elkind, D. (1976). *Child development and education: A Piagetian perspective.* New York: Oxford University Press.

Erikson, E. H. (1950). *Childhood and society.* New York: Norton.

Erikson, E. H. (1968). Life cycle. In D. L. Sills (Ed.), *The international encyclopedia of the social sciences* (Vol. 9, pp. 286-292). (Reprinted in M. Bloom, Ed., *Life span development: Bases for preventive and interventive helping,* 2nd ed., New York: Macmillan).

Ernest, J. (1976). Mathematics and sex. *American Mathematical Monthly, 83,* 595-614.

Eron, L. D. (1982). Parent-child interaction, television violence, and aggression of children. *American Psychologist, 37*(2), 197-211.

Freud, A. (1958). Adolescence. In *The psychoanalytic study of the child.* New York: International Universities Press.

Garmezy, N., Masten, A., Nordstrom, L., & Ferrarese, M. (1979). The nature of competence in normal and deviant children. In M. W. Kent & J. E. Rolf (Eds.), *The primary prevention of psychopathology: Promoting social competence and coping in children* (Vol. 3). Hanover, NH: University Press of New England.

Getzels, J. W., & Jackson, P. W. (1962). *Creativity and intelligence: Explorations with gifted students.* New York: John Wiley.

Gilligan, C. (1982). *In a different voice: Psychological theory and women's development.* Cambridge, MA: Harvard University Press.

Goetting, A. (1986). The developmental tasks of siblingship over the life cycle. *Journal of Marriage and the Family, 48,* 703-714.

Hauser, S. T., Vieyra, M. A. B., Jacobson, A. M., & Wertlieb, D. (1985). Vulnerability and resilience in adolescence: Views from the family. *Journal of Early Adolescence, 5*(1), 81-100.

Havighurst, R. (1972). *Developmental tasks and education* (3rd. ed.). New York: McKay.

Hirsch, E. D. Jr. (1987). *Cultural literacy: What every American needs to know.* New York: Houghton Mifflin.

Kohlberg, L. (1983). *The psychology for moral development.* New York: Harper & Row.

LeCroy, C. W., & Rose, S. D. (1986). Evaluation of preventive interventions for enhancing social competence in adolescents. *Social Work Research and Abstracts, 22*(2), 8-16.

Maccoby, E., & Jacklin, C. N. (1974). *The psychology of sex differences.* Palo Alto, CA: Stanford University Press.

McAnarney, E. R., & Schreider, C. (1984). *Identifying social and psychological antecedents of adolescent pregnancy: The contributions of research to concepts of prevention.* New York: William T. Grant Foundation.

Mussen, P., & Eisenberg-Berg, N. (1977). *Roots of caring, sharing, and helping: The development of prosocial behavior in children.* San Francisco: Freeman.

Noble, K. D. (1987). The dilemma of the gifted woman. *Psychology of Women Quarterly, 11,* 367-378.

Perlman, D., & Cozby, P. C. (1983). *Social psychology.* New York: Holt, Rinehart & Winston.

Perry, C. L., & Murray, D. M. (1982). Enhancing the transition years: The challenge of adolescent health promotion. *Journal of School Health, 52*(5), 307-311.

Rosenberg, M. (1965). *Society and the adolescent self-image.* Princeton, NJ: Princeton University Press.

Rotter, J. B. (1966). Generalized expectancies for internal versus external control of reinforcement. *Psychological Monographs, 80,* 1-28.

Rutter, M. J. (1987). Psychosocial resilience and protective mechanisms. *American Journal of Orthopsychiatry, 57*(3), 316-331.

Schinke, S., & Gilchrist, L. (1984). *Life skills counseling with adolescents.* Baltimore: University Park Press.

Stolberg, A. L. (1987). Prevention programs for divorcing families. In L. Bond (Ed.), *Families in transition: Primary prevention programs that work.* Hanover, HN: University Press of New England.

Tanner, J. M. (1971). Sequence, tempo, and individual variation in the growth and development of boys and girls aged twelve to sixteen. *Daedalus, 4*(100), 907-930.

Tanner, J. M. (1987). Issues and advances in adolescent growth and development. *Journal of Adolescent Health Care, 8,* 470-478.

Tapp, J. L., & Levine, F. J. (Eds.). (1977). *Law, justice, and the individual in society: Psychological and legal issues.* New York: Holt, Rinehart & Winston.

Toffler, A. (1970). *Future shock.* New York: Random House.

2. The Social Environmental Constructs of Social Competency

Steven P. Schinke
Columbia University

Alfred L. McAlister
University of Texas

Mario A. Orlandi
American Health Foundation

Gilbert J. Botvin
Cornell University Medical College

Social environmental constructs offer insights for understanding adaptive and problem behavior among adolescents and for designing and carrying out effective intervention strategies aimed at enhancing adolescent social competency. This chapter reviews and critically examines the social environmental constructs related to social competency during adolescence. After a summary of recent theoretical and empirical research on social environmental constructs, there is discussion of social networks, friendships, and role formulations among adolescents; physical, cross-cultural, and historical perspectives; the transition from elementary school into junior high; and media and television influences. An applied research example is used to illustrate and amplify the chapter's major points about intervention development. Implications for further research and conclusions about social constructs and social competency among adolescents close the chapter.

This chapter focuses on the powerful and pervasive role social environmental constructs play in determining social competency among adolescents. Social environmental constructs as presented and discussed here offer insights into designing and carrying out effective intervention strategies aimed at reducing problem behavior and deviance during adolescent years. To illustrate this intervention process, we will describe an example of intervention

AUTHORS' NOTE: *The preparation of this chapter was made possible with support from the William T. Grant Foundation, the Pew Charitable Trusts, and the Henry J. Kaiser Family Foundation.*

research. The chapter concludes with guidelines for the design and execution of interventions that employ social environmental constructs to promote social competency among adolescents.

Social environmental construct variables provide a useful practical, theoretical, and empirical framework for understanding and guiding such interventions. For example, intervention programming applications of social environmental constructs would include efforts by clinical investigators to alter or improve an adolescent's surroundings, family relationships, problem-solving skills, communication skills, friendships, role formulations, youth perceptions of external forces and influences, and alternative recreational activities.

THEORY

Cooper and Ayers-Lopez (1985) delineate three conceptual approaches to explicate conceptions and skills adolescents garner from experiences with their families: individuation in relationships, construction of self through social means, and development of the capacity for mutuality in negotiation.

Individuation concerns "a property of dyadic relationships . . . observable in children's assertions of independence from the influence of their parents" (p. 15). Expanding their discussion of individuation, Cooper and Ayers-Lopez (1985, pp. 15-16) went on to write,

> The dimensions of individuation are operationalized in terms of patterns of communication that reflect individuality and connectedness. . . . Individuality is reflected in expressions of self-assertion and separateness, and connectedness, by mutuality and permeability. *Self-assertion* is seen when individuals communicate their point of view clearly, and *separateness*, when they express differences between themselves and others. *Mutuality* is seen when they demonstrate sensitivity to the views of others, and *permeability*, when they show responsiveness or openness to the ideas of others. (italics in original)

The construction of self through social means indicates the aspects of adolescent development that allow young people to "reflect upon and integrate their experiences in . . . relational contexts" (p. 17). Also regarding the construction of self, Coopers and Ayers-Lopez (1985, p. 17) noted, "Although not focused on individual differences, this approach [the construction of the self through social means] provides the groundwork for tracing commonalities in individualization from family to peer systems."

Finally, Coopers and Ayers-Lopez (1985, p. 18) described the development of the capacity for mutuality in negotiation as including "four levels of development, with higher levels indicating increasing appreciation of the thoughts, feelings, and wishes of both the self and the other person as well as of contextual factors."

The above approaches provide a foundation for understanding the connections between various social environmental influences that affect adolescents. This foundation holds special meaning for adolescents who are beginning to develop peer systems based on family-oriented systems.

Other inquiries into adolescent development show the greater influence of family on youths' behavior, attitudes, and perceptions relative to peer and interpersonal influences (Attie, Brooks-Gunn, & Peterson, in press; Baumrind, 1985; Gottman & Mettetal, in press; McCubbin, Needle, & Wilson, 1985). Constantine (1987) noted that issues pertinent to adolescents with authoritarian traditional parents may not be as relevant to adolescents raised with more permissive styles.

Puberty and diverse developmental factors, as explicated in other chapters in this volume and elsewhere, cannot be overlooked or discounted in understanding an adolescent's social competence within social environmental contexts (see Alderman & Doverspike, 1988; Peterson, in press; Peterson & Ebata, in press; Peterson & Hamburg, 1986; Silbereisen, Noack, & Eyferth, 1986; Whittaker, Schinke, & Gilchrist, 1986).

Social Networks

Over the past decade a considerable body of research in the area of psychology referred to as social networks or informal social supports has emerged. This research elucidates a range of social, behavioral, and emotional problems. For example, among other findings, a study by Fischer, Sollie, and Morrow (1986) found major differences in the social networks of female and male adolescents.

Similarly ethnic-racial variables are apt to influence an adolescent's social networks. In an illustrative study, Coates (1985) studied the relationship between social network characteristics and self-concept dimensions for middle-income, African American adolescents. In addition to noting strong and positive relationships between self-concept and social network characteristics, Coates suggested that social networks and social supports among adolescents vary by ethnicity and race. The implications of these findings are clear for investigations in cross-cultural settings or with heterogeneous populations of youths.

Another study of social networks, reported by Cairns, Perrin, and Cairns (1985) investigated the relationship between adolescents' perceptions of their social structures and affiliated patterns. The major findings were stated as follows:

> Adolescents who were co-members in social clusters not only interacted with each other, they tended to return consent forms as a unit and drop out of school together. It seems reasonable to expect that such peer-defined clusters would also produce a mutual influence among adolescents in their attitudes about behavior, scholastic achievement, and social values. (Cairns, Perrin, & Cairns, 1985, p. 352)

Cairns, Perrin, and Cairns found high levels of accuracy among adolescents regarding their conceptualizations of their social systems. Two implications they drew from these findings follow:

> First, under some conditions, a small set of adolescent respondents can provide a window into the nature of the peer networks that exist within a given social system. . . . Second [youths'] perceptions of the social structure—including the individual's own placement in it—were impressively validated by outside informational sources. (Cairns, Perrin, & Cairns, 1985, pp. 352-353)

Another area that has a close relationship to social networks concerns friendship in adolescence.

Friendships

Similar to social networks, dimensions of friendships among adolescents have been subjected to theoretical and empirical inquiry. For example, after reviewing and examining current theory and research findings, Reisman (1985) noted wide variations in definitions and criteria of friendship during adolescence. Despite a lack of consensus about the nature and functions of friendship, Reisman was able to draw some conclusions. Perhaps the most important finding suggested by Reisman's (1985, p. 389) review concerns social competence:

> A growing and persistent body of research indicates that few or no friendships in adolescence or disturbed peer relations are associated with psychological difficulties, social incompetence, and subsequent poor adjustment in adulthood.

Yet, Reisman pointed out that changing an adolescent's ability to make friends is not a straightforward task. Regarding past attempts to modify adolescent behavior, for instance, Reisman continued to draw from his investigation, offering this warning:

> The behavioral model has stimulated a variety of clever and resourceful social skills training programs to enhance social competence. However, much of this research has proceeded on the assumptions that peer reactions and social incompetence are two sides of the same coin, and that being inept in social situations is merely a function of being ignorant about how to behave. A long history of psychopathology in personality should remind us of the distinction between learning and performance, or the significance of the interfering and inhibiting effects of anxiety, and of the importance of the child's perception of the situation. (Reisman, 1985, p. 389)

To cite an example, Berndt and Das (1987) examined popularity and friendship perceptions among fourth and eighth graders. Berndt and Das found that changes in friendships between autumn and spring of the academic year were associated with the frequency of positive and negative comments about peers. Furthermore, these changes were linked with prosocial and aggressive behavior among peers. Ratings of academic ability among subjects in this study were unrelated to changes in friendship. However, Berndt and Das found that less popular children and adolescents were judged by their peers as less able academically.

Role Formulations

In a seminar paper Peterson (1987) put forth three conclusions about role transitions and identity development during the adolescent years, as follows: High levels of role complexity and ambiguity may impede identity development; premature identities with roles may result from low levels of role complexity, which may be a function of the few alternatives available to youths; and moderate levels of role complexity among adolescents may be ideal for providing climates for identity development.

According to these conclusions, moderate levels of role complexity allow youths to explore and experiment with alternatives. These explorations and the experimentation, if done within the proper context, will not unduly complicate the process of role transition.

Below we discuss other developmental forces within the context of social environmental constructs that additionally affect the manner in which adolescents reach and attain social competence.

Physical, Cross-Cultural, and Historical Perspectives

Nottelmann and Welsh (1986) found that adolescents' perceptions of physical stature and competence vary depending on the social context. In particular, the authors concluded that

> (a) early adolescent self-ratings were related to their physical stature;
> (b) social and general competence self-ratings were related to physical stature; and (c) the relationship between self-ratings and physical stature varied within the larger social context, the school in which the ratings were obtained. (Nottelmann & Walsh, 1986, p. 22)

In addition to the physical changes common to all adolescents, a number of other influences affect American youth compared with young people from other industrialized Western cultures. A report from West Germany compared North American and West German research perspectives (Hubner-Funk, 1987). Semi-structured interviews with adolescents in neighborhoods of Munich and its environs confirmed the value of an ecological perspective for research focusing on aspects of social competency during adolescence. In particular, Hubner-Funk found that inter-actions between gender, family background, level of schooling, and neighborhood generated distinctive coping patterns in the adolescents who were interviewed.

Others have also observed the value of including such demo-graphic factors as gender and family composition when studying adolescents' behavior within social contexts (see Craig-Bray & Adams, 1986; Delgado-Gaitan, 1986; Plake, 1987; Udry, Talbert, & Morris, 1986). For example, Dusek, Carter, and Levy (1986) found that the resolution of identity issues has important implications for self-esteem in late adolescence and that identity is differen-tially related to self-esteem for males and females. Studies that have attempted to control for multiple variables, including gen-der, ethnicity, and family background factors, have noted the importance of such multivariate investigations in adolescent re-search (see Simmons & Blyth, 1987; Van Hasselt & Hersen, 1987; Zayas, 1987).

Historical research further demonstrates the effects of environ-mental influences on adolescent social competency. Chronicling the changes in the social context surrounding American adoles-cents during the 1960s, Cross and Kleinhesselink (1985, p. 529) note:

> The opportunities that adolescents have in the 1980's . . . are many. However, opportunities are more severely limited than ever for those with poor social and work skills. Opportunities also bring pressure to achieve which is so intense that it is obviously associated with a great deal of youthful anxiety and psychopathology. . . . So adoles-cents with good skills are able to compete for myriad opportunities, against great odds, if they are not distracted by the available means to indulge themselves. The adolescents with limited skills will have more difficulty competing in the hi-tech society and will also be distracted by opportunities to self-indulge.

The corpus of material in the preceding sections lends theoreti-cal and empirical credence to the value of a perspective that includes social environmental forces when attempting to explain and alter an adolescent's behavior. Further proof of the value of this perspective consists of studies on the transition into junior high. This transition is associated with problem behavior and risk taking and is a potential source of positive change.

Transition to Junior High

The junior high transition period is often linked with students anxieties about changes they are about to face and the cognitive and behavioral disruptions that occur once they have made the move into junior high (Doueck, Schinke, Gilchrist, & Snow, 1988; McAlister, 1983; Snow, Gilchrist, Schilling, Schinke, & Kelso, 1986a).

In a longitudinal study of about 2,200 early adolescents, Midgley and Feldlaufer (1987) found a "developmental mismatch" between maturing adolescents and the classroom environments they experience before and after the transition to junior high school. Midgley and Feldlaufer (1987, p. 225) concluded, "This [developmental] mismatch may be related to the negative changes in student beliefs and behaviors that have been observed when students enter junior high school." These findings closely mirror what others have discovered when studying the junior high transitional procedures (McAlister, 1981; Schinke, Schilling, & Snow, 1987; Snow, Gilchrist, Schilling, Schinke, & Kelso, 1986b).

Media and Television Influences

To conclude this review of literature on the social environmental construct variables that affect an adolescent's social competence, we highlight findings on the influence of media and television. Pioneer research in this field has been executed by Greenfield et al. (1987) in three studies on the effects of rock music lyrics and music videos.

Briefly, the investigators established that rock music lyrics are often misunderstood by youth and that rock music elicits more affective responses from adolescents when heard without an accompanying video presentation. Considering the pervasiveness of television and media in the lives of American adolescents, the video medium has vast potential for promoting social competence among adolescents.

Harwood and Weissberg (1987) noted this potential in areas of pedagogy as applied to teaching adolescents adaptive behavior. In addition, the investigators suggested that research could profit from video applications to control intervention protocols. They pointed out the interest that adolescents have in the video medium, thereby providing motivation. Video and audio formats also generate opportunities for positive peer and adult modeling. Finally, Harwood and Weissberg drew attention to the portability of video for classroom and other didactic use.

IMPLICATIONS FOR INTERVENTION

The diverse theoretical and empirical research reviewed above reflects the importance of considering social environmental constructs when designing preventive interventions to enhance adolescent social competency. For example, according to the Berndt and Das (1987) study reviewed earlier, friendship and popularity have contrasting patterns of effects on perceptions of peers. Berndt and Das went on to elaborate their ideas about the design of effective interventions:

> Interventions designed to increase the frequency of prosocial behavior and reduce the frequency of aggressive behavior may facilitate friendship formation more than they increase overall popularity. Conversely, interventions designed to increase academic achievement may contribute more to popularity than to the formation of close relationships. (Berndt & Das, 1987, p. 438)

We need new approaches to develop interventions to promote social competency among adolescents within social environmental constructs. Those new approaches should attend to such areas as self-regulation (Bandura, in press), problem solving (Covington, 1986), and school-based skills training (Weissberg, Caplan, & Sivo, 1989).

The following paragraphs present a research example that illustrates the process of designing an intervention to enhance adolescent social competency using social environmental constructs. The prevention intervention research application is drawn from our current work with high-risk youth.

INTERVENTION RESEARCH APPLICATION

In our research we have focused on black and Hispanic adolescents from low-socioeconomic communities and neighborhoods in the Southwestern United States who are at above-average risk for later and habitual substance use by virtue of their membership in defined socioeconomic groups and their environmental surroundings. Specific negative behaviors targeted in our research are the use of tobacco, alcohol, and marijuana—the so-called gateway substances that antecede subsequent problems with substance abuse.

Concurrently our research focuses on culturally sensitive strategies for promoting adaptive and healthy behavior among high-risk adolescents. Some of these strategies include teaching skills for resisting media pressures and other types of social influences to smoke, drink, or take drugs; teaching adaptive life skills as a means of decreasing general vulnerability and providing adolescents with the skills to achieve desired goals; altering individual attitudes and perceived social norms; and increasing knowledge of adverse consequences.

High-risk youth are taught problem-solving skills, self-defense, verbal and nonverbal communication, and ways to seek out and interact with positive role models. Typically the intervention includes teaching adolescents not only what to say, that is, the specific content of the refusal message, but also how to deliver the refusal message in a way that will be maximally effective. The intervention uses older or same-age peer leaders to implement many of these prevention programs. Students observe other students and then practice the skills through role-playing.

Material has also been included in the programs to combat the perception that tobacco, alcohol, and drug use are widespread. This is accomplished simply by providing students with the rates of tobacco, alcohol, and drug use among their age group.

Specifically we will test several intervention components drawing heavily from our past research in the Life Skills Training (LST) approach to prevent substance abuse (Botvin, 1985, 1986; Botvin, Baker, Renick, Filazzola, & Botvin, 1984) and from our research in tobacco prevention and intervention (Orlandi, 1986; Schinke et al. 1986).

Conceptual Framework

Increasingly the focus in problem behavior prevention and health promotion during the past decade has shifted from the individual to the community. This shift is due, at least in part, to the recognition that the sociocultural environment exerts a significant influence on the shaping of an adolescent's values, behaviors, and competencies. Accordingly, individual behavior changes brought about by focused individual or group intervention approaches are more likely to be sustained if such changes are facilitated by a supportive environment within an adolescent's everyday life. Thus the intervention concurrently addresses high-risk youth and the institutions within which these individuals function, namely, the family, church, schools, alternative recreational centers, schools, and neighborhoods. The intervention is designed to help institutions assess and monitor their members' specific needs, implement skills development programs, and evaluate progress and provide feedback. Social environmental construct changes that have the greatest impact on social competency enhancement and on problem behavior reduction in the everyday lives of most American adolescents will occur in youths' homes, schools, and peer groups.

With the growing awareness of social environmental constructs as venues for health promotion and problem prevention, the objective of such social competency-promoting interventions is to create and maintain a variety of synergistic effects. To achieve synergism, this approach to competency building among adolescents draws on concepts from social learning theory, community psychology, diffusion and adoption research, communication research, community organizations, and community-based health promotion research.

SUMMARY AND CONCLUSIONS

This chapter has outlined major themes and related theories of social environmental constructs that affect social competency among American adolescents. These theories focus on the importance of biological, developmental, familial, and peer variables in understanding and intervening in adolescent behavior. Yet extant theories alone cannot sufficiently explain the complex forces that shape adolescents' cognition, values, and actions in America today.

Rather empirical data from diverse and varied areas are needed to complete this explanation, namely, on family influences, friendships, and other social networks and role formulations; on physical, cross-cultural, and historical perspectives; on the junior high transition; and on the popular media.

The theories and data reported here supply the groundwork for guidelines in the development of responsive interventions to help American adolescents acquire and maintain social competence. The chapter includes material on current research and the design of such interventions. Specifically, we noted the wisdom of interventions that combine tested and available skills-based approaches with environmentally oriented approaches.

Meanwhile, much more work remains to be done. Investigators must pay particular attention to interventions for adolescents who face the greatest likelihood of having problem behaviors in later adolescence and adulthood. Finally, we reiterate the need for synergistically combined interventions that utilize the best skills approaches and the latest versions of environmentally and community-based interventions to advance the social competence of American adolescents.

REFERENCES

Alderman, M. K., & Doverspike, J. E. (1988). Perceived competence, self-description, expectation, and successful experience among students in grades seven, eight, and nine. *Journal of Early Adolescence, 19,* 119-131.

Attie, I., Brooks-Gunn, J., & Peterson, A. C. (in press). A developmental perspective on eating disorders and eating problems. In M. Lewis & S. M. Miller (Eds.), *Handbook of developmental psychopathology.* New York: Plenum.

Bandura, A. (in press). Self-regulation of motivation and action which have great impact on social competency enhancement and on problem behavior reduction through goal systems. In V. Hamilton, G. H. Bower, & N. H. Fryda (Eds.), *Cognition, maturation, and affect: A cognitive science view.* Dordrecht: Martinus Nigholl.

Baumrind, D. (1985). Familial antecedents of adolescent drug use: A developmental perspective. In C. L. Jones & R. J. Battjes (Eds.), *Etiology of drug abuse: Implications for prevention* (Research Monograph No. 56, pp. 13-44). Rockville, MD: National Institute on Drug Abuse.

Berndt, T. J., & Das, R. (1987). Effects of popularity and friendship on perceptions of the personality and social behavior of peers. *Journal of Early Adolescence, 7,* 429-439.

Botvin, G. J. (1985). The development of life skills as a health promotion strategy: Theoretical issues and empirical findings. *Special Services in the Schools, 1,* 9-23.

Botvin, G. J. (1986). Substance abuse prevention research: Recent developments and future directions. *Journal of School Health, 56,* 369-374.

Botvin, G. J., Baker, E., Renick, N., Filazzola, A. D., & Botvin, E. M. (1984). A cognitive-behavioral approach to substance abuse prevention. *Addictive Behaviors, 9,* 137-147.

Cairns, R. B., Perrin, J. E., & Cairns, B. D. (1985). Social structure and social cognition in early adolescence: Affiliative patterns. *Journal of Early Adolescence, 5,* 339-355.

Coates, D. L. (1985). Relationships between self-concept measures and social network characteristics for Black adolescents. *Journal of Early Adolescence, 5,* 319-338.

Constantine, L. L. (1987). Adolescent process and family organization: A model of development as a function of family paradigm. *Journal of Adolescent Research, 2,* 349-366.

Cooper, C. R., & Ayers-Lopez, S. (1985). Family and peer systems in early adolescence: New models of the role of relationships in development. *Journal of Early Adolescence, 5,* 9-21.

Covington, M. V. (1986). Instruction in problem solving and planning. In S. L. Friedman, E. K. Scholnick, & R. R. Cocking (Eds.), *Blueprints for thinking: The role of planning in cognitive development.* Cambridge, MA: Cambridge University Press.

Craig-Bray, L., & Adams, G. R. (1986). Measuring social intimacy in same-sex and opposite-sex contexts. *Journal of Adolescent Research, 1,* 95-101.

Cross, H. J., & Kleinhesselink, R. R. (1985). The impact of the 1960's on adolescence. *Journal of Early Adolescence, 5,* 517-531.

Delgado-Gaitan, C. (1986). Teacher attitudes on diversity affecting student socio-academic responses: An ethnographic view. *Journal of Adolescent Research, 1(1),* 103-114.

Doueck, H. J., Schinke, S. P., Gilchrist, L. D., & Snow, W. H. (1988). School-based tobacco use prevention. *Journal of Adolescent Health Care, 9,* 301-304.

Dusek, J., Carter, O. B., & Levy, G. (1986). The relationship between identity development and self-esteem during the later adolescent years. Sex differences. *Journal of Adolescent Research, 1,* 251-265.

Fischer, J. L., Sollie, D. L., & Morrow, K. B. (1986). *Journal of Adolescent Research, 6,* 1-14.

Gottman, J., & Mettetal, G. (in press). Speculations about social and affective development: Friendship and acquaintanceship through adolescence. In J. M. Gottman & J. Parker (Eds.), *Conversations of friends.* New York: Cambridge.

Greenfield, P. M., Bruzzone, L., Koyamatsu, K., Satuloff, W., Nixon, K., Brodie, M., & Kingsdale, D. (1987). What is rock music doing to the minds of our youth? A first experimental look at the effects of rock music lyrics and music videos. *Journal of Early Adolescence, 7,* 315-329.

Harwood, R. L., & Weissberg, R. P. (1987). The potential of video in the promotion of social competence in children and adolescents. *Journal of Early Adolescence, 7,* 345-363.

Hubner-Funk, S. (1987). Major career transitions of youth: The status passage from school to work in neighborhood context. *Journal of Adolescent Research, 2,* 143-160.

McAlister, A. (1981). Social and environmental influences on health behavior. *Health Education Quarterly, 8,* 25-31.

McAlister, A. (1983). Social-psychological approaches. In T. Glynn, C. Leukefeld, & J. P. Ludford (Eds.), *Preventing adolescent drug abuse: Intervention strategies* (Monograph Series No. 47). Washington, DC: National Institute on Drug Abuse.

McAlister, A., Perry, C., & Maccoby, N. (1979). Adolescent smoking: Onset and prevention. *Pediatrics, 63,* 650-658.

McCubbin, H. I., Needle, R. H., & Wilson, M. (1985). Adolescent health risk behaviors: Family stress and adolescent coping as critical factors. *Family Relations, 34,* 51-62.

Midgley, C., & Feldlaufer, H. (1987). Students' and teachers' decision-making fit before and after the transition to junior high school. *Journal of Early Adolescence, 7,* 225-241.

Nottelmann, E. D., & Welsh, C. J. (1986). The long and the short of physical stature in early adolescence. *Journal of Early Adolescence, 6,* 15-27.

Orlandi, M. A. (1986). Community-based substance abuse prevention: A multicultural perspective. *Journal of School Health, 56,* 394-401.

Peterson, A. C. (1987). The nature of biological-psychosocial interactions: The sample case of early adolescence. In R. M. Lerner & T. T. Foch (Eds.), *Biological-psychosocial interactions in early adolescence: A life-span perspective.* Hillsdale, NJ: Lawrence Erlbaum.

Peterson, A. C. (in press). Pubertal change and psychosocial development. In P. Baltes, D. L. Featherman, & R. M. Lerner (Eds.), *Life-span development and behavior* (Vol. 9). New York: Academic Press.

Peterson, A. C., & Ebata, A. T. (in press). Developmental transitions and adolescent problem behavior: Implications for prevention and intervention. In K. Hurrelmann (Ed.), *Social prevention and intervention.* New York: de Gruyter.

Peterson, A. C., & Hamburg, B. A. (1986). Adolescence: A developmental approach to problems and psychopathology. *Behavior Therapy, 17,* 480-499.

Peterson, G. W. (1987). Role transitions and role identities during adolescence: A symbolic interactionist view. *Journal of Adolescent Research, 2,* 237-254.

Plake, B. S. (1987). Sex differences in early adolescents: Measurement and methodology review. *Journal of Early Adolescents, 7,* 139-142.

Reisman, J. M. (1985). Friendship and its implications for mental health or social competence. *Journal of Early Adolescence, 5,* 383-391.

Schinke, S. P., Schilling, R. F., Gilchrist, L. D., Whittaker, J. K., Kirkham, M. A., Senechal, V. A., Snow, W. H., & Maxwell, J. S. (1986). Definitions and methods for prevention research with youth and families. *Children and Youth Services Review, 8,* 257-266.

Schinke, S. P., Schilling, R. F., & Snow, W. H. (1987). Stress management with adolescents at the junior high transition: An outcome evaluation of coping skills intervention. *Journal of Human Stress, 13,* 6-22.

Silbereisen, R. K., & Noack, P. (in press). On the constructive role of problem behavior in adolescence. In N. Bolger, A. Casp, G. Downey, & M. Moorhouse (Eds.), *Person and context: Developmental processes.* Cambridge, MA: Cambridge University Press.

Silbereisen, R. K., Noack, P., & Eyferth, K. (1986). Place for development: Adolescents, leisure settings, and developmental tasks. In R. K. Silbereisen, K. Eyferth, & G. Rudinger (Eds.), *Development as action in context* (pp. 87-108). New York: Springer-Verlag.

Simmons, R. G., & Blyth, D. A. (1987). *Moving into adolescence: The impact of pubertal change and school context.* New York: Aldine.

Snow, W. H., Gilchrist, L. D., Schilling, R. F., Schinke, S. P., & Kelso, C. (1986a). Preparing for junior high school: A transition training program. *Social Work in Education, 9,* 33-43.

Snow, W. H., Gilchrist, L. D., Schilling, R. F., Schinke, S. P., & Kelso, C. (1986b). Preparing students for junior high school. *Journal of Early Adolescence, 6,* 127-137.

Udry, J. R., Talbert, L. M., & Morris, N. M. (1986). Biosocial foundations for adolescent family sexuality. *Demography, 23,* 217-230.

Van Hasselt, V. B., & Hersen, M. (Eds.). (1987). *Handbook of adolescent psychology.* New York: Pergamon.

Weissberg, R. P., Caplan, M. Z., & Sivo, P. J. (1989). A new conceptual framework for establishing school-based social competence promotion programs. In L. A. Bond, B. E. Compas, & C. Swift (Eds.), *Primary Prevention and Promotion in the schools.* Newbury Park, CA: Sage.

Whittaker, J. K., Schinke, S. P., & Gilchrist, L. D. (1986). The ecological paradigm in child, youth and family services: Implications for policy and practice. *Social Service Review, 60,* 483-503.

Zayas, L. H. (1987). Toward an understanding of suicide risks in young Hispanic females. *Journal of Adolescent Research, 2,* 1-11.

3. The Social Biological Constructs of Social Competency

A. Chris Downs
University of Houston—Clear Lake

This chapter focuses on the biological antecedents and consequences of social competence. Broad biological phenomena—including the timing of puberty, general hormonal changes, and genital/sexual developments—and specific issues—including physical attractiveness, menarche, asynchronous growth, and late/early maturity—are reviewed. Implications and directions for future inquiry are discussed.

Historically, most theories of adolescent development have addressed, in varying degrees and for diverse purposes, the impact of biological processes on personal and social attributes (e.g., Freud, 1946; Gesell, Ilg, & Ames, 1956; Hall, 1904; Hollingworth, 1928). Indeed, Sprinthall and Collins (1988, p. 31) suggest that "if adolescence has a single defining characteristic, it is the dramatic bodily changes that occur in the second decade of life." Several excellent reviews of the specific biological and constitutional changes associated with adolescence have been offered by M. Faust (1977), Petersen and Taylor (1980), and Tanner (1962, 1971).

As theorists and researchers have speculated on the impact of biological change on adolescents, large bodies of research have grown around the timing of puberty, weight and height, body build, physical attractiveness, menarche, and, more recently, spermarche (first ejaculation for boys). Further, these developments have been examined in light of various social and personal characteristics.

AUTHOR'S NOTE: *I am grateful to Phillip M. Lyons, Jr., Bryan D. Neighbors, and Donald K. Pennell for their helpful suggestions on earlier drafts of this manuscript and to Gay Carter for her help in securing much-needed reference materials. This manuscript is dedicated to Martin Crone, with the hope that his adolescence will be filled with social competence.*

The extent to which each of the various biological and constitutional changes influences adolescent *social competence* is a relatively old concern but one that has only recently received direct empirical examination. For example, Hall (1904) placed significant emphasis on puberty as a factor in feelings of social adequacy, normalcy, and skill. However, in previous research only certain *aspects* of social competence have typically been examined. For instance, some research has focused on how the timing of puberty mitigates popularity with peers and leadership responsibilities. Although not directed specifically at social competence, holding the leadership of a group or attaining some measure of popularity would certainly require that an individual engage in conversation easily, listen to and respond to the needs of others, show an ease of interaction, accept responsibility, adapt to varying social circumstances, and adequately handle decision-making processes, all of which would seem to reflect social competence. This chapter will focus on the biological and constitutional concomitants of those personal and interpersonal variables that seem most germane to social competence.

Previous research on the biological and constitutional underpinnings of adolescent social development can be sorted into two groups. The first focuses on the process of puberty, wherein both the timing of pubertal events and the events themselves (e.g., menarche) are examined in light of social and personal variables. The second area focuses on the importance of physical appearance on self-perception and social functioning. Researchers in this area have typically examined the importance of overall physical attractiveness, body image, height, and weight as these attributes relate to competence issues.

However, given the wide range of social and personal variables to which pubertal processes and appearance have been related in previous research, it seems prudent to demarcate the parameters of social competency relevant to this review. A socially competent adolescent would probably possess certain personal and interpersonal qualities. On a personal level, the socially competent adolescent would show a reasonable amount of emotional control, positive personality traits and a corresponding lack of psychopathology, a willingness to make well-thought-out decisions, a good self-concept and high self-esteem, motivation to achieve a viable identity status, an appropriate behavioral style, a general acceptance of the physical self (i.e., body image and attractiveness), and an understanding of societally determined standards of morality (with a corresponding lack of delinquent or criminal behavior).

On an interpersonal level, the socially competent adolescent would exhibit ease in conversation, the ability to listen to and respond appropriately to the concerns of others including mediating disputes between age-mates, good status with the peer group with accompanying strivings for leadership and popularity, a reasonable degree of interest in intimate relationships (via dating, sexual exploration, and so on), a healthy respect for the desires of others, good success at handling the social tasks associated with the cultural demands of adolescence, reasonable academic achievement with an accompanying interest in extracurricular activities, willingness to accept responsibility and follow through on assigned tasks, comfort in asking for help when unsure, and an ability to adapt to varying social circumstances. In addition, the socially competent adolescent would show some desire for independence from parents including limit testing, but relations with family members would be generally viable and positive. In a recent call for renewed research on adolescent mental health, Powers, Hauser, and Kilner (1989) described mentally healthy adolescents in ways that closely parallel the description of social competence outlined above. Moreover, they call for a careful examination of how to promote mental health by looking at its various social, psychological, cultural, and biological concomitants. The review that follows seems to address this call for an emphasis on the biological aspects of adolescent social competence. Evidence of the impact of biological processes on social competence will be examined first for the pubertal processes literature and subsequently for the physical appearance literature.

PUBERTAL PROCESSES

Numerous questions have been raised about defining and measuring both the onset and the process of pubertal change. These questions have generally focused on (a) whether puberty is a series of somatic and endocrinological events or a socially defined and fairly subjective construction (e.g., Boxer, Tobin-Richards, & Petersen, 1983; Brooks-Gunn & Petersen, 1984; Petersen, Crockett,

Richards, & Boxer, 1988); (b) the relationship of types of pubertal events (primarily endocrine and somatic changes) to cognition, affect, and social behaviors (e.g., Brooks-Gunn, Petersen, & Eichorn, 1985; Petersen, Crockett, Richards, & Boxer, 1988); (c) the quality of indices currently used to appropriately measure pubertal change (e.g., Brooks-Gunn, 1984; Brooks-Gunn & Warren, 1985; Nottelmann et al., 1987; Petersen, Crockett, Richards, & Boxer, 1988); and (d) the extent to which chronological age appropriately gauges pubertal change (e.g., Tanner, 1962, 1971). Of these issues only the last has reached a clear result: Chronological age is a very poor indicator of adolescent physical development.

While theorists and researchers scrutinize the definitions and measurements of pubertal change, it is quite clear that adolescents themselves are aware of the changes taking place. For instance, in one study with 1,006 15- to 18-year-old Senegalese subjects, most adolescents reported that they noticed pubertal changes in themselves and in their peers (D'Hondt & Vandewiele, 1982). These perceptions appear to be based on genuine, objective biological change rather than on misperception. Morris and Udry (1980) asked 47 girls and 48 boys, aged 12-16, to indicate into which of five levels of pubertal development they would place themselves. The levels were based on illustrations of five stages of development each for male genitalia, testicular size, male pubic hair, female breasts, and female pubic hair. The adolescents' self-placements (with the exception of boys' judgments of testicular size) correlated at and beyond +.60 with assessments of them made by physicians. Moreover, when Petersen, Tobin-Richards, and Boxer (1983) asked 337 sixth graders to rate themselves on each of seven indices of pubertal change, they accurately reported the changes. Petersen, Crockett, Richards, and Boxer (1988) recently reported a follow-up of those subjects and again noted that adolescents' self-reports of pubertal change (as measured by the Pubertal Development Scale) showed strong psychometric properties, with both high internal consistency and high external validity. In addition, Petersen's self-report measure appears to correlate very nicely with physicians' ratings of pubertal change. Namely, Brooks-Gunn, Warren, Rosso, and Gargiulo (1987) asked 151 eleven-, twelve-, and thirteen-year-old girls to rate their pubic hair and breast development using illustrations and Petersen's scale. When these self-ratings were compared with physicians' ratings, the correlations were reasonably high (+.61-.67).

In sum, adolescents appear to recognize the fact that changes in body and facial hair, skin condition, voice, height, physical appearance, and sexual organs have occurred. However, technical, definitional, and measurement issues in research on the effects of puberty remain problematic. In the review that follows, studies with larger sample sizes and those employing carefully defined and multiply determined indicators of pubertal change will be emphasized. Readers interested in the relative merits of the varying definitions and anthropomorphic criteria are referred to Petersen, Crockett, Richards, and Boxer (1988), Nottelmann et al. (1987), Brooks-Gunn (1984), and Brooks-Gunn and Warren (1985).

Investigations of pubertal processes have typically produced very different patterns of results for adolescent girls and boys. Indeed, given that pubertal change occurs about two years earlier for girls than boys, that it is a radically different biological process for girls and boys, and that it raises differential cultural expectations for the two genders (e.g., Petersen & Taylor, 1980), it is not at all surprising that strong gender differences are found for the impact of puberty. Consequently, the impact of pubertal processes on social competence will be discussed separately for adolescent girls and boys.

Pubertal Processes for Girls

Menarche is typically used as the primary benchmark for pubertal status among girls. The physiological, attitudinal, psychological, sociocultural, cross-cultural, and group difference aspects of menarche have been extensively reviewed elsewhere (e.g., Brooks-Gunn, 1984; Brooks-Gunn & Petersen, 1983; Brooks-Gunn & Ruble, 1982; Clarke & Ruble, 1978; Clausen, 1975; M. Faust, 1977; Greif & Ulman, 1982; Hamilton, Brooks-Gunn, & Warren, 1985; Logan, 1980; Rierdan & Koff, 1980, 1981, 1985) and will not be reviewed here. However, one critical factor in understanding the literature on pubertal processes in girls is the distinction between (a) the timing of menarche (early, on time, late) and (b) the importance of menarche as an event. In the former type of literature, research has focused on the psychosocial impact of experiencing menarche ahead of, with, or later than age-mates. The latter literature examines the impact of menarche regardless of its timing vis-à-vis peers. This distinction is an important one that will be maintained as appropriate in the discussion of girls' pubertal processes below.

As noted earlier, social competence would seem to have both personal and interpersonal dimensions. Although direct evidence of an impact of pubertal processes on girls' social competence is lacking, there is a good deal of research that focuses on attributes that are relevant to both the personal and the interpersonal dimensions of adolescent social competence.

Personal Social Competence

On the personal level of adolescent social competence, a positive self-image would seem to be a salient attribute. Moreover, that self-image would likely correlate highly with other measures of the self-system, including self-concept, self-consciousness, and self-esteem. With few exceptions, the previous research suggests that pubertal timing has little significant impact on girls' *self-image*. Ruble and Brooks-Gunn (1982) studied 639 fifth- to twelfth-grade girls and an additional longitudinal sample of 120 fifth- and sixth-grade girls, all of whom responded to questions concerning their reactions to menarche and their overall self-image. Using a self-image measure by Simmons, Rosenberg, and Rosenberg (1973), Ruble and Brooks-Gunn (1982) were able to tap feelings of self-worth, self-reflection, and self-consciousness. Overall, these researchers discovered that self-image scores were lower only for those girls who were unprepared for menarche or who reached menarche early as compared with on-time maturers or prepared girls. In contrast, Apter, Galatzer, Beth-Halachmi, and Laron (1981) administered the Offer Self-Image Questionnaire to 56 adolescents (girls and boys) who had experienced varying degrees of pubertal delay and growth retardation. They found that delays in maturation were unrelated to self-image.

One study examined the event (as opposed to the timing) of menarche with respect to self-concept among adolescent girls. Garwood and Allen (1979) studied self-concept and reported difficulties with menarche among 232 girls from middle- and lower- socioeconomic-status backgrounds. An examination of self-concept scores across four menarcheal status levels suggested that, although postmenarcheal girls reported more personal problems, they tended to have higher scores on both self-concept and adjustment than premenarcheal or menarcheal girls.

Another key factor in self-image, as it relates to social competence, would seem to be *self-esteem*. Socially competent adolescents would probably have high levels of self-worth and self-value. It is interesting that repeated examinations of the relationship between girls' pubertal timing and self-esteem have produced little connection between these variables.

Simmons, Blyth, Van Cleave, and Bush (1979) interviewed and conducted pubertal assessments (menarche for girls, height growth for boys) on 798 Caucasian children from Milwaukee during the course of grades six and seven. These researchers used a version of the Simmons, Rosenberg, and Rosenberg (1973) self-image instrument and discovered no simple impact of girls' pubertal processes on self-esteem. However, they found that early-maturing girls who had begun "dating-like behavior" (Simmons, Blyth, Van Cleave, & Bush, 1979, p. 957) had the lowest levels of self-esteem as compared with later-maturing girls and girls who showed less dating behavior. Indeed, 50% of early-maturing girls who went out on social occasions with boys showed low self-esteem and this percentage increased substantially (to 61%) for those early-maturing girls who were dating and who also were in a junior high school environment (as opposed to a kindergarten to eighth-grade school structure). The authors suggest that among girls the combination of entering junior high school, dating, and maturing early leads to lower levels of self-esteem. Follow-up investigations by these researchers, including longitudinal scrutiny of these subjects through the tenth grade, however, have repeatedly produced a lack of association between self-esteem or self-consciousness and pubertal timing for girls (Blyth, Simmons, & Zakin, 1985; Simmons & Blyth, 1987). One other study directly examined the relationship between global self-esteem and pubertal timing. Jaquish and Savin-Williams (1981), in a naturalistic study on the ecology of adolescent self-esteem with 40 seventh graders from various socioeconomic backgrounds, found that self-esteem levels did not vary by girls' pubertal standing.

Also on a personal level, a socially competent adolescent would be likely to exhibit a host of *positive personality attributes*. Research examining the relationship of girls' pubertal processes to various personality traits has provided an intriguing pattern with respect to puberty, especially for girls who mature earlier than their peers.

Among the earliest investigations of the impact of pubertal processes on personality was the longitudinal Oakland Growth Study (see especially H. E. Jones, 1949). In that study, early-maturing girls were typically rated as more withdrawn and submissive, less assured, and less expressive than late-maturing peers. Moreover, late maturers were rated as more active and expressive.

Other research has suggested that differences in the timing of puberty during adolescence can lead to personality differences for women in adulthood. Shipman (1964) studied 82 twenty- to fifty-year-old women who varied in the timing of the occurrence of menarche as adolescents (as determined by retrospective reports). Using the Cattell 16 Personality Factor Test, early maturers scored higher on dependency, on-time maturers higher on femininity, and late maturers higher on dominance. This suggests that the timing of menarche may lead to personality differences for women later in life.

Peskin (1973) essentially replicated the earlier Oakland study results (e.g., H. E. Jones, 1949) with 11 early- and 10 late-maturing girls who were found at the lowest and highest quartiles of physical maturity in the Berkeley Growth Study sample. He compared behavior ratings for these girls when they were adolescents and once again at age 30. Peskin found that during adolescence the early maturers showed more angry outbursts and whining and were more likely than late maturers to show a desire for social isolation (as evidenced by higher scores on indices of introversion, dream recall, and irritability). Moreover, the early-maturing girl was characterized as "cheerless, ill poised, socially vulnerable, easily disorganized under stress, and preoccupied with her early sexual image" while the late-maturing girl was viewed as "gregarious, socially poised and aware, as well as assertive and active" (Livson & Peskin, 1980, p. 72). As adults, however, the early maturers showed greater levels of self-direction while late maturers were more inclined to withdraw when confronted with obstacles. Peskin (1973) suggests that late-maturing girls, as compared with their earlier-maturing counterparts, may be at greater psychological risk during adulthood.

Other research relating girls' pubertal timing to personality traits has focused on depression, impulse control, and psychopathology. Simmons and Blyth (1987), studying 924 adolescents as part of their longitudinal effort in Milwaukee, found no timing of puberty differences for depressive affect as indexed by the modified Rosenberg-Simmons Depression Scale. However, Susman et al. (1985) reported a higher degree of sad affect and emotional tone among early- compared with later-maturing girls. In their study, 52 girls aged 9-14 were studied using the Psychopathology and Emotional Tone subscale from the Offer Self-Image Questionnaire. Although the results for the Simmons and Blyth (1987) and Susman et al. (1985) studies differ, the two sets of researchers employed markedly different measures of both pubertal timing and depression. That is, Simmons and Blyth (1987) used menarche as the primary index of pubertal growth and the Rosenberg-Simmons Depression Scale, and Susman et al. (1985) employed a variety of indices of pubertal growth with hormone level as the primary index and the Offer Self-Image instrument to measure depression.

It is interesting that Susman et al. (1985) also reported higher psychopathology scores on the Offer questionnaire among early compared with later maturers. This pattern was corroborated by Petersen and Crockett (1985), who studied 335 sixth graders (boys and girls) and their families longitudinally for three years. These researchers used age at peak height velocity as the primary index of pubertal timing and portions of the Self-Image Questionnaire for Young Adolescents (SIQYA; Petersen, Schulenberg, Abramowitz, Offer, & Jarcho, 1984) as the measure of psychopathology. They found that early maturers (both boys and girls) showed the most psychopathology compared with peers who matured later. In addition, Petersen and Crockett (1985) found that *late* maturers (boys and girls) exhibited more impulse control as measured by the SIQYA than early or on-time maturers.

In conjunction with positive self-image and personality traits, a socially competent adolescent would be likely to act in a mature and relatively independent manner, would show a concern for acting in competent ways, and would exhibit some normal psychological crisis associated with the formation of a workable identity. Two early investigations suggested that menarche as an event (rather than the timing of menarche) may be related to *level of maturity*. Stone and Barker (1937) compared 175 girls who had not yet experienced menarche with 175 who had. They found that postmenarcheal girls gave more mature responses on the Pressey Interest Attitude Test and the Sullivan Scale. M. Faust (1960), using the Guess Who Test and Prestige Questionnaire, found similarly high levels of more mature responses among postmenarcheal compared with premenarcheal girls. Here it seems important to underscore that these findings are based on the event rather than on the timing of menarche.

One large study focused on the relationship of sixth- through tenth-grade girls' pubertal processes to *independence* and *concern for acting in competent ways*. Simmons and Blyth (1987), in a longitudinal follow-up to their Milwaukee study (Simmons, Blyth, Van Cleave, & Bush, 1979), discovered that early-maturing girls were more likely to be willing to take a bus unaccompanied (sixth grade only), go places without parental permission (ninth grade only), and be left alone at home (seventh grade only). However, there were no *timing of menarche* differences for other independent activities including not seeking parental approval to be out after dark, baby-sitting, and working at a part-time job as well as perceived independence from parents and in decision making. A few *menarcheal status* differences for independence were also found: Postmenarcheal girls were more willing than premenarcheal girls to take a bus unaccompanied (sixth grade only), be left at home (sixth and seventh grades), and baby-sit (sixth and seventh grade), and were also more likely to believe that they made independent decisions (sixth grade only). There were no menarcheal status differences for other independence variables including going places without permission, not seeking parental approval to be out after dark, holding a part-time job, or perceiving oneself as independent from parents.

Simmons and Blyth (1987) also asked a series of questions concerning subjects' concerns for acting in competent ways. Early maturers were more likely than on-time or later maturers to perceive themselves as smart but this finding was obtained only among the sixth graders (not at the seventh, ninth, or tenth grades in their sample). There were no pubertal timing effects for seeing oneself as good at sports or schoolwork, in caring about being smart, in caring about being good at school or sports, or in valuing competence vis-à-vis popularity and independence. In addition, postmenarcheal girls were more likely than premenarcheal girls to care about schoolwork but again this applied only to the sixth graders. There were no other menarcheal status differences for perceptions of competence.

A great deal of theory and research has focused on *identity formation* in adolescents and young adults (e.g., Adams & Montemayor, 1983; Marcia, 1980). In brief, a significant period of psychological crisis is apparently requisite for the eventual formation of a workable and viable identity as an adult. Crisis then would be an important, and quite natural, component of the socially competent adolescent's psychological makeup. Berzonsky and Lombardo (1983) speculated that early-maturing girls would address adolescent stressors at an earlier age and would be more likely to engage in an identity-related crisis late in adolescence, compared with later maturers. These researchers used a standard identity status interview that covered four topic areas (politics, religion, sex, occupation) with 59 first-semester college women. Pubertal timing was assessed by asking subjects at what age they had matured. Despite the retrospective and imprecise nature of the criterion for pubertal timing, they found that pubertal timing was strongly related to identity-based crisis: Women who reported earlier menarche were more often found in crisis whereas those who reported later menarche were more often in a noncrisis status.

One other constellation of personal issues seems especially relevant to social competence. Namely, the socially competent adolescent would possess a reasonable awareness of the physical self, including body awareness and satisfaction with physical features including weight and height. The literature concerning the impact of puberty on *physical self-satisfaction* is substantial and relatively clear.

Menarche, aside from its developmental timing, seems to have a major impact on girls' physical self-satisfaction and self-recognition. Collins and Propert (1983) photographed 157 girls, aged 11-17.9 years, who were premenarcheal, menarcheal, or postmenarcheal. The subjects were asked to identify themselves from a set of five photos grouped on the basis of height and linearity. The researchers discovered a developmental ordering of self-identification, with 59% of premenarcheal, 66% of menarcheal, and 84% of postmenarcheal girls accurately selecting themselves from the array of photos. The results of this study suggest that menarche leads to an increased awareness and recognition of the physical self.

In addition, postmenarcheal girls appear to be more aware of being women. Rierdan and Koff (1981) compared the human figure drawings of 49 premenarcheal and 45 postmenarcheal seventh- and eighth-grade girls. The scored drawings were different for the two groups with postmenarcheal girls showing greater sexual differentiation and sexual identification. The groups did not differ, however, in level or class of anxiety.

Stone and Barker (1939), in their study of 1,000 girls in grades seven to nine also found differences for concern with the physical self on the basis of menarche. Namely, postmenarcheal girls showed much more interest in self-adornment as compared with premenarcheal girls.

One other study of menarcheal status seems relevant to girls' physical self-satisfaction. Simmons and Blyth (1987) discovered that postmenarcheal girls are generally less satisfied with their weight than premenarcheal girls at the sixth and seventh grades, were more concerned with their height and body build in the sixth grade, and less satisfied with height in the seventh grade. There were no menarcheal status differences for perception of the self as good-looking, satisfaction or concern with looks, or satisfaction with body build. Simmons and Blyth (1987) suggest that the dissatisfaction expressed concerning weight is related to the fact that postmenarcheal girls tend to gain weight.

The timing of puberty for girls also seems to lead to specific consequences for girls' physical self-satisfaction. Simmons and Blyth's ongoing longitudinal work (Blyth, Simmons, & Zakin, 1985; Simmons & Blyth, 1987) seems to shed the most light in this area. Specifically, they have found that early-maturing girls (as indicated by an earlier timing of menarche) are *less satisfied* with specific physical characteristics: weight (all grades six to ten), height (grades seven and nine), and body build (grades nine and ten). Moreover, early maturers express more *concern* about weight (grades nine and ten), height (grade seven only), and body build (grades six, nine, and ten).

Petersen and Crockett's (1985) study of girls in the sixth through eighth grades complements the results of Simmons and Blyth's Milwaukee research. Namely, Petersen and Crockett found that the body image scores (as determined by one component of the SIQYA) of early-maturing girls declined over the three school grades while comparable scores for on-time and late maturers remained relatively constant.

Duncan, Ritter, Dornbusch, Gross, and Carlsmith (1985) also predicted that early-maturing girls (who tend to gain weight earlier) would express greater dissatisfaction with how much they weighed. Their data consisted of that from 5,735 adolescents associated with the National Health Examination Survey (collected from 1966 to 1970). They found that early-maturing girls were far more likely to want to be thinner. In fact, 69% of early-maturing girls wanted to be thinner but only 27% of late maturers wanted to lose weight. It is interesting that timing of maturation was not related to satisfaction with height.

In sum it would appear that, at least on a personal level of social competence, girls' pubertal timing is not strongly related either to self-image or to other measures of the self-system including self-concept, self-consciousness, and self-esteem. However, there is some evidence that maturing early is related to general psychopathology, less impulse control, greater willingness to engage in independent activities, and an earlier involvement in identity crisis issues. In addition, girls who have experienced menarche may show higher levels of maturity compared with girls who have yet to have the experience. Both the event of menarche and the timing of puberty (typically gauged with reference to menarche) seem related to girls' physical self-satisfaction. Girls who have already experienced menarche and those who do so early seem particularly vulnerable to lowered satisfaction with the body. This may be primarily due to heightened awareness of physical cues associated with menarche and to increased weight accompanying that event.

Interpersonal Social Competence

On the interpersonal level, the socially competent adolescent would seem to possess good relationships with peers, family members, and the school system. Girls' peer relationships seem far more influenced by the timing of menarche than by its occasion. Indeed menarche, as an event, appears to have little impact on relations with peers. The early work of Stone and Barker (1937, 1939) indicated that postmenarcheal girls showed more heterosexual behavior compared with premenarcheal girls. And Simmons and Blyth (1987) reported greater dating behavior among post- compared with premenarcheal sixth graders. However, a recent study by Gargiulo, Attie, Brooks-Gunn, and Warren (1987) suggests that group membership may have just as much or more to do with heterosexual dating interests than menarcheal status. These researchers examined the self-reports and maternal reports of the dating behavior of seventh- to ninth-grade girls aged 12-15, of whom 59 were enrolled in national classical ballet company schools and 328 were not. The results indicated that menarcheal status was related to dating among the dancers but not among the subjects in the normative sample. Consequently, the impact of menarche on heterosexual dating interests may be fairly group specific.

A couple of additional studies have focused on peer prestige and number of friends girls have as a function of menarcheal status. M. Faust (1960), in her study of 731 sixth- to ninth-grade girls, found that menarche was associated with greater perceptions of prestige with peers. In contrast, Harper and Collins (1972) studied 631 Australian girls aged 10-17. Rather than employing a questionnaire as Faust (1960) did, Harper and Collins (1972) used a peer nomination technique to determine which girls were most desirable as friends (and presumably were more prestigious). They discovered no differences in peer desirability on the basis of menarcheal status. Moreover, Simmons and Blyth (1987) found no menarcheal status differences for the extent to which girls cared about popularity with either gender or valued popularity over competence or independence. Further, they discovered no menarcheal status differences for perceived parental or peer expectations of subjects' dating or opposite-sex interests. Finally, Brooks-Gunn, Warren, Samuelson, and Fox (1986) studied the friendship characteristics of 120 middle- to upper-class girls in the fifth to seventh grades using interviews. They found that premenarcheal and postmenarcheal girls had a similar number of friends. It is interesting that premenarcheal girls believed that they were behind their friends in terms of physical maturation whereas postmenarcheal girls reported that they were ahead of their friends.

Although menarcheal status seems generally unrelated to girls' peer relations, the *timing* of girls' puberty seems very important in peer relations. For instance, early-maturing girls may have more close friends than later maturers. When Brooks-Gunn, Warren, Samuelson, and Fox (1986) compared the breast development of their subjects with self-reported number of close friends, they found that those with the least and the most advanced development generally had fewer close friends than girls with an average breast development. Moreover, among premenarcheal girls, the number of close friends was higher among girls with more advanced development.

It is not surprising that early-maturing girls' increased level of intimacy with others may be directed at older peers. Magnusson, Strattin, and Allen (1985), in a longitudinal study with Swedish adolescent girls, found that, although early maturers were more likely to drink and engage in sexual exploration than later maturers, the effects were primarily due to the fact that early maturers were more likely to have older friends who were already engaged in such behavior. M. Faust (1960) noted that earlier maturers tended to have older friends and experienced greater peer prestige compared with later maturers. Simmons and Blyth (1987) found that early and on-time maturers were likely to perceive female friends as expecting them to date as compared with the expectations of late maturers' friends.

Curiously, although earlier-maturing girls may have more close, and perhaps older, friends, they do not necessarily seem to have more heterosexual dates. Dornbusch et al. (1981) used data from the National Health Examination Survey of 12- to 17-year-old black and white adolescents to determine whether the development of dating is more closely associated with pubertal maturation or with grade in school. They discovered that neither pubertal processes nor the timing of puberty accounted for heterosexual dating interests once chronological age was considered. They suggest that age-based social pressures for girls are more likely to account for dating than sexual maturation.

Three very different, though all longitudinal, investigations have focused on adolescent girls' tendencies to join clubs and to seek out social contacts. In an early investigation, M. C. Jones and Mussen (1958), using adolescents in the Oakland Growth Study, suggested that early-maturing girls are not likely to be popular or to seek leadership positions. However, in Simmons and Blyth's (1987) longitudinal study, there were no timing of puberty differences for girls' self-reported club behaviors, leadership responsibilities, or value placed on same-gender popularity. However, Simmons and Blyth (1987) did note that those ninth-grade girls who were the most mature reported they were more popular with boys. In contrast, Peskin's (1973) study with the small Berkeley Growth Study sample of 21 girls suggested that early maturers, during adolescence, are more likely to *withdraw* from social contacts and to be less sociable than later maturers. As 30-year-old adults, however, it was the late maturers who were more likely to withdraw in the face of frustration and adversity as compared with those who had matured early.

Savin-Williams (1979) conducted an ingenious study of the relationship of pubertal timing to peer status. Using both behavioral observations and sociometric indices, he studied 40 adolescents aged 12-14 at a summer camp. Girls' peer status in small peer group hierarchies was significantly correlated with rank orderings of pubertal maturation (based on Tanner's stages of pubic hair and genitalia development), which suggests that the more mature-for-age girls were more likely to be found in group leadership positions.

There are at least three major research exceptions to the pattern of closer, and perhaps more intimate and prestigious, relations with peers for early-maturing girls. Susman et al. (1985) examined a variety of indices of peer relations with respect to timing of puberty (as judged by hormone levels). They found that, although early maturers spent *fewer* hours with friends, there were no timing of puberty differences for interest in dating, actual number of heterosexual dates, or number of friends. Moreover, Duncan, Ritter, Dornbusch, Gross, and Carlsmith (1985) found that teachers' reports of 12- to 17-year-old girls' popularity was unrelated to pubertal timing and Petersen and Crockett (1985) found no association between girls' pubertal timing and reported relations with peers.

Several investigations are relevant to the apparent impact of girls' pubertal processes on elements of social competence within the family unit. The early results of the Milwaukee study (see especially Simmons, Blyth, & McKinney, 1983) suggested that early-maturing sixth- and seventh-grade girls were slightly more likely than late maturers to report that they perceived themselves as growing independent from parents. However, these differences were not apparent for the ninth and tenth graders. In a more recent and thorough report, however, Simmons and Blyth (1987) underscore that almost no pubertal timing differences were found for girls' perceived evaluations by parents, for perceived affective relations with parents, or for most of a very large number of questions focusing on adolescents' perceptions of parents. The results for family relationships from the Milwaukee study should be taken only as they relate to adolescents' *perceptions* of family relations because parents were not studied directly and adolescents were not actually observed in interactions with parents.

Savin-Williams and Small (1986) administered questionnaires to 64 Caucasian adolescent daughter-parent (mother *or* father) dyads, all from upper-middle-income, well-educated backgrounds. Adolescent boys in this study ($N = 69$) will be discussed later. The questionnaires for parents tapped parents' expressions of affection, perceptions of their adolescents' affection, conflict, stress, concern over their adolescents' behaviors, and control over decisions concerning their adolescents. The adolescents responded to questionnaires gauging expression of affection to parents, reports of parents' affection toward them, conflict, desire for autonomy, nonadherence to parents' advice, and perceptions of parental control. Level of puberty was determined using the anthropometric methods described by Tanner (Marshall & Tanner, 1969, 1970). The parents reported significantly more conflict with early-maturing girls *than boys* and less with late-maturing girls *than boys*. Mothers reported greater stress from early-maturing boys and girls; parents of early-maturing girls, compared with parents of on-time or late-maturing girls, reported more stress. In addition, although they found no timing of puberty effect for most of the adolescents' responses (including adolescents' feelings of affection for parents, perceptions of support from their parents, nonadherence to parental advice, perceptions of parents as controlling, or desire for autonomy), early-maturing girls reported more conflict with parents than on-time or late-maturing peers. Savin-Williams and Small (1986) note that the sample of parents was well educated, which may have led to responses unlike those found in the general population.

Building on their earlier work (Papini & Sebby, 1987), Papini and Sebby (1988) studied 40 adolescent girl- and 23 adolescent boy-parent triads. The families were Caucasian and pubertal timing was assessed using criteria based on the earlier work of Tanner (1962). Each family member responded to a 44-item checklist designed to gauge intensity of disputes with other family members during the previous month. The disputes could have focused on a variety of issues, including drugs and home responsibilities. Using factor analyses, the set of specific issues was reduced to conflict over persistent concerns and over issues pertaining to school, household, room care, appearance, leisure, and time schedule. Unfortunately, because of small cell sizes, analyses of gender by pubertal status for the issues were impossible. However, Papini and Sebby (1988) found (for the sample as a whole) that pubertal timing had no relationship to conflict over household issues. In addition, families with adolescents who had not yet *or* were currently encountering puberty reported more conflict over leisure and time management issues than families with adolescents who had already experienced puberty. Moreover, adolescent girls reported more conflict over "persistent concerns" (Papini & Sebby, 1988, p. 9) including sex, who the adolescent's friends were, and coming home on time.

Finally, Hill, Holmbeck, Marlow, Green, and Lynch (1985a) studied the relationship between menarcheal status and a number of parenting and adolescent-parent dyad variables for both father-daughter and mother-daughter dyads using questionnaires administered to all family members. The general finding from their investigation was that postmenarcheal girls seemed more inclined to elicit and perhaps request greater liberties from parents compared with premenarcheal girls.

Girls' interpersonal social competence levels would also seem to be evidenced in their conduct and success in academic settings. Simmons and Blyth's (1987) study suggested that earlier maturers may be expected by teachers to act older. In grades six and seven, teachers were more often perceived by early and on-time maturers as expecting older behaviors compared with the perceptions of late maturers. In contrast, when teachers were studied directly, few timing of puberty effects were observed by Duncan, Ritter,

Dornbusch, Gross, and Carlsmith (1985). Namely, they found that there were no timing of puberty effects for teachers' reports of school absence, need for discipline, grade repetition, deviant behavior, or adjustment. Unfortunately, little other evidence of a relationship between girls' pubertal processes and behavior in school settings seems available.

Summary

Are girls' pubertal processes related to their levels of social competence? Probably, but certainly not in a general, systematic fashion. Menarche may enhance self-concept and lead to greater maturity, but at the same time this event seems to elicit both positive (concerning being a woman) and negative (especially regarding weight) views concerning some physical attributes. Relations with peers, parents, and school personnel do not seem heavily influenced by menarcheal status. The timing of puberty may affect social competence a bit more than the event of menarche, especially in personality functioning, identity struggles, and peer relationships.

Pubertal Processes for Boys

Boys' pubertal changes have been measured by a variety of indices including changes in the body, pubic and facial hair, voice, skin, height, weight, and hormone levels. Although Tanner (1962) originally emphasized the need for measuring genital growth, such measurements are typically not possible (e.g., Petersen, Crockett, Richards, & Boxer, 1988). The relative merits of various indices are described at length by Petersen and Taylor (1980), Petersen, Crockett, Richards, and Boxer (1988), Brooks-Gunn, Petersen, and Eichorn (1985), and Brooks-Gunn and Warren (1985).

First ejaculation, or spermarche, for boys has only recently been seriously discussed as a potential counterpart to the occurrence of menarche. Gaddis and Brooks-Gunn (1985) broke important new ground when they examined boys' psychological reactions and preparation for and discussions with peers about spermarche. Of 13 subjects, 11 had experienced spermarche, 55% thought they were informed prior to the event, and 3 had ejaculation explained to them by an adult male. The majority of the boys had strong positive feelings at spermarche and, unlike some of the findings for menarche, boys were not upset or ashamed over the event. Despite the small sample involved, Gaddis and Brooks-Gunn's (1985) study underscores the need for more research in this area. Indeed, spermarche, like menarche, is a concrete event in time. And because boys appear to react favorably to the event, it is entirely possible that spermarche has a positive impact on self-esteem, peer relationships, and so on, some of which may enhance boys' feelings of overall social competence. Although difficult to conduct because of the private nature of the issue, a great deal more research is needed on spermarche.

Boys' social competence, like that of girls, would seem to have personal and interpersonal dimensions. On a personal level, self-image, personality attributes, maturity, independence, concern over competence, identity strivings, and physical self-satisfaction would all seem to be important contributors to social competence.

Personal Social Competence

Aside from the relatively routine finding that boys tend to have higher levels of self-esteem, self-stability, and other aspects of *self-image* than girls (e.g., Jaquish & Savin-Williams, 1981; Simmons & Blyth, 1987), there appears to be little relationship between boys' pubertal processes and these variables. In an early report from the Milwaukee study, with approximately 335 (predominately Caucasian) boys, it appeared that the fastest-growing seventh-grade boys had higher self-esteem levels than slower-growing boys (Simmons, Blyth, Van Cleave, & Bush, 1979). However, in their later, more thorough report (Simmons & Blyth, 1987), it was clear that boys' levels of self-image were unrelated to pubertal development (as indexed by height growth velocity) at any of the grades studied (six, seven, nine, and ten). Unfortunately, little additional evidence bearing on a possible relationship between self-image and boys' pubertal timing seems to exist.

A comparatively larger body of evidence is available for the relationship of boys' pubertal processes to personality attributes. The early research in this area came from the Oakland Growth Study (e.g., Clausen, 1975; Jones & Bayley, 1950; Mussen & Jones, 1957). Essentially, early-maturing boys were rated as more happy, relaxed, attractive, and poised than late maturers and late maturers were rated as more anxious, dependent, and rejected and less self-confident and adequate than early maturers. Moreover, longitudinal assessment of these subjects suggested that early-maturing boys continue to demonstrate more positive personality attributes into adulthood (M. C. Jones, 1957).

Peskin (1967) challenged the Oakland study results citing various methodological and interpretation of results difficulties. Using the Berkeley Guidance Study data, Peskin selected the 22 earliest- and 18 latest-maturing boys. Large differences in responses to the Thematic Apperception Test were reported. Early maturers were more likely to express primitive aggression and coercion and late maturers more often expressed strivings for independence, coping via newer learning strategies, and constructive progress toward goals. Behavior ratings for these groups also suggested differences based on pubertal timing with early maturers more likely to exhibit socially submissive behavior, "somberness" (Peskin, 1967, p. 10), behavioral anxiety, and more frequent and severe temper tantrums. In contrast, late maturers evidenced more overall activity, exploratory behavior, intellectual curiosity, and selfishness. In addition, Livson and Peskin (1980) report that boys' personality patterns as adolescents were typically mirrored and enhanced in adulthood.

Other research on the relationship of boys' pubertal timing has not confirmed Peskin's results. For instance, Carron and Witzel (1975) administered the High School Personality Questionnaire and Gough's Adjective Checklist to 75 fifteen-old boys. Timing of maturation was based on extreme scores for skeletal development and peak height velocity. Early and late maturers differed on only 2 of the 15 possible personality dimensions. Namely, late maturers showed more assertiveness and expedience and early maturers evidenced more humility and conscientiousness. Timing of maturing was unrelated to the balance of the personality constructs indexed.

Furthermore the results of the Milwaukee study yielded no evidence of a pubertal timing effect for boys' depressive affect as determined by the Rosenberg-Simmons Depression Scale (Simmons & Blyth, 1987). In contrast, using hormone levels as the primary pubertal indices with 56 nine- to fourteen-year-old boys, Susman et al. (1985) found mixed evidence for both emotional tone and psychopathology as determined by portions of the Offer Self-Image Questionnaire. That is, both psychopathology and emotional tone scores for early and late maturers varied depending on the type of hormonal assessment utilized. When estradiol levels or testosterone-to-estradiol ratios were used as the criteria for pubertal status, early maturers (as judged by higher totals on these indices) showed lower psychopathology and emotional tone scores compared with later maturers. When androstenedione was used, the pattern reversed: Boys higher in androstenedione (and thus who were presumably earlier in maturing) showed higher levels of both psychopathology and emotional tone than boys showing lower levels of androstenedione. Although the relative merits of the varying types of hormonal assessments remain unclear, the pattern for androstenedione receives support from Petersen and Crockett's (1985) study. Namely, they found that early-maturing boys (as indexed by peak height velocity) were higher on psychopathology as determined by the SIQYA. In addition, Petersen and Crockett (1985) found more impulse control among later compared with early and on-time maturers.

In addition to personality attributes, boys' pubertal levels have also been examined in association with *maturity, independence,* and *concern for competence.* The early Oakland study results suggested that early-maturing boys were more likely to exhibit mature, adultlike behavior (e.g., Clausen, 1975). However, Simmons and Blyth (1987) reported virtually no timing of puberty differences for boys' perceived self-confidence, concern with competence, independence from parents, or perceptions that others expected mature behaviors. One curious finding emerged for seventh graders: Early-maturing boys reported more positive feelings about being boys compared with later maturers. This may suggest that earlier maturers are more pleased with becoming men, at least in the early phases of puberty.

In light of Berzonsky and Lombardo's (1983) finding of a potential relationship between girls' pubertal timing and crisis associated with *identity formation,* it would seem reasonable to expect a similar association for boys. As part of the same investigation with college-age women, these researchers administered identity status interviews to 46 college-age men. In contrast to the results for women, they found that men in identity crisis reported a *later* age at maturity compared with men not in identity crisis. This curious finding deserves careful additional research prior to speculation on how it might fit into an overall pattern for early- and late-maturing boys.

Similar to the evidence for girls, it appears that *physical self-satisfaction* may be an important factor in emerging social competence for boys and one that seems heavily affected by pubertal processes. Petersen and Crockett (1985) found that boys' body image scores were substantially above those for girls and that early-maturing boys tended to retain a positive body image over the course of grades six to eight whereas on-time and late maturers showed decreases in body image, especially between the sixth and seventh grades. It is interesting that, by the eighth grade, the body image scores across the pubertal timing groups were equivalent.

Simmons and Blyth's (1987) Milwaukee study seems to clarify the pattern noted by Petersen and Crockett (1985). Namely, timing of maturity was related to overall body image at grades six, seven, and nine whereas early maturers had a higher body image at those grades. This is essentially what Petersen and Crockett (1985) found in their sample. Simmons and Blyth (1987) also found, however, that in the sixth grade early maturers were more satisfied with height and in the seventh grade they were more satisfied with both height and body build. In contrast, in the seventh grade, later maturers reported more satisfaction with overall appearance. In addition, by the tenth grades, early maturers showed a slightly greater concern over body image with more concern over weight and less concern over body build than later maturers. Early-maturing boys then seem to have a somewhat greater degree of satisfaction with their bodies but vary in the extent to which they are happy with the specific aspects of bodily growth: greater satisfaction with height and body build and less satisfaction with weight than later maturers.

Duncan, Ritter, Dornbusch, Gross, and Carlsmith (1985) also examined satisfaction with body image for boys in the National Health Examination Survey of 5,735 adolescents. Although the sample of boys overall were generally satisfied with their weight, early maturers seemed more satisfied than later maturers. These researchers also noted increasing dissatisfaction with height as puberty was delayed: Later maturers were generally less satisfied with height than earlier maturers.

Interpersonal Social Competence

On an interpersonal level of social competence, boys' pubertal processes have been examined in terms of relations with peers, families, and schools. The early evidence from the Oakland study indicated that early-maturing boys were more often rated as leaders in their peer groups and as more popular (e.g., Jones & Bayley, 1950; Mussen & Jones, 1957). The results of Simmons and Blyth's (1987) investigation complements this early finding. Specifically, they found that early-maturing sixth-grade boys believed they were more popular with peers and cared more about popularity with girls than later-maturing peers. These differences were absent at the later grades, however. It is interesting that late-maturing tenth graders reported greater concern over being good at sports, compared with on-time but not early maturers, but early-maturing tenth graders thought they were good at sports compared with their later-maturing counterparts. Indeed, late-maturing tenth-grade boys seemed to have the lowest self-estimates of athletic abilities.

These earlier investigations have received mixed corroboration from later research. For instance, Petersen and Crockett (1985) found no timing of puberty effects on boys' self-reported peer relations. But Savin-Williams (1979) noted a strong association of level of physical maturity with relative peer group rank for 20 adolescent boys: Early-maturing boys were typically found at the higher ranks of the peer group hierarchy.

Simmons and Blyth (1987) examined interest in heterosexual dating. Although differences were absent for the later grades (seven, nine, ten), early-maturing sixth-grade boys reported greater dating behavior than later maturers. In the seventh grade, early and on-time maturers reported greater expectations by other boys to date compared with late maturers, and in the ninth grade early maturers expressed similar expectations of them by their parents.

A similar level of interest in dating was reported by Susman et al. (1985). They discovered that early-maturing boys were more interested than later maturers in heterosexual dating. However, the actual number of dates early and late maturers had was unclear due to different patterns found for pubertal timing as based on follicle stimulating hormone (early maturers had more dates) or estradiol (early maturers had fewer dates). And, although there were no pubertal timing differences for number of friends, early maturers reportedly spent more time with their friends than did later maturers. These findings are made even less clear when considering Dornbusch et al.'s (1981) finding that pubertal processes fail to account for dating once age is taken into account.

Although dating may or may not be influenced by pubertal timing, boys' sexual arousal levels are clearly affected by hormonal changes. Udry, Billy, Morris, Gruff, and Raj (1985) studied gonadotropin and sexual arousal levels among adolescent boys and discovered a direct, linear effect of androgen on sexual arousal, curiosity, and interest. Apparently as boys' hormonal levels fluctuate with the onset of puberty, their sexual interests increase.

Boys' pubertal processes appear to be generally unrelated to perceptions of interactions with parents. For example, Petersen and Crockett (1985) found no timing of puberty effects for boys' reports of family relations on the SIQYA. Moreover, Simmons and Blyth (1987) found that pubertal processes were unrelated to boys' perceptions of independence from parents. However, early-maturing tenth graders were *less* likely to believe that their parents liked their friends compared with the perceptions of later maturers.

In addition, in Savin-Williams and Small's (1986) questionnaire investigation, 69 adolescent son-parent dyads were studied. Fathers of early-maturing sons were more inclined to view sons as supportive compared with fathers of late-maturing sons. Parents reported less conflict with early-maturing sons. Parents also reported *more* conflict with later-maturing sons *than daughters.* There were no pubertal timing differences for boys for *parents'* expression of affection, reported stress, concerns over adolescent behavior, or control over decisions involving the adolescents. Further, there were no timing of puberty differences for *boys'* expression of affection to parents, reports of parents' affection, conflict with parents, desires for autonomy, nonadherence to parental advice, or perceptions of parental control. Finally, Papini and Sebby (1988) report several pubertal timing effects in terms of adolescents' and parents' reports of intrafamilial conflict, but their results are not reported by gender.

Perhaps boys' pubertal processes are more linked to actual, as opposed to perceived, interactions with parents. In a series of important investigations, Steinberg and Hill have noted a pattern of increasing conflict between sons and their mothers. In an initial report Steinberg and Hill (1978) examined the verbal interactions of 31 middle-income adolescent boys and their parents. Boys' interruptions of both parents were correlated with level of maturity and parents' and boys' explanations to each other were inversely correlated with boys' maturity. They concluded that as boys develop they interrupt their parents more and explain themselves less and consequently may assert themselves more as they mature.

In a second study Steinberg (1981) conducted in-home observations of 27 triads of adolescent boys and their parents on three occasions during a one-year period. Steinberg found that mother-son conflict increased until after sons passed the peak of puberty. Specifically, until near the end of puberty, mothers and sons interrupted each other with increasing frequency and explained themselves less often, sons deferred to their mothers with decreasing frequency, and the pattern of family interaction seemed progressively more rigid. Near the end of puberty, however, the conflict and rigidity lessened. Steinberg (1981) also noted that father-son interaction showed increased deference on the part of sons and greater assertiveness on the part of fathers over the course of pubertal change.

Finally, Hill, Holmbeck, Marlow, Green, and Lynch (1985b) administered questionnaires in the home setting to 100 seventh-grade boys and their parents. Pubertal status was based on raters' judgments of various physical characteristics following the method developed earlier by Steinberg (1981). Hill, Holmbeck, Marlow, Green, and Lynch (1985b) found that mothers were most likely to be accepting and satisfied with the more mature boys compared with the less mature boys. These researchers suggest that, prior to the conclusion of pubertal changes, the adolescent son is most likely to encounter difficulties with the mother but not with the father.

Early- and late-maturing boys' interactions with school officials may be slightly different as a consequence of pubertal timing. For instance, Petersen and Crockett (1985) found that early-maturing boys *and* girls had higher literature grades than later maturers, although there were no differences for four other academic subjects.

Moreover, Duncan et al. (1985) reported that early-maturing boys, especially those early maturers from low-socioeconomic backgrounds, were more likely to engage in deviant behavior than later maturers. However, they found no timing effect for teachers' reports of absence, adjustment, need for discipline, or grade repetition.

Simmons and Blyth (1987) also found no pubertal timing effect for boys' perceptions of their academic performance, problem behaviors in school, or school participation. Tenth-grade early and on-time maturers were more likely to care about being smart than late maturers.

Summary

Similar to the earlier discussion of social competence for girls, boys' pubertal processes do not appear to be directly or systematically related to social competence. Timing of maturity seems unrelated to self-image correlates, concern with competence, or reports of family interactions. Further, the evidence concerning personality characteristics, dating activities, and relations with school personnel is mixed. Early maturers *do* seem happier about certain physical characteristics, especially height, and report more popularity and leadership roles with peers and more short-term conflict with mothers.

PHYSICAL APPEARANCE

Physical appearance has often been touted by social and developmental psychologists as a salient factor in socialization processes (e.g., Adams, 1977; Berscheid & Walster, 1974; Langlois, 1986, in press; Langlois & Stephan, 1981; Lerner, 1982; Udry, 1977). This emphasis seems to be justified. Appearance socializers, at least in Western cultures, are pervasive, forceful, and diverse and they include teachers, peers, media, significant others, strangers, friends, acquaintances, and (potentially) family members (e.g., Adams, 1977; Berscheid & Walster, 1974; Downs & Harrison, 1985; Langlois & Stephan, 1981). These socializers, certainly in varying degrees, extol to the virtues of tall, mesomorphic bodies for males; shorter, ectomorphic bodies for females; and attractive faces for both genders. Indeed, these "ideal" types, at least according to the stereotypes, possess highly favorable interpersonal skills, personality attributes, and other qualities associated with successful living. Unattractive persons and those with body types unlike the gender-based "ideals" are often viewed less favorably.

The evidence of the existence of appearance stereotypes and the extent to which socializers maintain them is formidable (e.g., Adams, 1977; Adams & Crossman, 1978; Berscheid & Walster, 1974; Downs & Currie, 1983; Downs, Reagan, Garrett, & Kolodzy, 1982; Langlois & Stephan, 1981). Moreover, objective raters show very high agreement on appearance criteria, particularly on who is and who is not facially attractive (e.g., Alicke, Smith, & Klotz, 1986; Downs & Abshier, 1982; Downs & Wright, 1982; Korthase & Trenholme, 1982; Mathes, Brennan, Haugen, & Rice, 1985). A comparatively smaller body of evidence indicates that socializers *act* on these perceptions and dispense differential consequences (e.g., Downs & Lyons, 1989; Kleck & DeJong, 1983; Langlois & Downs, 1979). And, in turn, there are a few studies that suggest that persons with different levels of attractiveness, height, and weight may think, feel, and behave in specific ways, although not always in ways that mirror the stereotypes of them (e.g., Agnew, 1984; Baum & Forehand, 1984; Bull, 1982; Langlois & Downs, 1979; Moran & McCullers, 1984; Ogundari, 1985).

The relationship between appearance and social competence may be robust, especially among adolescents. Appearance-based socialization occurs from infancy onward (e.g., Adams, 1977; Langlois & Stephan, 1981) and there is a great deal of evidence that such socialization affects *children's* feelings of social competence (in the form of self-esteem and so on). During adolescence, major constitutional changes occur in height, weight, body build, and attractiveness levels. Whether differential socialization based on appearance is consistent with the adolescent's *earlier* appearance as a child or whether it changes in accordance with the newer, adolescent appearance remains, unfortunately, an open question. That adolescents' levels of social competence *are* affected by their appearance *as adolescents* is clear, however. Height, weight, body type, and attractiveness have all been empirically related to attributes gauging elements of adolescent social competence. In the review of the impact of appearance variables on aspects of adolescent social competence below, height, weight/body type, and attractiveness will be addressed sequentially. Within each, attention will first focus on perceptions and stereotypes. Then differential treatment by socializers will be examined briefly. Finally, specific differences in behaviors, emotions, and personality qualities related to the social competence levels of adolescents varying in physical characteristics will be addressed.

Height

One of the most common findings in the psychological literature during the last 60 years has been the sociocultural advantages taller males and shorter females have over shorter males and taller females, respectively. Social expectations for taller males include greater motivation, achievement, access to rewards and power, occupational and social status, intelligence, maturity, self-esteem, prestige, and general competence (e.g., Brackbill & Nevill, 1981; Ehrhardt & Meyer-Bahlburg, 1975; Holmes, Hayford, & Thompson, 1982b; Holmes, Karlsson, & Thompson, 1985; Morrow, 1984; Nottelmann & Welsh, 1986; Prieto & Robbins, 1975). The expected advantages for shorter compared with taller females are typically less pronounced and are often linked with specific sex-typed variables such as dating and marriage prospects (e.g., Jones & Mussen, 1958). Consequently, cultural expectations for the two genders based on stature are probably not similar (e.g., Nottelmann & Welsh, 1986).

Societal perceptions based on height may increase for adolescents during the growth spurt. Height growth is recognized by parents, teachers, peers, and adolescents themselves as a primary index of adolescent physical maturity (e.g., Brooks-Gunn & Warren, 1985). Moreover, significant socializers probably recognize the fact that the end of height growth during adolescence represents a close final approximation of adult height. Consequently, expectations based on stature might be expected to be particularly evident during the growth spurt.

Previous investigations have generally demonstrated socializers' differential perceptions based on adolescents' stature. Adults (not necessarily the parents of adolescents) appear to expect greater intellectual expertise from taller compared with shorter boys *and* girls (Brackbill & Nevill, 1981) and perceive them to be more generally competent (Ehrhardt & Meyer-Bahlburg, 1975). Parents may share these views. In one study (Holmes, Hayford, & Thompson, 1982b) parents of children and adolescents with constitutional delay, growth hormone deficiency, or Turner's syndrome evaluated their offspring using the Problem Behavior Checklist and Social Competence Scale. Parents, particularly those of adolescent girls, were inclined to rate their children as behaviorally immature and emotionally inhibited. These adolescents' teachers shared the parents' perceptions. Although Holmes, Hayford and Thompson's (1982b) subjects' short statures were due to genetic, physiological, and/or hormonal problems, the results nonetheless suggest that parents may hold differential perceptions of shorter-for-age children and adolescents. Holmes, Karlsson, and Thompson's (1985) follow-up study with parents of similarly affected adolescents corroborated the earlier findings and added that shorter adolescents were perceived as having poorer adjustment at ages 12-14. However, these adolescents were perceived by parents as adjusting quite well at earlier and later ages. During ages 12 to 14, parents reported that their short-for-age adolescents tended to prefer solitary activities and individual sports (e.g., swimming) and avoided group activities with peers.

Adolescents' peers and teachers may share the general cultural expectations based on height, although the evidence is scant. Prieto and Robbins (1975) asked 69 twelve- to fifteen-year-old boys to evaluate themselves and their peers on a variety of bipolar adjectives including *self-esteem*. Subjects' teachers also rated the boys using the same instrument. Teachers' and peers' ratings of self-esteem and height of the target subjects were highly and positively correlated. However, there were no associations between subjects' levels of self-esteem and their *actual* height. In contrast, Nottelmann and Welsh (1986) asked the teachers of 64 sixth- and 62 seventh-grade boys and girls to complete the Teacher's Rating Scale of Child's Actual Competence. They found that teachers rated sixth-grade boys more competent than sixth-grade girls but seventh-grade girls more competent than seventh-grade boys. Teachers' evaluations were unrelated to adolescents' stature.

The actual characteristics of adolescents varying in height seem to reflect some of these expectations but certainly not to the extent one might expect given the generalized nature of sociocultural expectations based on stature. Shorter adolescents with constitutional delay and/or growth hormone deficiency tend not to show atypical personality traits (Holmes, Hayford, & Thompson, 1982a) but do seem to have lower grades in school (Holmes, Thompson, & Hayford, 1984) and seem to avoid large groups (Holmes, Karlsson, & Thompson, 1985). Shorter adolescents without biological impairment also evidence atypical patterns including diminished social judgment (e.g., Stabler, Whitt, Moreault, D'Ercole, & Underwood, 1980). For instance, Stabler, Whitt, Moreault, D'Ercole, and Underwood (1980) used the Picture Arrangement subtest of the WISC-R to tap social judgment and adaptive competitiveness with 31 very short boys, aged 6-16, and 29 age-matched controls. They found that shorter boys tended to respond competitively to tasks and, according to the investigators, in ways that suggested a lack of social judgment.

Drotar, Owens, and Gotthold (1981) found a corroborating pattern with 16 children and adolescents of extremely short stature as compared with age-matched peers. Specifically, shorter children showed much greater reactions to frustration and tended to use less adaptive or mature solutions in a problem-solving task. It is interesting that shorter and control children did *not* differ on measures of general adjustment, body image, sex role development, or sex-related fantasy.

Despite an apparent lack of difference in self-esteem levels between tall and short adolescents (Prieto & Robbins, 1975), shorter adolescents may still rate themselves as lower in social competence. Brooks-Gunn and Warren (1985) indicate that, among young adolescents, shorter compared with taller peers rated themselves lower on a variety of indices designed to gauge social competence.

Finally, adolescents, especially shorter boys, may link height and occupational prestige. Morrow (1984) asked 314 boys aged 15-18 to rate 12 occupations in terms of prestige and physical height. As in previous research, subjects linked occupational prestige with stature. However, this link was much stronger for boys who perceived themselves as short compared with peers who perceived themselves as average or tall in height.

In addition to actual height, concern and satisfaction *with* height seem related to adolescents' levels of self-esteem. Simmons and Blyth (1987) report that those sixth-grade girls in their Milwaukee study who were satisfied with their height *and* who cared about their stature had the highest level of self-esteem compared with girls who were less satisfied and/or did not care much about their height. A comparable but far less significant pattern was found for sixth-grade boys. It is interesting that the relations among satisfaction with and care about height and self-esteem were not significant for the seventh-grade boys *or* girls in their study.

Easily the best investigation to date concerning height and competence was reported by Nottelmann and Welsh (1986). In addition to teachers' perceptions of competence, the sixth- and seventh-grade participants took the Harter (1982) Perceived Competence Scale for Children. The Harter measure produces four subscales of competence evidenced on the cognitive, social, physical, and general levels. Among sixth graders, tall boys rated themselves higher in social competence than tall girls and the pattern of means suggested that shorter boys and girls tended to have lower (but not significantly lower) levels of self-rated social competence than taller boys. There were no stature differences for sixth graders' ratings of general, cognitive, or physical competence. The pattern of results for the seventh graders was entirely different than that for the sixth graders. Namely, shorter girls rated themselves as much less generally competent than taller girls or shorter boys. Because Harter's general competence subscale may be taken to reflect global self-esteem, these differences seem to point to strong self-esteem-level differences. Moreover, taller girls who were seventh graders in a middle school (compared with a junior high school structure) rated themselves as much more socially competent than shorter girls in the same environment rated themselves. Other differences for cognitive and physical competence were absent for the seventh graders.

Weight and Body Image

Stereotypes based on weight, like those for height, are broadly shared, particularly in American culture (Collins & Plahn, 1988; Staffieri, 1967). Generally, more positive attributes are assigned to mesomorphic compared with ectomorphic or endomorphic boys (e.g., Cavior & Lombardi, 1973; Dwyer & Mayer, 1968) and to ectomorphic rather than mesomorphic or endomorphic girls (e.g., Dwyer & Mayer, 1968). That adolescents share these expectations has been demonstrated primarily by Lerner's work. Indeed, Lerner has demonstrated these patterns of expectations based on body types among adolescents in the United States (Lerner, 1969), Mexico (Lerner & Pool, 1972), and Japan (Lerner & Iwawaki, 1975). Moreover, Collins and Plahn (1988) recently replicated the same findings with Australian adolescents.

Given the generalized nature of perceptions based on body types, it seems important to understand where adolescents receive weight/body type information and how that information affects their self-perceptions of their bodies. Desmond, Price, Gray, and O'Connell (1986) investigated adolescents' sources of information about weight. First-year high school boys (*N* = 93) indicated that their sources of weight control information were family members, television, and the school coach. Girls (*N* = 101) received weight control information primarily from family members, magazines, and friends. Teachers and school counselors were rarely mentioned as weight information sources. Similarly, Levinson, Powell, and Steelman (1986) noted the important influence parents have on adolescents' self-perceptions of weight with 6,500 adolescents from the National Health Examination Survey.

Desmond, Price, Gray, and O'Connell (1986) also discovered that at least one-third of adolescents who were thin and half of those who were normal weight were engaged in exercise and/or dieting to lose weight. This suggests that the societal emphasis on being thin or muscular-average works. And Desmond, Price, Gray, and O'Connell's (1986) study replicates the reports of several other investigators indicating that a large percentage of adolescents, especially girls, are unsatisfied with their body image and want to alter their weight or change their body shape (e.g., Clifford, 1971; Collins & Plahn, 1988; Forehand, Faust, & Baum, 1985; Storz & Greene, 1983).

Research on personality, self-image, and behavioral differences among adolescents and adults varying in body type and body image has an old and controversial history. Sheldon (e.g., Sheldon, Stevens, & Tucker, 1940) outlined a major theory, accompanied by highly controversial supporting evidence, on the three primary somatotypes and their relations to social and personal attributes. Despite the controversy over Sheldon's research methodology, later research has, in fact, demonstrated some differences among persons with differing body types, although perhaps not to as generalized a degree as Sheldon had proposed.

Among adolescents, body image and body type seem strongly related to self-esteem and self-concept. Several investigations have linked adolescent endomorphic body types with lower body esteem (e.g., Allon, 1979; Hendry & Gillies, 1978) and self-esteem (e.g., Felker & Kay, 1971; Stager & Burke, 1982). For instance, Stager and Burke (1982) asked 406 Caucasian 9- to 16-year-olds from middle-class backgrounds to complete the Piers-Harris Children's Self-Concept Scale and semantic differential ratings of global and specific aspects of both self-concept and body build concepts. They also took weight measurements of the subjects. Heavier children tended to endorse body type stereotypes more often and had lower self-esteem scores than average weight or thin children. Further, Mendelson and White (1985) studied 47 girls and 50 boys aged 8-17. Half of these Canadian subjects were overweight and half were normal weight. Using the Coopersmith Self-Esteem Inventory and Body-Esteem Scale, they found that, among 11- to 14-year-olds, overweight boys (but not overweight girls) had lower self-esteem levels. Among 14- to 17-year-olds, however, the pattern was reversed: Overweight girls, but not boys, had lower self-esteem. This reversal may be due to increasing pressure in later adolescence for girls to conform to cultural expectations for weight, but the emphasis on weight for boys may decrease during the same period. In any case, Mendelson and White (1985) noted that at all ages being overweight was correlated with having lower body esteem, which, in turn, was associated with lower self-esteem.

Pomerantz (1979) also noted a strong relationship between self-esteem and body self-satisfaction but among girls, not boys. Namely, sixth, eighth, tenth, and twelfth graders completed the Rosenberg Self-Esteem Scale, the Body Cathexis Scale, and a supplemental questionnaire. Girls' but not boys' self-esteem levels were strongly associated with body satisfaction. Supplementing these findings, Simmons and Blyth (1987) found, among sixth-grade girls (and less so for boys and seventh graders), that girls who were more *satisfied with* their weight *and* were more *concerned about* their weight had higher levels of self-esteem than those sixth-grade girls who were less satisfied or concerned.

The relationship between weight and self-image may not be a simple one, however. For instance, Toriola and Igbokwe (1985) discovered a low correlation between self- and objectively-rated somatotypes among 352 male and 300 female Nigerian high school students. Indeed, as Forehand, Faust, and Baum (1985) have suggested, adolescents may often have misperceptions of their weight and body type and the misperceptions may be just as likely (or even more likely) to be related to self-concept and personal adjustment as actual weight. Forehand, Faust, and Baum (1985) administered the Piers-Harris Children's Self-Concept Scale and the Childhood Depression Inventory to 99 sixth- and seventh-grade girls from lower- and lower-middle-income, rural homes. They discovered that those girls who inaccurately over- or underestimated their weight had poorer self-concept levels and greater depression scores than girls who gave more accurate weight estimations. This specific finding complements the results of an earlier study by Teri (1982), who discovered that, among 568 high school students, body image was a strong predictor of depression, with over- and underweight adolescents showing greater depression than average-weight peers.

Accuracy of weight perception in the Forehand, Faust, and Baum (1985) study was not related to popularity as determined by sociometric measures. A few other studies *have* found such a link. For example, in their earlier study, Baum and Forehand (1984) used sociometric assessments of peer relations for 220 sixth and seventh graders and found that overweight subjects tended to have more negative peer relations.

Actual and/or perceived (over- or under-) weight has also been implicated in intelligence levels (e.g., Clifford, 1971), conflict in family relations (e.g., J. Faust, 1987), intentions to smoke cigarettes (Tucker, 1983), and critical behavior/delinquency (e.g., Jurich & Andrews, 1984).

Physical Attractiveness

General societal stereotypes and expectations based on physical attractiveness (typically measured on the basis of facial rather than bodily attractiveness) are clearly directed at adolescents. Teachers and school counselors tend to expect greater academic achievement and better social skills from attractive compared with unattractive students (e.g., Clifford, 1975; Clifford & Walster, 1973; Lerner & Lerner, 1977; Mercado & Atkinson, 1982).

Moreover, parents may also hold attractiveness-based expectations of their adolescent offspring, but the evidence is scant and mixed. Felson and Reed (1986) found that mothers and fathers of 22 fourth to seventh graders made relatively high attractiveness judgments of their children—ratings that were much higher than those held by the children of themselves. This complements identical findings with parents and younger children (Downs & Reagan, 1983). Nonetheless, Elder, Nguyen, and Caspi (1985) noted that fathers tended to reject, exploit, and be less emotionally supportive of less attractive daughters during the Depression in the United States. And there is tangential evidence that unattractive adolescents may more often be targets of parental abuse (McCabe, 1984). Thus parents *may* direct appearance-based attributes at their own offspring, but the evidence is mixed.

Peers tend to perceive attractive compared with unattractive adolescents as popular (e.g., Cavior & Dokecki, 1973; Kleck & DeJong, 1983), as socially adjusted (Lerner & Lerner, 1977), as more similar to themselves in attitudes (e.g., Cavior, Miller, & Cohen, 1975), as more likely to be successful academically (Johnson & MacEachern, 1985), as better leaders (Weisfeld, Bloch, & Ivers, 1984), and as better potential friends (e.g., Zakin, 1983). Peer perceptions may be particularly important in any socialization based on appearance. Specifically, in three separate studies using a measure of attractiveness-based stereotypy—the Attitudes Toward Physical Attractiveness Scale (ATPAS)—my colleagues and I have reported that adolescents tend to hold much more extreme positions on attractiveness than children (Downs & Currie, 1983) or adults (Downs & Abshier, 1982; Downs, Reagan, Garrett, & Kolodzy, 1982).

Given the social pressure to look good, it does not seem surprising that adolescents care a great deal about how attractive they are (Simmons & Blyth, 1987). However, unlike the earlier pubertal timing and height literatures, adolescents do *not* seem to hold self-judgments of attractiveness that are similar to more objective, rater-based judgments of them. Felson and Reed (1986) noted that parents tend to rate adolescents higher than adolescents rate themselves. Moreover, we (Downs & Abshier, 1982) asked 314 male and 351 female eighth to tenth graders to complete a simplified Personal Attributes Questionnaire with self-ratings of attractiveness and physical appeal to others embedded in it. Objective (adult and adolescent) rater-based judgments, although quite similar among the independent raters, were completely unrelated to adolescents' self-ratings (average r = .00). It is surprising that a second administration of the self-ratings two weeks after the first indicated substantial stability in self-ratings over time. Finally, as has been reported with other samples (e.g., Simmons & Blyth, 1987), boys tended to rate themselves higher in attractiveness and physical appeal to others than did girls. Given the apparent disparity between objective ratings of attractiveness and adolescents' self-ratings, it seems important to note attractiveness-based differences in personality, behavior, and so on, first for studies using objective ratings and subsequently for those employing self-ratings.

Objective ratings of attractiveness have been examined in association with adolescents' personality styles, achievement and intelligence, self-esteem, peer relations, and involvement in criminal activity. The evidence relating objective attractiveness to personality attributes is sparse. Shea, Crossman, and Adams (1978) administered Marcia's Ego Identity Status Questionnaire, Rotter's Internal-External Locus of Control Scale, and a sentence-completion measure of ego functioning to 294 late adolescents who were also objectively rated on facial attractiveness. These researchers discovered no relationship between the personality measures and appearance. In contrast, in our research with both adults and adolescents, objectively rated attractiveness has generally been related to traditional sex-typed roles, with attractive males more often scoring high in masculinity, and attractive females more often scoring high in femininity, compared with their unattractive counterparts (Downs & Abshier, 1982; Downs, Reagan, Garrett, & Kolodzy, 1982). Further, Lerner and Lerner (1977) found a positive correlation between attractiveness levels and adjustment with 56 fourth- and 48 sixth-grade boys.

Furthermore, objective attractiveness and both intelligence and achievement may be related but in an unexpected manner. Moran and McCullers (1984) examined the achievement and IQ test scores of attractive and unattractive high school students and found that *un*attractive adolescents performed better than attractive adolescents on both measures. The authors suggest that this finding may be due to a compensation effect wherein unattractive adolescents compensate for their appearance by concentrating on schoolwork. A comparable study by Clifford (1975), however, failed to find an association between attractiveness and either IQ or achievement with sixth graders.

Zakin, Blyth, and Simmons (1984) studied a sample of 286 sixth-grade Caucasian girls drawn from Simmons and Blyth's Milwaukee sample. They were concerned with the impact of pubertal processes on the self-esteem levels of attractive and unattractive girls. They discovered that, among girls who had not yet begun pubertal changes, unattractive and average girls had lower self-esteem levels than attractive girls. However, among girls encountering pubertal changes, a reverse pattern was found: Unattractive and average girls had higher self-esteem levels than attractive girls. Unfortunately, only one rater of attractiveness was used to gauge the girls' attractiveness levels and consequently the reliabilities of the ratings are open to question.

Attractive and unattractive adolescents also seem different in their peer relationships and interpersonal styles. Dion and Stein (1978), employing an experimental manipulation, examined the attempts of attractive and unattractive male and female fifth and sixth graders to influence their peers. They found that attractive subjects with opposite-gender peers and unattractive males with other males were the most successful in influence attempts.

Other research on attractiveness and peer relations has demonstrated a strong relationship between these variables. Using a peer nomination technique, Lerner and Lerner (1977) noted a strong association between attractiveness and positive peer relations with their sample of fourth- and sixth-grade boys. Moreover, Zakin, Blyth, and Simmons (1984) found that unattractive girls perceived themselves as less popular with boys and girls than girls who were attractive or average.

Friendship selection may also be moderated by objective attractiveness levels. Ayers and Clark (1985) studied 136 seventh and eighth graders and assessed the similarity in attractiveness of friendship pairs that appeared to be reciprocal or nonreciprocal. Attractive adolescents tended to be more often found in reciprocal friendships; they more often had friendships with other attractive persons and these friendships were based on reciprocity.

Objective attractiveness has also been associated with involvement in criminal activity. Cavior's early work (Cavior & Howard, 1973) demonstrated that black and white male and female juvenile delinquents tended to be unattractive. Further, the less attractive the delinquent, the more often she or he continued exhibiting deviant behaviors, even after incarceration. More recently Agnew (1984), using the National Youth in Transition Survey, reported the results of interviews with each of 1,886 eleventh-grade boys, all of whom had been objectively rated for attractiveness. Attractiveness bore a direct relationship to the seriousness of the delinquent acts in which the adolescents engaged and to the frequency of delinquent acts both in school and at home. Moreover, Agnew (1984) reported that unattractive boys showed lower forms of social control, more frustration, and lower self-concepts than more attractive boys.

The evidence associating objectively rated unattractiveness with various personality and interpersonal relationships has not been replicated in the small body of research employing adolescents' *self-ratings* of attractiveness. Simmons and Rosenberg (1975) examined the relationships among satisfaction with physical appearance, self-consciousness, and self-esteem with 1,900 children and adolescents from the third to the twelfth grades. They discovered that those individuals with lower satisfaction with their physical appearance were more self-conscious and had lower levels of self-esteem than those adolescents with greater satisfaction with their appearance. These findings mesh well with our work (Downs & Abshier, 1982) in which higher self-esteem levels were found among adolescents judging themselves low *or* high in attractiveness. The lowest levels of self-esteem were found among adolescents who rated themselves only moderately attractive. Indeed, we speculated that those lowest and highest in self-judged attractiveness may have a greater degree of acceptance of physical appearance than those in the middle range of attractiveness. In contrast, those who believe themselves to be average in looks may engage in a social comparison with idealized images of attractive persons and may engage in a struggle to match these images. If (or when) they are unsuccessful, their self-esteem levels drop. Together with comparable findings for adults (Downs, Reagan, Garrett, & Kolodzy, 1982; Downs & Wright, 1982) and for physical satisfaction in the Simmons and Rosenberg (1975) study, it would appear that adolescents who believe themselves to be only moderately attractive may be at greatest psychological risk.

Summary

The case for a *probable* link between physical appearance and (elements of) social competence has been advanced often (e.g., Adams, 1977; Langlois & Stephan, 1981). Moreover, it is clear how theorists have been led to this conclusion: Stereotypes based on attractiveness, body type, height, and weight are pervasive. This, coupled with evidence that socializers actually dispense differential treatment based on appearance, seems to lead to an inevitable theoretical conclusion. Namely, stereotypes, acted on by socializers, are very likely to be mirrored in the personalities, self-images, and behaviors of adolescents varying in appearance. Thus far these conclusions are *not* warranted. Despite the evidence of varying self-image levels based on adolescents' height, weight, and body type, a *pervasive* pattern of personality characteristics, emotional attributes, and behaviors all varying because of appearance simply is not evident.

Important caveats are in order here. Initially adolescents' self-perceptions of how they look may be extraordinarily important in resulting social competence levels, but most of the literature focuses on more objective estimates of appearance. Because subjective and objective indices are often not correlated, social competence could be uniquely related to each. Moreover, *direct* evidence on the personal and social attributes of adolescents varying in appearance, particularly with reference to attractiveness, is surprisingly scarce.

CONCLUSIONS AND OBSERVATIONS

Demonstrating a causative impact of biological and constitutional factors on adolescent social competence is very much like mining for gold on the basis of a seemingly reliable rumor. The gold probably exists in the areas in which digging occurs, and yet only small and not very lucrative strikes are made. Like the hopeful miner, a reviewer sifting through the earlier research is led to suspect a strong, even pervasive, biological-constitutional basis for social competence. Yet only rare nuggets have been secured thus far.

The largest difficulty in determining links between biological factors and social competence in adolescence is a dearth of research *directly* examining possible links. Instead, researchers have focused on correlates of competence, such as self-image, personality, and interpersonal variables. That focus has provided some intriguing patterns that suggest that social competence does, in fact, have some biological and constitutional precursors in adolescence. Evidence on timing of maturation, weight, and height provides the most complete picture thus far and suggests that self-image, some personality attributes, and both peer and family relations are influenced by these factors.

It is tempting to try to assemble the current evidence into a probable pattern for social competence in light of its biological/constitutional concomitants. Yet I am hesitant to do so with so very many parts of the overall pattern still missing. Thus, rather than attempt to create a scenario based on the earlier evidence, it seems far more productive to suggest more concrete ways in which research should examine adolescent social competence in light of biological and constitutional constructs.

Initially it is imperative to underscore the fact that social competence as a personal and interpersonal variable has been emphasized by theorists for a very long time (e.g., Hall, 1904). However, until only recently, researchers have focused on other attributes that are only moderately relevant to social competence. In my opinion, Susan Harter's (e.g., 1982) research should serve as a model for more direct inquiry. Indeed, Harter has painstakingly developed competence scales that seem broad enough to encompass most of the aspects typically thought relevant to several types of competence, including the social domain. Use of her competence scales, with appropriate revisions for (especially older) adolescents, could serve as an outstanding springboard for later inquiry on adolescent competence. Moreover, measures like Harter's will help researchers avoid the task of assembling portraits of competence based on *elements of* the construct rather than on the construct as a whole. Indeed, at the moment, virtually nothing is known about the biological or constitutional underpinnings of certain elements of personal and interpersonal social competence. For instance, on a personal level of competence, the moral standards and judgments used by the socially competent adolescent as they relate to that adolescent's pubertal processes or appearance seem unknown. Moreover, on an interpersonal level of competence, a full understanding of adolescents' relations with peers, family members, and schools is warranted.

The lack of evidence linking biological/constitutional factors with family processes is especially disheartening. The likelihood of an association seems strong, particularly in light of the work of Steinberg, Hill, and their colleagues. Yet little of this work has incorporated the tantalizing suggestions of Montemayor (e.g., 1986) concerning family conflict. Because numerous theorists have postulated that pubertal processes could lead to ongoing, substantial intrafamily conflict, Montemayor's prescriptions for further work in this area seem paramount. Similar suggestions, focusing on parameters of intimacy in peer relations (e.g., Roscoe, Kennedy, & Pope, 1987), should similarly receive greater attention. Finally, across all of the research on the interpersonal aspects of social competence, researchers simply *must* begin employing observations of adolescents with their families, peers, and school personnel. There is an abundance of questionnaire and sociometric data on these processes; actual, in vivo observations in the home and school are now critical.

Although empirical research using social competence as a construct seems to be fairly recent, work on biological and constitutional variables is comparatively old. However, there are large numbers of problems with that research as well. Some of these problems have been adequately addressed by Brooks-Gunn, Petersen, and others, and they relate to definitional and methodological concerns over pubertal processes. Other research issues in this area seem equally troublesome, however. For instance, a persistent difficulty in the appearance literature is the omission of the typical, or "average," adolescent. That is, most research examines attractive *or* unattractive, over- *or* underweight, or tall *or* short adolescents. The few important exceptions to this type of research suggest that moderately attractive, and average-height or weight adolescents are not necessarily found at the midpoints of graphs linking their more extreme counterparts. Indeed, our research has repeatedly suggested that there may be specific and unique outcomes for moderately attractive compared with either very attractive or very unattractive adolescents. In addition, as Simmons and Blyth's (1987) work has demonstrated, levels of appearance may also be greatly affected by adolescents' concern over and satisfaction with physical attributes. And the situation of appearance is complicated even further by the growing evidence that adolescents do *not* tend to perceive their levels of appearance in the same ways others see them. In short, a full range of appearance levels (high, moderate, low), as viewed objectively and subjectively, coupled with adolescents' satisfaction with and concern over these levels, all need careful inspection, preferably all together, in studies employing large samples of subjects with diverse backgrounds.

An additional, enduring difficulty in understanding the relationship of biological and constitutional factors to social competence is a serious lack of attention to the multicollinearity of biological and constitutional factors. For instance, pubertal processes and events are very likely to affect both the actual and the perceived attractiveness levels adolescents possess. These perceptions, in turn, may enhance or suppress adolescents' satisfaction with the pubertal processes themselves. For instance, an objectively very attractive 10-year-old girl may experience biological changes that lead her to believe that she has become less attractive. Her belief may lead to a negative attitude both about her attractiveness level and also about what the pubertal processes have done to her. Consequently, pubertal processes research and appearance issues should *jointly* receive additional attention.

Other biologically relevant factors deserve more scrutiny as well. For example, health concerns and the ability of the body to perform certain tasks (e.g., athletic feats) appear to be very important to some but not to all adolescents (e.g., Downs & Neighbors, 1989; Sobol, 1987), and yet it is exceedingly rare for these concerns to be viewed in light of either biological/constitutional processes or social competence.

In sum, there is a great deal of additional empirical work to be done on the interface of biological processes and social competence. Like the miner who has found a few precious gold nuggets, it is likely that more concentrated efforts on these constructs will reap a very rich strike.

REFERENCES

Adams, G. R. (1977). Physical attractiveness research: Toward a developmental social psychology of beauty. *Human Development, 20,* 217-239.

Adams, G. R., & Crossman, S. (1978). *Physical attractiveness: A cultural imperative.* Roslyn Heights, NY: Libra.

Adams, G. R., & Montemayor, R. (1983). Identity formation during early adolescence. *Journal of Early Adolescence, 3,* 193-202.

Agnew, R. (1984). Appearance and delinquency. *Criminology: An Interdisciplinary Journal, 22,* 421-440.

Alicke, M. D., Smith, R. H., & Klotz, M. L. (1986). Judgments of physical attractiveness: The role of faces and bodies. *Personality and Social Psychology Bulletin, 12,* 381-389.

Allon, N. (1979). Self-perceptions of the stigma of overweight in relationship to weight-losing patterns. *American Journal of Clinical Nutrition, 32,* 470-480.

Apter, A., Galatzer, A., Beth-Halachmi, N., & Laron, Z. (1981). Self-image in adolescents with delayed puberty and growth retardation. *Journal of Youth and Adolescence, 10,* 501-505.

Ayers, M., & Clark, M. L. (1985, March). *Reciprocity and junior high school friendships.* Paper presented at the meeting of the Southeastern Psychological Association, Atlanta.

Baum, C., & Forehand, R. (1984). Social factors associated with adolescent obesity. *Journal of Pediatric Psychology, 9,* 293-302.

Berscheid, E., & Walster, E. (1974). Physical attractiveness. In L. Berkowitz (Ed.), *Advances in experimental social psychology.* New York: Academic Press.

Berzonsky, M. D., & Lombardo, J. P. (1983). Pubertal timing and identity crisis: A preliminary investigation. *Journal of Early Adolescence, 3,* 239-246.

Blyth, D. A., Simmons, R. G., & Zakin, D. F. (1985). Satisfaction with body image for early adolescent females: The impact of pubertal timing within different school environments. *Journal of Youth and Adolescence, 14,* 207-225.

Boxer, A. M., Tobin-Richards, M., & Petersen, A. C. (1983). Puberty: Physical change and its significance in early adolescence. *Theory into Practice, 22,* 85-90.

Brackbill, Y., & Nevill, D. D. (1981). Parental expectations of achievement as affected by children's height. *Merrill-Palmer Quarterly, 27,* 429-441.

Brooks-Gunn, J. (1984). The psychological significance of different pubertal events to young girls. *Journal of Early Adolescence, 4,* 315-327.

Brooks-Gunn, J., & Petersen, A. C. (Eds.). (1983). *Girls at puberty: Biological and psychosocial perspectives.* New York: Plenum.

Brooks-Gunn, J., & Petersen, A. C. (1984). Problems in studying and defining pubertal events. *Journal of Youth and Adolescence, 13,* 181-196.

Brooks-Gunn, J., Petersen, A. C., & Eichorn, D. (1985). The study of maturational timing effects in adolescence. *Journal of Youth and Adolescence, 14,* 149-161.

Brooks-Gunn, J., & Ruble, D. N. (1982). The development of menstrual-related beliefs and behaviors during early adolescence. *Child Development, 53,* 1567-1577.

Brooks-Gunn, J., & Warren, M. P. (1985). Measuring physical status and timing in early adolescence: A developmental perspective. *Journal of Youth and Adolescence, 14,* 163-189.

Brooks-Gunn, J., Warren, M. P., Rosso, J., & Gargiulo, J. (1987). Validity of self-report measures of girls' pubertal status. *Child Development, 58,* 829-841.

Brooks-Gunn, J., Warren, M. P., Samuelson, M., & Fox, R. (1986). Physical similarity of and disclosure of menarcheal status to friends: Effects of grade and pubertal status. *Journal of Early Adolescence, 6,* 3-14.

Bull, R. (1982). Physical appearance and criminality. *Current Psychological Reviews, 2,* 269-292.

Carron, A. V., & Witzel, H. D. (1975). Comparisons of personality for selected groups of fifteen-year-old males. *Perceptual and Motor Skills, 40,* 727-734.

Cavior, N., & Dokecki, P. R. (1973). Physical attractiveness, perceived attitude similarity and academic achievement as contributors to interpersonal attraction among adolescents. *Developmental Psychology, 9,* 44-54.

Cavior, N., & Howard, I. R. (1973). Facial attractiveness and juvenile delinquency among Black and White offenders. *Journal of Abnormal Child Psychology, 1,* 202-213.

Cavior, N., & Lombardi, D. (1973). Developmental aspects of judgments of physical attractiveness and children. *Developmental Psychology, 8,* 67-71.

Cavior, N., Miller, K., & Cohen, S. H. (1975). Physical attractiveness, attitude similarity and length of acquaintance as contributors to interpersonal attraction among adolescents. *Social Behavior and Personality, 3,* 132-141.

Clarke, A. E., & Ruble, D. N. (1978). Young adolescents' beliefs concerning menstruation. *Child Development, 49,* 231-234.

Clausen, J. A. (1975). The social meaning of differential physical and sexual maturation. In S. E. Dragastin & G. H. Elder (Eds.), *Adolescence in the life cycle: Psychological change and social context* (pp. 25-47). Washington, DC: Hemisphere.

Clifford, E. (1971). Body satisfaction in adolescence. *Perceptual and Motor Skills, 33,* 119-125.

Clifford, M. M. (1975). Physical attractiveness and academic performance. *Child Study Journal, 5,* 201-209.

Clifford, M. M., & Walster, E. (1973). Research note: The effects of physical attractiveness on teachers' perceptions. *Sociology of Education, 46,* 248-258.

Collins, J. K., & Plahn, M. R. (1988). Recognition accuracy, stereotypic preference, aversion, and subjective judgment of body appearance in adolescents and young adults. *Journal of Youth and Adolescence, 17,* 317-334.

Collins, J. K., & Propert, D. S. (1983). A developmental study of body recognition in adolescent girls. *Adolescence, 18,* 767-774.

Desmond, S. M., Price, J. H., Gray, N., & O'Connell, J. K. (1986). The etiology of adolescents' perceptions of their weight. *Journal of Youth and Adolescence, 15,* 461-474.

D'Hondt, W., & Vandewiele, M. (1982). Attitudes and behavior at the time of adolescence perceived by secondary school students in Senegal. *Journal of Genetic Psychology, 140,* 319-320.

Dion, K. K. & Stein, S. (1978). Physical attractiveness and interpersonal influence. *Journal of Experimental Social Psychology, 14,* 97-108.

Dornbusch, S. M., Carlsmith, J. M., Gross, R. T., Martin, J. A., Jennings, D., Rosenberg, A., & Duke, P. (1981). Sexual development, age and dating: A comparison of biological and social influences upon one set of behaviors. *Child Development, 52,* 179-185.

Downs, A. C., & Abshier, G. R. (1982). Conceptions of physical appearance among young adolescents: The interrelationships among self-judged appearance, attractiveness stereotyping and sex-typed characteristics. *Journal of Early Adolescence, 2,* 255-265.

Downs, A. C., & Currie, M. (1983). Indexing elementary school-age children's views of attractive and unattractive people: The Attitudes Toward Physical Attractiveness Scale—Intermediate version. *Psychological Documents, 13,* 23 (MS 2579).

Downs, A. C., & Harrison, S. K. (1985). Embarrassing age spots or just plain ugly? Physical attractiveness stereotyping as an instrument of sexism on American television commercials. *Sex Roles, 13,* 9-19.

Downs, A. C., & Lyons, P. M. (1989, April). *The "real world" impact of physical attractiveness on misdemeanor judgments.* Paper presented at the meeting of the Southwestern Psychological Association, Houston, TX.

Downs, A. C., & Neighbors, B. D. (1989, April). *Adolescents' attributes of "normal" and "atypical" peers.* Paper presented at the meeting of the Southwestern Psychological Association, Houston, TX.

Downs, A. C., & Reagan, M. A. (1983, April). *Recognition, development and correlates of self-defined attractiveness among young children.* Paper presented at the meeting of the Western Psychological Association, San Francisco.

Downs, A. C., Reagan, M. A., Garrett, C., & Kolodzy, P. (1982). The Attitudes Toward Physical Attractiveness Scale (ATPAS): An index of stereotypes based on physical appearance. *Catalog of Selected Documents in Psychology, 12,* 44-45. (MS 2502).

Downs, A. C., & Wright, A. D. (1982). Differential conceptions of attractiveness: Comparison of subjective versus objective sources of ratings. *Psychological Reports, 50,* 282.

Drotar, D., Owens, R., & Gotthold, J. (1981). Personality adjustment of children and adolescents with hypopituitarism. *Annual Progress in Child Psychiatry & Child Development,* pp. 306-314.

Duncan, P. D., Ritter, P. L., Dornbusch, S. M., Gross, R. T., & Carlsmith, J. M. (1985). The effects of pubertal timing on body image, school behavior and deviance. *Journal of Youth and Adolescence, 14,* 227-235.

Dwyer, J., & Mayer, J. (1968). Psychological effects of variations in physical appearance during adolescence. *Adolescence, 3,* 353-380.

Ehrhardt, A. A., & Meyer-Bahlburg, H. F. L. (1975). Psychological correlates of abnormal pubertal development. *Clinics in Endocrinology and Metabolism, 4,* 207-222.

Elder, G. H., Nguyen, T. V., & Caspi, A. (1985). Linking family hardship to children's lives [Special Issue: Family development]. *Child Development, 56,* 361-375.

Faust, J. (1987). Correlates of the drive for thinness in young female adolescents. *Journal of Clinical Child Psychology, 16,* 313-319.

Faust, M. S. (1960). Developmental maturity as a determinant in prestige of adolescent girls. *Child Development, 31,* 173-184.

Faust, M. S. (1977). Somatic development of adolescent girls. *Monographs of the Society for Research in Child Development, 42*(1, Serial No. 169).

Felker, D. W., & Kay, R. S. (1971). Self-concept, sports interests, sports participation and body type of seventh- and eighth-grade boys. *Journal of Psychology, 78,* 223-228.

Felson, R. B., & Reed, M. (1986). The effects of parents on the self-appraisals of children. *Social Psychology Quarterly, 49*, 302-308.

Forehand, R., Faust, J., & Baum, C. G. (1985). Accuracy of weight perception among young adolescent girls: An examination of personal and interpersonal correlates. *Journal of Early Adolescence, 5*, 239-245.

Freud, A. (1946). *The ego and the mechanisms of defense.* New York: International Universities Press.

Gaddis, A., & Brooks-Gunn, J. (1985). The male experience of pubertal change. *Journal of Youth and Adolescence, 14*, 61-69.

Gargiulo, J., Attie, I., Brooks-Gunn, J., & Warren, M. P. (1987). Girls' dating behavior as a function of social context and maturation. *Developmental Psychology, 23*, 730-737.

Garwood, S. G., & Allen, L. (1979). Self-concept and identified problem differences between pre- and postmenarcheal adolescents. *Journal of Clinical Psychology, 35*, 528-537.

Gesell, A., Ilg, F. L., & Ames, L. B. (1956). *Youth: The years from ten to sixteen.* New York: Harper.

Greif, E. G., & Ulman, K. J. (1982). The psychological impact of menarche on early adolescent females: A review of the literature. *Child Development, 53*, 1413-1430.

Hall, G. S. (1904). *Adolescence: Its psychology and its relations to physiology, anthropology, sociology, sex, crime, religion and education* (Vols. 1-2). New York: Appleton.

Hamilton, L. H., Brooks-Gunn, J., & Warren, M. P. (1985). Sociocultural influences on eating disorders in female professional dancers. *International Journal of Eating Disorders, 4*, 465-477.

Harper, J. F., & Collins, J. K. (1972). The effects of early or late maturation on the prestige of the adolescent girl. *Australian and New Zealand Journal of Sociology, 8*, 83-88.

Harter, S. (1982). The Perceived Competence Scale for Children. *Child Development, 53*, 87-97.

Hendry, L. B., & Gillies, P. (1978). Body type, body esteem, school and leisure: A study of overweight, average and underweight adolescents. *Journal of Youth and Adolescence, 7*, 181-195.

Hill, J. P., Holmbeck, G. N., Marlow, L., Green, T. M., & Lynch, M. E. (1985a). Menarcheal status and parent-child relations in families of seventh-grade girls. *Journal of Youth and Adolescence, 14*, 301-316.

Hill, J. P., Holmbeck, G. N., Marlow, L., Green, T. M., & Lynch, M. E. (1985b). Pubertal status and parent-child relations in families of seventh-grade boys. *Journal of Early Adolescence, 5*, 31-44.

Hollingworth, L. S. (1928). *The psychology of adolescence.* New York: Appleton.

Holmes, C. S., Hayford, J. T., & Thompson, R. G. (1982a). Personality and behavior differences in groups of boys with short stature. *Children's Health Care, 11*, 61-64.

Holmes, C. S., Hayford, J. T., & Thompson, R. G. (1982b). Parents' and teachers' differing views of short children's behavior. *Child Care, Health & Development, 8*, 327-336.

Holmes, C. S., Karlsson, J. A., & Thompson, R. G. (1985). Social and school competencies in children with short stature: Longitudinal patterns. *Journal of Developmental & Behavioral Pediatrics, 6*, 263-267.

Holmes, C. S., Thompson, R. G., & Hayford, J. T. (1984). Factors related to grade retention in children with short stature. *Child Care, Health & Development, 10,* 199-210.

Jaquish, G. A., & Savin-Williams, R. C. (1981). Biological and ecological factors in the expression of adolescent self-esteem. *Journal of Youth and Adolescence, 10,* 473-485.

Johnson, R. W., & MacEachern, R. (1985). Attributions of physical attractiveness: Tests of social deviance and social identity hypotheses. *Journal of Social Psychology, 125,* 221-232.

Jones, H. E. (1949). Adolescence in our society. In *The family in a democratic society.* New York: Columbia University Press.

Jones, M. C. (1957). The later careers of boys who were early- or late-maturing. *Child Development, 28,* 113-128.

Jones, M. C., & Bayley, N. (1950). Physical maturing among boys as related to behavior. *Journal of Educational Psychology, 41,* 129-148.

Jones, M. C., & Mussen, P. H. (1958). Self-conceptions, motivations, and interpersonal attitudes of early- and late-maturing girls. *Child Development, 29,* 491-501.

Jurich, A. P., & Andrews, D. (1984). Self-concepts of rural early adolescent juvenile delinquents. *Journal of Early Adolescence, 4,* 41-46.

Kleck, R. E., & DeJong, W. (1983). Physical disability, physical attractiveness, and social outcomes in children's small groups. *Rehabilitation Psychology, 28,* 79-91.

Korthase, K. M., & Trenholme, I. (1982). Perceived age and perceived physical attractiveness. *Perceptual and Motor Skills, 54,* 1251-1258.

Langlois, J. H. (1986). From the eye of the beholder to behavioral reality: The development of social behaviors and social relations as a function of physical attractiveness. In C. P. Herman, M. P. Zanna, & E. T. Higgins, (Eds.), *Physical appearance, stigma, and social behavior: The Ontario Symposium* (Vol. 3, pp. 23-51). Hillsdale, NJ: Lawrence Erlbaum.

Langlois, J. H. (in press). The origins and functions of appearance-based stereotypes: Theoretical and applied implications. In R. A. Eder (Ed.), *Developmental perspectives on craniofacial problems.* New York: Springer-Verlag.

Langlois, J. H., & Downs, A. C. (1979). Peer relations as a function of physical attractiveness: The eye of the beholder or behavioral reality? *Child Development, 50,* 409-418.

Langlois, J. H., & Stephan, C. W. (1981). Beauty and the beast: The role of physical attractiveness in the development of peer relations and social behavior. In S. S. Brehm, S. M. Kassin, & F. X. Gibbons (Eds.), *Developmental social psychology: Theory and research.* New York: Oxford University Press.

Lerner, R. M. (1969). The development of stereotyped expectancies of body build-behavior relations. *Child Development, 40,* 127-141.

Lerner, R. M. (1982). Children and adolescents as producers of their own development. *Developmental Review, 2,* 342-370.

Lerner, R. M., & Iwawaki, S. (1975). Cross-cultural analyses of body-behavior relations: II. Factor structure of body build stereotypes of Japanese and American adolescents. *Psychologia: An International Journal of Psychology in the Orient, 18,* 83-91.

Lerner, R. M., & Lerner, J. V. (1977). Effects of age, sex and physical attractiveness on child-peer relations, academic performance and elementary school adjustment. *Developmental Psychology, 13,* 585-590.

Lerner, R. M., & Pool, K. B. (1972). Body-build stereotypes: A cross cultural comparison. *Psychological Reports, 31,* 527-532.

Levinson, R., Powell, B., & Steelman, L. C. (1986). Social location, significant others and body image among adolescents. *Social Psychology Quarterly, 49,* 330-337.

Livson, N., & Peskin, H. (1980). Perspectives on adolescence from longitudinal research. In J. Adelsen (Ed.), *Handbook of adolescent psychology* (pp. 47-98). New York: John Wiley.

Logan, D. D. (1980). The menarche experience in twenty-three foreign countries. *Adolescence, 15,* 247-256.

Magnusson, D., Strattin, H., & Allen, V. L. (1985). A longitudinal study of some adjustment processes from mid-adolescence to adulthood. *Journal of Youth and Adolescence, 14,* 267-283.

Marcia, J. (1980). Identity in adolescence. In J. Adelsen (Ed.), *Handbook of adolescent psychology* (pp. 159-187). New York: John Wiley.

Marshall, W. A., & Tanner, J. M. (1969). Variations in pattern of pubertal changes in girls. *Archives of Disease in Children, 44,* 291-303.

Marshall, W. A., & Tanner, J. M. (1970). Variations in pattern of pubertal changes in boys. *Archives of Disease in Children, 45,* 13-23.

Mathes, E. W., Brennan, S. M., Haugen, P. M., & Rice, H. B. (1985). Ratings of physical attractiveness as a function of age. *Journal of Social Psychology, 125,* 157-168.

McCabe, V. (1984). Abstract perceptual information for age level: A risk factor for maltreatment. *Child Development, 55,* 267-276.

Mendelson, B. K., & White, D. R. (1985). Development of self-body-esteem in overweight youngsters. *Developmental Psychology, 21,* 90-96.

Mercado, P., & Atkinson, D. R. (1982). Effects of counselor sex, student sex and student attractiveness on counselors' judgments. *Journal of Vocational Behavior, 20,* 304-312.

Montemayor, R. (1986). Family variation in parent-adolescent storm and stress. *Journal of Adolescent Research, 1,* 15-31.

Moran, J. D., & McCullers, J. C. (1984). A comparison of achievement scores in physically attractive and unattractive students. *Home Economics Research Journal, 13,* 36-40.

Morris, N. M., & Udry, J. R. (1980). Validation of a self-administered instrument to assess stage of adolescent development. *Journal of Youth and Adolescence, 9,* 271-280.

Morrow, J. (1984). Deviational salience: Application to short stature and relation to perception of adolescent boys. *Perceptual and Motor Skills, 59,* 623-633.

Mussen, P. H., & Jones, M. C. (1957). Self-conceptions, motivations, and interpersonal attitudes of late- and early-maturing boys. *Child Development, 28,* 243-256.

Nottelmann, E. D., Susman, E. J., Blue, J. H., Inoff-Germain, G., Dorn, L. D., Loriaux, D. L., Cutler, G. B., & Chrousos, G. P. (1987). Gonadal and adrenal hormonal correlates of adjustment in early adolescence. In R. M. Lerner & T. T. Foch (Eds.), *Biological-psychological interactions in early adolescence: A life-span perspective.* Hillsdale, NJ: Lawrence Erlbaum.

Nottelmann, E. D., & Welsh, C. J. (1986). The long and the short of physical stature in early adolescence. *Journal of Early Adolescence, 6,* 15-27.

Ogundari, J. T. (1985). Somatic deviations in adolescence: Reactions and adjustments. *Adolescence, 20,* 179-183.

Papini, D. R., & Sebby, R. A. (1987). Adolescent pubertal status and affective family relationships: A multivariate assessment. *Journal of Youth and Adolescence, 16,* 1-15.

Papini, D. R., & Sebby, R. A. (1988). Variations in conflictual family issues by adolescent pubertal status, gender and family member. *Journal of Early Adolescence, 8,* 1-15.

Peskin, H. (1967). Pubertal onset and ego functioning. *Journal of Abnormal Psychology, 72,* 1-15.

Peskin, H. (1973). Influence of the developmental schedule of puberty on learning and ego functioning. *Journal of Youth and Adolescence, 2,* 273-290.

Petersen, A. C., & Crockett, L. (1985). Pubertal timing and grade effects on adjustment. *Journal of Youth and Adolescence, 14,* 191-206.

Petersen, A. C., Crockett, L., Richards, M., & Boxer, A. (1988). A self-report measure of pubertal status: Reliability, validity, and initial norms. *Journal of Youth and Adolescence, 17,* 117-133.

Peterson, A. C., Schulenberg, J. E., Abramowitz, R. M., Offer, D., & Jarcho, H. D. (1984). A Self-Image Questionnaire for Young Adolescents (SIQYA): Reliability and validity studies. *Journal of Youth and Adolescence, 13,* 93-111.

Peterson, A. C., & Taylor, B. (1980). The biological approach to adolescence: Biological change and psychological adaptation. In J. Adelson (Ed.), *Handbook of adolescent psychology* (pp. 117-155). New York: John Wiley.

Peterson, A. C., Tobin-Richards, M., & Boxer, A. M. (1983). Puberty: Its measurement and its meaning. *Journal of Early Adolescence, 3,* 47-62.

Pomerantz, S. C. (1979). Sex differences in the relative importance of self-esteem, physical self-satisfaction and identity in predicting adolescent satisfaction. *Journal of Youth and Adolescence, 8,* 51-61.

Powers, S. I., Hauser, S. T., & Kilner, L. A. (1989). Adolescent mental health. *American Psychologist, 44,* 200-208.

Prieto, A. G., & Robbins, M. C. (1975). Perceptions of height and self-esteem. *Perceptual and Motor Skills, 40,* 395-398.

Rierdan, J., & Koff, E. (1980). The psychological impact of menarche: Integrative versus disruptive changes. *Journal of Youth and Adolescence, 9,* 49-58.

Rierdan, J., & Koff, E. (1981). The psychological impact of menarche: Integrative versus disruptive changes. *Annual Progress in Child Psychiatry & Child Development,* pp. 483-493.

Rierdan, J., & Koff, E. (1985). Timing of menarche and initial menstrual experience. *Journal of Youth and Adolescence, 14,* 237-244.

Roscoe, B., Kennedy, D., & Pope, T. (1987). Adolescents' views of intimacy: Distinguishing intimate from nonintimate relationships. *Adolescence, 22,* 511-516.

Ruble, D. N., & Brooks-Gunn, J. (1982). The experience of menarche. *Child Development, 53,* 1557-1566.

Savin-Williams, R. C. (1979). Dominance hierarchies in groups of early adolescents. *Child Development, 50,* 923-935.

Savin-Williams, R. C., & Small, S. A. (1986). The timing of puberty and its relationship to adolescent and parent perceptions of family interactions. *Developmental Psychology, 22,* 342-347.

Shea, J., Crossman, S. M., & Adams, G. R. (1978). Physical attractiveness and personality development. *Journal of Psychology, 99,* 59-62.

Sheldon, W. H., Stevens, S. S., & Tucker, W. B. (1940). *The varieties of human physique: An introduction to constitutional psychology.* New York: Harper & Row.

Shipman, W. G. (1964). Age of menarche and adult personality. *Archives of General Psychiatry, 10,* 155-159.

Simmons, R. G., & Blyth, D. A. (1987). *Moving into adolescence: The impact of pubertal change and school context.* New York: Aldine de Gruyter.

Simmons, R. G., Blyth, D. A., & McKinney, K. D. (1983). The social and psychological effects of puberty on white females. In J. Brooks-Gunn & A. Petersen (Eds.), *Female puberty.* New York: Plenum.

Simmons, R. G., Blyth, D. A., Van Cleave, E. F., & Bush, D. M. (1979). Entry into early adolescence: The impact of school structure, puberty, and early dating on self-esteem. *American Sociological Review, 44,* 948-967.

Simmons, R. G., & Rosenberg, F. (1975). Sex, sex roles, and self-image. *Journal of Youth and Adolescence, 4,* 229-258.

Simmons, R. G., Rosenberg, F., & Rosenberg, M. (1973). Disturbance in the self-image at adolescence. *American Sociological Review, 38,* 553-568.

Sobol, J. (1987). Health concerns of young adolescents. *Adolescence, 22,* 739-750.

Sprinthall, N. A., & Collins, W. A. (1988). *Adolescent psychology: A developmental view* (2nd ed.). New York: Random House.

Stabler, B., Whitt, J. K., Moreault, D. M., D'Ercole, A. J., & Underwood, L. E. (1980). Social judgments by children of short stature. *Psychological Reports, 46,* 743-746.

Staffieri, J. R. (1967). A study of social stereotype of body image in children. *Journal of Personality and Social Psychology, 7,* 101-104.

Stager, S. F., & Burke, P. J. (1982). A reexamination of body build stereotypes. *Journal of Research in Personality, 16,* 435-446.

Steinberg, L. D. (1981). Transformations in family relations at puberty. *Developmental Psychology, 17,* 833-840.

Steinberg, L. D., & Hill, J. P. (1978). Patterns of family interaction as a function of age, the onset of puberty and formal thinking. *Developmental Psychology, 14,* 683-684.

Stone, C. P., & Barker, R. G. (1937). Aspects of personality and intelligence in post-menarcheal and pre-menarcheal girls of the same chronological age. *Journal of Comparative Psychology, 23,* 439-455.

Stone, C. P., & Barker, R. G. (1939). The attitudes and interests of premenarcheal and postmenarcheal girls. *Journal of Genetic Psychology, 54,* 27-71.

Storz, N. S., & Greene, W. H. (1983). Body weight, body image and perception of fad diets in adolescent girls. *Journal of Nutrition Education, 15,* 15-18.

Susman, E. J., Nottelmann, E. D., Inoff-Germain, G. E., Dorn, L. D., Cutler, G. B., Jr., Loriaux, D. L., & Chrousos, G. P. (1985). The relation of relative hormonal levels and physical development and social-emotional behavior in young adults. *Journal of Youth and Adolescence, 14,* 245-264.

Tanner, J. M. (1962). *Growth at adolescence* (2nd ed.). Oxford: Blackwell Scientific.

Tanner, J. M. (1971, Fall). Sequence, tempo, and individual variation in the growth and development of boys and girls aged twelve to sixteen. *Daedalus*, pp. 907-930.

Teri, L. (1982). Depression in adolescence: Its relationship to assertion and various aspects of self-image. *Journal of Clinical Child Psychology, 11*, 101-106.

Toriola, A. L., & Igbokwe, N. U. (1985). Relationship between perceived physique and somatotype characteristics of 10- to 18-year-old boys and girls. *Perceptual and Motor Skills, 60*, 878.

Tucker, L. A. (1983). Cigarette smoking intentions and obesity among high school males. *Psychological Reports, 52*, 530.

Udry, J. R. (1977). The importance of being beautiful: A reexamination and racial comparison. *American Journal of Sociology, 83*, 154-160.

Udry, J. R., Billy, J. O. G., Morris, N. M., Gruff, T. R., & Raj, M. H. (1985). Serum androgenic hormones motivate sexual behavior in boys. *Fertility and Sterility, 43*, 90-94.

Weisfeld, G. E., Bloch, S. A., & Ivers, J. W. (1984). Possible determinants of social dominance among adolescent girls. *Journal of Genetic Psychology, 144*, 115-129.

Zakin, D. F. (1983). Physical attractiveness, sociability, athletic ability, and children's preference for their peers. *Journal of Psychology, 115*, 117-122.

Zakin, D. F., Blyth, D. A., & Simmons, R. G. (1984). Physical attractiveness as a mediator of the impact of early pubertal changes for girls. *Journal of Youth and Adolescence, 13*, 439-450.

PART II

INFLUENCES ON SOCIAL COMPETENCY

4. The Family and Social Competence in Adolescence

Gary W. Peterson
Arizona State University

Geoffry K. Leigh
Ohio State University

The purpose of this chapter is to examine the parent-youth relationship and the larger family system as contexts for the development of social competence during adolescence. Consistent with this objective, social competence is conceptualized as a developmental phenomenon that is a product of social interaction in families. As such, social competence is difficult to define and both general and specific definitions are necessary to clarify its meaning. Important subdimensions of social competence include (a) internal or cognitive resources, (b) a balance between sociability and individuality, and (c) social skills in reference to peers. The meaning of socially competent or adaptive behavior varies in terms of ethnicity and cultural variables, developmental period, situational factors, and gender role expectations. Important aspects of parent-adolescent relationships that either predict or are associated with adolescent social competence include parental styles, behavior, modeling, and power. Dimensions of family process, structure, and communication that are drawn from systems perspectives are examined for their association with adolescent social competence. Other topics include the reciprocal effect of adolescent social competence on parents and families, with additional attention to social-structural variables that have impact on parent-adolescent relationships.

EXAMINING SOCIAL COMPETENCE

The belief that it is normal for adolescents to become "disturbed" is one of the most common themes used to characterize the years between childhood and adulthood. The dramatic metaphor of "storm and stress" is often used to portray the inner psychic and biological forces that are supposed to reappear with the onset of puberty. According to this "traditional" perspective, adolescents are expected to experience heightened discord among the major personality components, increased interpersonal conflict, and a process of "separation" from parents (Blos, 1979; Freud,

1965; Hall, 1904). Contrasting with this traditional perspective, however, is recent scholarship presenting a less turbulent view in which the majority of youth progress through adolescence without serious disturbances. That is, most adolescents are portrayed as traversing this period with considerable competence while managing to balance parental ties with expanding peer relationships (Kandel & Lesser, 1972; Offer & Offer, 1975; Youniss & Smollar, 1985). Consistent with more recent scholarship, the purpose of this chapter is to describe how aspects of the parent-youth relationship and the larger family system are associated with the development of social competence during adolescence.

Although it may be perilous to identify particular interpersonal experiences as the primary sources of social competence, an even more unwise strategy would be to underestimate the role of families in the development of youthful capacities for social adaptation. Virtually no one in the social sciences, of course, would claim that families are the exclusive cradles of social competence in the young. In fact, families may accomplish just the opposite by serving as primary wellsprings for social "incompetence" in the form of debilitating dependencies, alienation, violent behavior, substance abuse, juvenile delinquency, and antisocial behavior (Haley, 1980; Leigh & Peterson, 1986; Steinberg, 1987; Steinmetz, 1987). Despite these pitfalls, however, social competence is often encouraged by family experiences that foster the knowledge, attitudes, values, and behaviors predisposing adolescents to function effectively in social relationships (Peterson & Rollins, 1987).

The Nature of Social Competence

Defining what is meant by the "social competence" of adolescents is perhaps the greatest challenge in writing this chapter. Ironically social competence is an interpersonal phenomenon that we observe on a daily basis, but one whose complexities are difficult to capture in a concise definition. Although social scientists often desire precise and/or measurable definitions of concepts, the great complexity of the concept of "social competence" has caused many scholars to formulate very general definitions that lack scientific rigor. Consequently, the failure to use "operational" in favor of "global" definitions has meant that a lack of clarity has hindered the empirical investigation of social competence.

Such general definitions include Zigler and Trickett's (1978) proposal that social competence is determined by the extent to which societal expectations have been met and whether or not information is provided about the level of self-actualization experienced. Other commentators such as Foote and Cottrell (1955) describe "interpersonal competence" as the ability versus the inability to engage in normal human interaction. In a similar vein, White (1959) defines "competence" as the organism's capacity to interact effectively with its environment. Finally, Waters and Sroufe (1983) describe "competent individuals" as those who make use of environmental and personal resources to achieve good developmental outcomes.

A second and contrasting definitional strategy is to describe the specific components of social competence. According to this "atomistic approach," social skills such as "knowing how and when to shake hands and follow directions" in various interpersonal settings (Burns & Farina, 1984) are primary indicators of social competence. Such specificity in defining social competence brings to mind the metaphor about the blind man who in studying an elephant could deal only with isolated pieces of the pachyderm's anatomy at a time, without being able to step back and visualize the whole. Perhaps the best definitional approach, however, recognizes that social competence is composed of many distinct components requiring a combination of general and specific strategies. Consequently, social competence is a useful construct because it illuminates important dimensions of social reality but does so only by defying the social scientist's inclination for parsimony. Another way of saying this is that social competence is a complex multidimensional concept requiring both general and specific statements of meaning.

Defining Social Competence

The most general definitions of social competence refer to adaptive functioning in which environmental and personal resources are used to achieve desirable developmental outcomes within interpersonal contexts (Waters & Sroufe, 1983). Individuals who develop these capabilities often possess sound judgment and the ability to manage circumstances to benefit themselves and others in social situations. Any general definition of social competence, therefore, must also consider the impact of the person on the social environment as well as the influence of the social context on the individual (Dodge, Pettit, McClaskey, & Brown, 1986). Such conceptions make it clear that social competence develops within the context of a transactional process between the developing person and the surrounding social context (Lerner, 1987). Competent adolescents, therefore, are neither passive recipients nor passive reactors to stimuli but are both active and reactive agents to their developmental and environmental circumstances.

Although general definitions begin to provide meaning, greater clarity is also provided by describing key subdimensions of adolescent social competence. Specifically, the major components of social competence consist of (a) internal or cognitive resources, (b) a balance between sociability and individuality, and (c) social skills in reference to peers.

One group of these qualities, *internal or cognitive capacities,* serves as resources or underlying bases for social skills that assist adolescents in establishing and maintaining positive interpersonal relationships. Specifically, such capacities include positive self-esteem, internal locus of control, social perspective taking, and interpersonal problem solving. The first internal capacity or resource for social competence, positive self-esteem, functions as a basis for socially adaptive behavior by providing adolescents with sufficient self-confidence to engage in and expand their social relationships (Openshaw & Thomas, 1986; Rollins & Thomas, 1979). An internal locus of control, or feelings of exercising control over one's life circumstances, serves as a second internal resource by encouraging self-initiative and the development of leadership skills in interpersonal settings (Adams, 1983). Social perspective taking (i.e., social role taking and empathy), on the other hand, is a third internal resource for social competence that encourages adolescents to understand and become sensitive to the feelings, intentions, and abilities of others (Adams, 1983; Grotevant & Cooper, 1986; Moore & Eisenberg, 1984). Closely associated with social perspective taking is a fourth internal resource—moral development. Prosocial responsiveness of this kind promotes an awareness of other's needs, an understanding of the impact of one's actions on others, and a willingness to accommodate one's behavior accordingly (Hoffman, 1977, 1982). Finally, social adaptation also requires the development of interpersonal problem-solving skills as a fifth internal resource. Specifically, socially competent adolescents are often more capable of (a) being sensitive to interpersonal problem situations, (b) generating alternative solutions, (c) planning for the attainment of interpersonal goals, (d) weighing consequences in terms of their effectiveness and social acceptability, and (e) perceiving cause-and-effect relations in interpersonal events (Shure, 1981).

In addition to "internal resources," a second major component of social competence is the paradoxical but necessary *balance between sociability (or togetherness) and individuality (or autonomy)*. These seemingly contradictory aspects of the human experience are actually complementary functions that contribute to interpersonal competence during all phases of the life course. The sociability function, on the one hand, involves the process of connecting and integrating with significant others—or tendencies toward "communion" that guide adolescents to form close relationships with others (Dyk & Adams, 1987). The individuality function, on the other hand, refers to becoming somewhat unique and differentiated and having freedom of action from others. Important aspects of this balance between sociability and individuality include the need to make progress toward such "agentic" qualities as autonomy and achievement while maintaining close parent-youth ties, conforming to parent's expectations, and developing successful friendship and peer relationships (Baumrind, 1975, 1978; Peterson & Rollins, 1987; Youniss & Smollar, 1986). Adolescents who are socially adaptive know themselves well enough to act independently while affiliating with and accommodating their behavior to the needs of others (Baumrind, 1978; Grotevant & Cooper, 1986; Waterman, 1984).

A third major component of social competence, the *social skills of adolescents in reference to peers*, refers to the application of previously specified interpersonal resources in a successful manner with age-mates. Specifically, such a focus examines the nature of the status, acceptance, and social skills demonstrated by adolescents within the peer group (Dodge, Pettit, McClaskey, & Brown,

1986). Such an approach focuses on the behavioral repertoires that adolescents acquire for adaptation and acceptance beyond family boundaries in reference to peers.

Variability in Social Competence

Before assuming that we have captured the "slippery" nature of social competence, several cautions underscore how difficult it is to define this concept. First, it is important to recognize that specific definitions of social competence will have cultural limitations. That is, societies and ethnic groups may vary widely in the extent to which specific aspects of social competence are valued and encouraged in the young (Baumrind, 1978). For example, there is greater emphasis on conformity to parents' expectations and less on individual autonomy within the Soviet Union and in Hispanic ethnic groups than in the mainstream culture of the United States (Baumrind, 1978, 1983; Bronfenbrenner, 1970; Thomas, Gecas, Weigert, & Rooney, 1974).

A second caution concerns the developmental nature of social competence to the extent that behavior considered adaptive during early adolescence may change dramatically in meaning by late adolescence (Healy & Stewart, 1984). In the case of behavioral autonomy, for example, it is appropriate for parents to monitor and supervise the dating activities of younger teenagers more closely than the more intimate activities of couples during their later teens and early twenties.

A third caution concerns the fact that the nature of social competence is best determined within the context of specific interpersonal situations (Goldfried & d'Zurilla, 1969; Schwartz & Gottman, 1976). Consider the situation, for example, in which a 17-year-old boy asks a 16-year-old girl for a date. The degree of competence demonstrated may depend upon whether the girl is standing alone in the school hallway or is taking an examination during class and does not wish to be disturbed. Any judgment about social competence, therefore, can be made only in terms of specific circumstances occurring within distinctive contexts.

Finally, it is important to be aware that gender role expectations continue to prescribe that some aspects of social competence differ for males and females (Baumrind, 1980; Gilligan, 1982). Studies continue to demonstrate that gender differences occur on several dimensions of social competence, including autonomy, conformity, connectedness, achievement, self-esteem, and peer relationships (see Baumrind, 1980; Gilligan, 1982; Peterson & Rollins, 1987, for reviews). The findings reflect the continued reality that males and females are socialized into attitudes, values, and behaviors composing sex-typed roles (Condry, 1984).

FAMILY STRUCTURED VARIABLES AS INFLUENCES

A serious error would be to limit our discussion of social competence to individual and personality variables. Although the psychological level of human development is an important aspect of social competence, many adaptive qualities are acquired within the context of experiences organized beyond the individual level of ontogeny. As previously indicated, families are one of the most important social environments that either facilitate or hinder the development of social competence in the young. Although much of this chapter deals with interpersonal processes within families that predict social competence, some attention is also given to social-structural variables, including socioeconomic status and family structure, as antecedents of social competence.

Socioeconomic Status

A long tradition of research indicates that parents with distinctive socioeconomic statuses (SES) often experience different conditions of life, develop disparate conceptions of social reality, and vary in the value systems they transmit to children (Gecas, 1979; Kohn, 1977; Peterson & Rollins, 1987). Parents who occupy white-collar positions, for example, learn the importance of working effectively with others and the need to exercise initiative and self-direction to meet the job expectations they face on a daily basis (Kohn, 1977; Kohn & Schooler, 1983). Many parents with prestigious employment and higher educational attainment use child-rearing approaches that emphasize self-direction (i.e., autonomy) and interpersonal skill as being components of social competence. Parents from such backgrounds often use reasoning and negotiation to encourage such qualities (Gecas, 1979; Kohn, 1983; Peterson & Rollins, 1987).

In contrast, parents who occupy blue-collar occupations often conduct their activities under conditions of close supervision and demands for conformity. One consequence of such experiences is the tendency for these parents to demonstrate greater responsiveness to authority and to use child-rearing practices that encourage such dimensions of social competence as obedience and conformity. Consequently the parenting repertoires of blue-collar adults tend to be more coercive, punitive, and authoritarian than those of their white-collar counterparts (Peterson & Rollins, 1987). An overall assessment of this research, therefore, is that SES is related to specific dimensions of adolescent social competence because different aspects of this concept are emphasized within families in particular socioeconomic levels (Kohn, 1977; Kohn & Schooler, 1983). Parents of a distinctive SES often use different child-rearing strategies to prepare their children for the unique challenges of social adaptation within each level of the social hierarchy.

Marital Status

Another aspect of family structure is concerned with the marital status of parents and its impact on parent-adolescent relationships and various dimensions of youthful social competence. As divorce rates have risen dramatically, increased concern has been expressed that adolescents from single-parent families are more likely to develop psychological and interpersonal problems (Blechman, 1982; Dornbusch et al., 1985; Jurich & Jones, 1986; Montemayor, 1984; Peterson, Leigh, & Day, 1984). Studies have tended to indicate that divorce trauma may contribute to coercive cycles within the parent-youth relationship and that parents use increased punitiveness, greater inconsistency, decreased support, and less reasoning with the young. Consequently researchers have linked these declines in the quality of parenting to such aspects of adolescent social competence as problems with interpersonal associations, heterosexual relationships, the independence process, self-esteem, and achievement as well as greater noncompliance and increases in aggressiveness, emotional turmoil, anxiety, and psychopathology (Hetherington, 1972; Hetherington, Cox, & Cox, 1978; Jacobson & Ryder, 1978; Montemayor, 1984; Patterson, 1982; Peterson, Leigh, & Day, 1984; Rashke, 1987). In contrast, others have reported that support systems exist outside the family (e.g., peers and adults other than parents) that make adolescents more capable than younger children of coping with parental divorce and may even predispose them to make gains in maturity (Brooks-Gunn, Warren, & Russo, in press; Crouter, Belsky, & Spanier, 1984; Hetherington, 1981, 1984; Steinberg & Silverberg, 1986; Wallerstein & Kelly, 1980; Zill & Peterson, 1983). Other investigators also provide evidence that many parents and adolescents recover from divorce and that the worst trauma and effects occur in the period one to two years following the dissolution of the marriage (Hetherington et al., 1978; Peterson, Leigh, & Day, 1984). Several reviewers also have concluded that marital status (e.g., divorce) has little separate influence, especially when critical psychological and relationship factors directly influencing adolescents are taken into account. Included among these efficacious phenomena are the coping skills of parents and youth, the self-esteem of the young, and the quality of the adolescent's relationship with both parents as well as the level of marital and postdivorce conflict between parents (Montemayor, 1984; Peterson, Leigh, & Day, 1984; Rashke, 1987). In short, one must go beyond an exclusive reliance on family structural variables to the domain of interpersonal processes as a means of understanding the impact of divorce on the social competence of adolescents.

Family Size, Birth Order, and Spacing

Other family structural variables such as family size, birth order, and the spacing of siblings also have consequences for various dimensions of adolescent social competence, including self-esteem, achievement, autonomy, and conformity to parents (Bossard & Boll, 1956; Elder & Bowerman, 1963; Kidwell, 1981; Leigh, 1986; Peterson & Rollins, 1987; Scheck & Emerick, 1976). For example, as family size increases through the addition of children and adolescents, parents often face more diverse demands from the increasing complexity of family relationships. Specifically, parents of large families become less capable of attending to individual needs, develop more direct means of control, and experience higher levels of frustration than those of smaller families. Consequently parents who have several offspring are reported to use more authoritarian techniques as efficient means to deal with these pressures, encourage conformity, and diminish autonomy in the young (Bossard & Boll, 1956; Elder & Bowerman, 1963; Gecas, 1979; Kidwell, 1981; Leigh, 1986; Scheck & Emerick, 1976).

Another structural variable, birth order, or the ordinal position of children in families, as a predictor of youthful social competence has a long tradition of scholarship (Adams, 1972; Adler, 1928; Ernst & Angst, 1983; Gecas & Pasley, 1984; Kidwell, 1981, 1982). Research on birth order often stems from the belief that youth in different ordinal positions in families may experience distinctive interactions with parents and, in turn, are influenced in terms of their social competence. The young may acquire aspects of their identity and individuality by developing roles, personalities, and behaviors that stand in contrast to parents and other siblings within families.

Several birth order studies comparing first- and last-borns have found that firstborns receive more parental attention, intrusive involvements, affectionate behavior, achievement pressure, and strict training. Last-borns, on the other hand, are exposed to more relaxed forms of discipline, less achievement pressure, and fewer maturity demands than those in other ordinal positions within families (Ernst & Angst, 1983; Kammeyer, 1967; Kidwell, 1981, 1982; Leigh, 1986; Peterson & Rollins, 1987). Although much less research exists about youth who occupy "middle" positions, Kidwell (1982) found that middle-born adolescents demonstrated lower self-esteem than either first- or last-borns. Such deficiencies, in turn, may have resulted from the inability of adolescents to establish their uniqueness and not experience the same status, recognition, or attention from parents as either first- or last-born youth.

Despite the fact that some consistencies exist in the research on birth order, other evaluators of the methodology and content of this research have concluded that little evidence exists supporting the idea that social competence is influenced by ordinal position (Ernst & Angst, 1983; Schooler, 1972; Schvaneveldt & Ihinger, 1979). Criticisms of birth order research have convinced researchers to use more complicated approaches and examine the influence of ordinal position in conjunction with other structural variables such as sibling number, child spacing, and gender composition on the parental behavior used with adolescents (Kidwell, 1981). Results from this research support the conclusions that sibling number and spacing have independent influences on such parental behaviors as punitiveness, reasoning, and support and that such behaviors may have important implications for adolescent social competence. Of special significance was the finding that positive parent-adolescent relationships were found to exist when children were spaced either close together (12 months or less) or very widely apart (four years or more), with the optimal spacing being about five years apart. Intermediate spacing (i.e., two to three years between siblings) was characterized by the highest levels of punitiveness and the lowest levels of support and reasoning by parents (Kidwell, 1981).

Additional studies using such multivariate models involving family size, birth order, and spacing are necessary. Future research should proceed further and determine whether or not variations in parental behavior associated with family structural variables actually translate into consequences for youthful social competence. Investigations also should be conducted to evaluate the relative influence of family structural and relationship variables on adolescent social competence. Such research should help to determine whether or not family structural variables are simply "marker" variables for more fundamental processes within family relationships (Leigh, 1986).

PARENTAL CHARACTERISTICS AND ADOLESCENT SOCIAL COMPETENCE

The most productive tradition of research on family influences has sought to examine interpersonal processes and attributes within the parent-adolescent relationship that contribute to various dimensions of adolescent social competence (Maccoby & Martin, 1983; Peterson & Rollins, 1987; Rollins & Thomas, 1979; Smith, 1986). Much of this research has been conducted from a "social mold" perspective in which various parental styles, behaviors, and characteristics (i.e., modeling and power) are conceptualized as antecedents of social and psychological "outcomes" in adolescents. Consequently this tradition of research takes the stance that socialization is a unidirectional process, with social agents (e.g., parents) functioning to influence or shape the young.

Contrasting with the social mold perspective, however, are alternative conceptions of socialization in which relationships between parents and adolescents are viewed as more dynamic, bidirectional, or even multidirectional (Bell & Harper, 1977; Lerner & Foch, 1987; Maccoby & Martin, 1983; Peterson & Rollins, 1987). Subsequent sections will deal with both the traditional and the more recent conceptualizations of family relationships that appear to be associated with youthful social competence.

Parental Styles and Adolescent Social Competence

The origins of youthful social competence can be examined in terms of the extent to which different parental styles either enhance or hinder the development of adaptive qualities in the young (Maccoby & Martin, 1983; Peterson & Rollins, 1987; Rollins & Thomas, 1979). Consequently a diverse assortment of "parenting styles" have been conceptualized in which complex collections or blends of control attempts, communication patterns, and nurturance are used to portray various patterns of child rearing.

Perhaps the most widely known set of parental styles from a "social mold" perspective is that developed by Baumrind (1975, 1978, 1980) through her identification of permissive, authoritarian, harmonious, and authoritative patterns of child rearing. The authoritarian style, for example, refers to the frequent imposition of parental authority through arbitrary or even punitive means in conjunction with low amounts of nurturance. Permissiveness, on the other hand, designates an approach to child rearing in which the parent serves as a resource for the young but refrains from controlling or shaping the present or future behavior of adolescents. Furthermore, the harmonious parent acquires influence without actually using control attempts and does so through equalitarian techniques and effective communication. Finally, authoritative parenting involves the application of firm control in a rational, issue-oriented manner in which verbal give-and-take is encouraged. Parents enforce an authoritative perspective by accommodating the individual interests of adolescents and providing the young with considerable amounts of nurturance (Baumrind, 1975, 1978).

According to Baumrind (1975, 1978) authoritative parenting fosters a particular kind of youthful social competence that is associated with success in Western societies. Specifically, social or "instrumental" competence is defined by such attributes as social responsibility, vitality, independence, achievement, friendliness, and cooperativeness with others. Although parents who use authoritative strategies tend to emphasize both autonomy and disciplined conformity in all phases of development, this style of child rearing is especially appropriate for facilitating the independence dimension of social competence as the parent-adolescent relationship becomes less asymmetrical and more egalitarian (Baumrind, 1978).

The work of Hauser, Powers, Noam, and Jacobson (1984) and Powers, Hauser, Schwartz, Noam, and Jacobson (1983), on the other hand, is a bidirectional approach to the study of styles of parent-adolescent interaction. Although focusing on a different aspect of adolescent ontogeny—the study of ego development— this work overlaps with social competence by considering the degree to which a person's interpersonal skills, awareness of self and others, and sense of mutuality and empathy become more differentiated and complex (Powers, Hauser, Schwartz, Noam, & Jacobson, 1983). Hauser and Powers have used the clinical observations of Stierlin (1974) in their research to conceptualize particular types of parent-adolescent relationships that either facilitate or hinder adolescent ego development. Specifically, these investigators examine "binding" and "enabling" interactions through which the expression of independent thoughts and perceptions are either encouraged or hindered. Binding or constraining interactions inhibit clear communication and adolescent ego development by distracting, withholding information, and showing indifference. Enabling interactions, on the other hand, enhance communication and youthful ego development through explaining, focusing on another person's perspective, problem solving, stimulating curiosity, and using affective expressions of acceptance and empathy (Hauser, Powers, Noam, & Bowlds, 1987; Hauser, Powers, Noam, & Jacobson, 1984; Powers, Hauser, Schwartz, Noam, & Jacobson, 1983). Of special importance for adolescent ego development are cognitive enabling interactions (e.g., stimulation of curiosity and problem solving) and communication that is affectively enabling (e.g., acceptance and empathy).

Adolescent ego development, therefore, is enhanced in family environments characterized by high amounts of noncompetitive sharing of perspectives, positive affection, and support as well as low levels of affectively based conflict and cognitively inhibiting behavior. Hauser and Powers suggest, therefore, that aspects of social competence are facilitated most effectively in family environments in which members are encouraged to understand one another's perspectives through interactions that foster clear communication (Hauser, Powers, Noam, & Jacobson, 1984; Powers, Hauser, Schwartz, Noam, & Jacobson, 1983).

A key aspect of Hauser and Powers's work is their effort to conceptualize influence within the parent-adolescent relationship as a mutual or reciprocal process. That is, adolescents are viewed as eliciting and responding to particular patterns of constraining and enabling behaviors, with parental actions being no more dominant or guiding than adolescent behavior. Changes in youthful ego development and social competence, therefore, are the result of either multiple "benign or constraining" interchanges within families.

Dimensions of Parental Behavior and Social Competence

Conceptually distinct from the study of parental styles is the related tradition of research that attempts to isolate dimensions of parental behavior for their separate influences on social competence during adolescence (Maccoby & Martin, 1983; Peterson & Rollins, 1987; Rollins & Thomas, 1979). Whereas "parental styles" consist of collections of several child-rearing behaviors, the study of parental behavior seeks to examine the efficacy of individual parental techniques separate from the predictive capacity of others. Although much of this research has been conducted from a "social mold" perspective (i.e., parental influence on adolescent outcomes), more recent studies and reinterpretations of older work have demonstrated the bidirectional nature of this tradition of scholarship (Baumrind, 1980; Bell & Harper, 1977; Patterson, 1982; Peterson & Rollins, 1987).

Since the 1940s numerous studies and reviews have identified two generic dimensions of parental behavior—support and control—as the principal aspects of child rearing that predict youthful social competence. The first of these dimensions, parental support, has received such labels as warmth, affection, nurturance, and acceptance (Becker, 1964; Martin, 1975; Rohner, 1986; Rollins & Thomas, 1979; Schaefer, 1959). Although parental support has been studied most often as a unitary dimension, recent investigators are beginning to identify several subdimensions of this variable, including companionship, physical affection, rejection, and general support. As yet, however, only a few studies have compared the relative predictive capacity of these subdimensions on various aspects of adolescent social competence (Barber & Thomas, 1986; Ellis, Thomas, & Rollins, 1976; Peterson, Rollins, Thomas, & Ellis, 1980).

The second child-rearing dimension, parental control, has been conceptualized in a variety of ways. For example, parental control has been defined as (a) a specific outcome or characteristic of adolescents that indicates whether or not particular control attempts by parents have been successful and (b) a general controlling atmosphere (or rule structure) for adolescent behavior that parents establish (Maccoby & Martin, 1983; Peterson & Rollins, 1987; Rollins & Thomas, 1979; Smith, 1983). The most common definition of control, however, refers to (c) actions used by parents while attempting to modify the behavior and internal states of adolescents (Peterson & Rollins, 1987).

Partly due to conceptual confusion, a continual problem has been the large number of inconsistent findings for parental control as a predictor of several dimensions of adolescent social competence (Rollins & Thomas, 1979; Thomas, Gecas, Weigert, & Rooney, 1974). As a result replication problems have stimulated efforts to reconceptualize the control dimension through the identification of different kinds of parental influence attempts and the manner in which they predict various aspects of youthful social competence (Hoffman, 1970; Maccoby & Martin, 1983; Peterson & Rollins, 1987; Rollins & Thomas, 1979; Smith, 1983; Staub, 1979). Subdimensions of parental control include coercion or power assertion, firm control, induction, love withdrawal, and commands. Consequently subsequent sections will review the existing research on subdimensions of parental control and support as predictors of adolescent social competence.

Firm Control and Induction

A common assumption in the literature on child rearing is that children and adolescents require some type of systematic guidance or "firm control" from parents. In recent years the most prominent advocate of firm control as a child-rearing strategy has been Diana Baumrind (1971, 1978, 1980, 1983), who defines this form of parental influence as "firm enforcement of rules, effective resistance to the child's coercive demands, and willingness to guide the child by regime and structured interventions" (Baumrind, 1971, p. 87).

According to several observers (Baumrind, 1978, 1983; Maccoby, 1980; Mussen, Conger, & Kagan, 1974), firm control is partially responsible for encouraging such aspects of adolescent social competence as social responsibility, self-control, independence, and self-esteem. Social responsibility and self-control, for example, are facilitated by parents who use firm control to encourage both external compliance and internalized conformity by the young to the expectations of others (Baumrind, 1978, 1983). At the same time, firm control combined with warmth and rational communication facilitates a gradual restructuring of the parent-adolescent relationship in which the young move step-by-step toward independence within a context of continued ties with parents (Baumrind, 1978; Peterson, 1986). Specific forms of firm control, therefore, seem to encourage a constructive balance between autonomy and continued responsiveness to parents (Peterson, 1986; Peterson & Stivers, 1987). Finally, higher self-esteem in adolescents is viewed as an outcome of parents using firm control through the enforcement of clearly defined limits (Coopersmith, 1967). Firm control is expected to facilitate self-esteem by contributing to inner controls, sets of values, and expectations that, in turn, lead to greater confidence in one's definition of the situation and standards for judging success and failure. Adolescents seem to gain a clearer concept of themselves when faced with forms of parental control that are viewed as being clear, consistent, and legitimate (Coopersmith, 1967; Openshaw & Thomas, 1986).

Standard interpretations of parental firm control and its effects on youthful social competence, however, have been challenged recently from the perspective of attribution theory (Lepper, 1981; Lewis, 1981). Advocates of this position believe that firm control often applies "functionally superfluous pressure" that is more likely to induce external compliance to authority rather than the internalization of norms and the attainment of self-responsibility. From this perspective, children and adolescents who are exposed to pressure that is "just sufficient" for compliance are viewed as being responsive to internal rather than external inducements (i.e., external control by parents) and, therefore, are less likely to deviate in the absence of external surveillance (Lepper, 1981). Consistent with this position, Lewis (1981) reinterprets much of Baumrind's (Baumrind, 1971; Baumrind & Black, 1967) early research as measures of child compliance rather than firm control. Furthermore, Lewis argues that firm control may not be the necessary antecedent of social competence because many of these outcomes also result from styles of parenting (i.e., harmonious and nonconforming styles) that do not include this form of influence as a component.

One means of reconciling these differing opinions is to consider the *specific kind* of control attempt used rather than simply the magnitude of control applied (Baumrind, 1983; Rollins & Thomas, 1979). *Parental induction*, for example, is one form of a parental control attempt in which reason is applied to influence the behavior and psychological characteristics of adolescents. This type of influence attempt is used by parents to explain how an adolescent's actions have either positive or negative consequences for both others and themselves (Hoffman, 1980; Maccoby & Martin, 1983; Rollins & Thomas, 1979; Staub, 1979). The lack of imposition of arbitrary authority is a special feature of induction that distinguishes it from punitive behaviors. This absence of forcefulness implies that adolescents have the opportunity to engage in two-way communication and express viewpoints that differ from their parents' perspectives. Consequently the use of induction creates a climate in which "social influence" becomes a bidirectional process between parents and adolescents (Peterson & Rollins, 1987).

Contrary to the use of more authoritarian behaviors by parents, induction is less likely to elicit feelings of hostility and resistance from the adolescent. Inductive techniques are more likely to be viewed as "minimally sufficient" control rather than the "functionally superfluous pressure" that is applied with punitive influence attempts (Baumrind, 1983; Rollins & Thomas, 1979; Smith, 1986). Correspondingly, parental induction is often viewed as predicting the development of reasoning abilities and dimensions of social competence involving concern for others. For example, prosocial behavior and moral development are facilitated by the use of inductive reasoning that focuses on the consequences of adolescents' action for others (Hoffman, 1970, 1980). Thus parental induction facilitates moral development and prosocial behavior through the process of internalizing the parent's rationales, by providing explanations about the experiences, and by stimulating sensitivity to the circumstances of others (Hoffman, 1980).

Current research also suggests that parental induction may facilitate higher self-esteem in adolescents (Coopersmith, 1967; Openshaw & Thomas, 1986; Openshaw, Thomas, & Rollins, 1983). The use of induction as a child-rearing behavior often transmits to adolescents a recognition of their ability (a) to engage in dialogues with parents, (b) to be treated with respect (i.e., not arbitrarily), (c) to evaluate the consequences of their behavior for others and themselves, and (d) to make decisions based on these judgments. In short, induction enhances adolescents self-esteem by communicating parental confidence in youthful abilities to understand and cope successfully with the social environment (Peterson & Rollins, 1987).

Parental induction also may be an important contributor to the balance that many adolescents establish between autonomy and conformity in reference to parents (Baumrind, 1978, 1980). The use of induction may enhance autonomy, on the one hand, because it is a form of control that refrains from imposing the will of parents on the young. As such, induction facilitates autonomy by allowing adolescents to assert their own will and offer perspectives that contrast with the viewpoints of parents. Yet, at the same time, induction also encourages conformity to parents through its use as a means of communicating expectations to adolescents (Rollins & Thomas, 1979). Consistent with this idea, investigators have reported that adolescents whose parents use rational control are often both compliant when parents are present and internally responsive to parent's expectations for various attitudes and behaviors (Elder, 1963; Peterson, Rollins, & Thomas, 1985).

Coercion or Punitiveness

Although the timeworn aphorism "spare the rod and spoil the child" continues to influence how we raise the young in our society, there is little evidence that coercive or punitive behaviors facilitate the development of social competence in the young. Specifically, coercive or punitive behavior consists of either verbal or physical attempts to apply firm control without the benefit of rational explanations (Hoffman, 1980; Peterson, Rollins, & Thomas, 1985). Child-rearing behaviors of this kind involve the application of arbitrary force that elicits hostility and tendencies in the young to resist parental influence (Cartwright, 1959; Rollins & Thomas, 1979). Although parents may use punitive approaches to change youthful behavior in the short term, there is mounting evidence that coercive strategies are counterproductive for encouraging long-term features of social competence (Hoffman, 1980; Martin, 1975; Peterson, Rollins, & Thomas, 1985). Furthermore, the efficacy of parental punitiveness diminishes considerably with older children and adolescents as cultural norms increasingly fail to legitimize its use and parents have less advantage in size and strength (Smith, 1986). As such, it is likely that parental coercion is perceived by adolescents as "functionally superfluous pressure" that encourages compliance to externally present authority rather than the attainment of self-responsibility through the internalization of norms (Kelman, 1961; Lepper, 1981; Lewis, 1983; Peterson, Rollins, & Thomas, 1985).

Although research indicates that parents who use coercive behavior may make their adolescents less responsive, this "turning away" does not mean that punitiveness promotes the dimension of social competence referred to as autonomy from parents (Peterson, 1986, 1987). Instead, the use of coercive behavior may promote a "separation process" in which there is failure to maintain a balance between progress toward autonomy and continual ties with parents. Parents who make consistent use of coercion often elicit feelings of rejection from adolescents rather than "guiding" the young toward independence within the context of positive relationships.

Coerciveness within the parent-child/early adolescent relationship also has been studied from a bidirectional perspective in the extended research program of Gerald Patterson and associates (Patterson, 1976, 1979, 1980, 1982, 1986; Patterson & Cobb, 1971, 1973). Specifically, this work has focused on families with children and preadolescents who are classified as antisocial or "out of control" by their parents, school authorities, and the court system. The central assumption of this work is that parents who fail to punish "everyday" or minor coercive behavior actually allow interaction sequences to develop that serve as the basis for training in more serious forms of aggression. As part of this escalating "coercion process," family members engage in patterned exchanges of behaviors that increasingly become aversive.

Several factors contributing to the onset of coercive processes include unskilled parenting, children or adolescents having difficult temperaments, stressful or disruptive events, and substance abuse by parents. Of special importance is the process of escalation that occurs within the parent-youth relationship as adverse behaviors of a trivial nature provide an initial learning base for the later development of high-amplitude aggressive exchanges (Patterson, 1982, 1986). For older children and younger adolescents, the escalation of coercion is enhanced most commonly through a three-step process of escape-avoidance conditioning (i.e., negative reinforcement) that consists of (a) an attack episode, (b) a counterattack episode, and (c) a positive outcome. Youngsters from distressed families show a regular progression from learning noncompliance to the acquisition of behavior that is physically assaultive. The effects of such coercive interchanges within distressed families, in turn, contribute to deficits in important aspects of social and cognitive competence such as lower self-esteem, antisocial behavior, problematic peer relationships, and poor academic performance (Patterson, 1982, 1986).

Other Forms of Control Attempts

Two additional forms of parental control attempts—love withdrawal and commands—have received some attention as predictors of adolescent social competence (Hoffman, 1970; Maccoby & Martin, 1983; Rollins & Thomas, 1979; Smith, 1983, 1986, 1988). Parental commands are imperative statements directed toward adolescents and not accompanied by punishment or overt threat of punishment (Smith, 1986). Love withdrawal, on the other hand, refers to disciplinary behavior used by parents that threatens to either withdraw or disconnect the affectionate bond with the adolescent (Hoffman, 1980; Steinmetz, 1979). Both of these control attempts may have implications for the delicate balance that many adolescents maintain between connectedness and autonomy in reference to parents.

Love withdrawal techniques such as scolding, isolating teenagers, and refusing to speak to the young are used to manipulate the adolescent's dependency needs and fears about losing the parent's emotional support. Consequently withdrawal of love often is used to keep adolescents responsive to parental perspectives (e.g., conformity and moral internalization), inhibit movements toward autonomy, and reverse youthful tendencies to deviate from parental expectations (Maccoby & Martin, 1983; Smith, 1983). Furthermore, love withdrawal is bidirectional in nature, due to its use by adolescents as well as parents (Smith, 1986). Just as parents seek to influence the young by manipulating dependency needs, teenagers may pout, communicate distance or avoidance, and play to the emotional bonds existing between parents and offspring.

Commands, on the other hand, are influence techniques used by parents for situations in which the primary goal is to gain compliance in the short term. Parents use commands for immediate impact during encounters concerning the independence behavior of adolescents. Although commands can be aversive to adolescents when parents are viewed as having a history of punitiveness, many of these control attempts are viewed as less repugnant than coercive behavior when parents are viewed as exercising "legitimate authority" and as avoiding the use of punitive behavior. Furthermore, the absence of an overtly punitive dimension to commands seems to evoke less hostility and resistance to parental authority from adolescents (Smith, 1986, 1988).

Despite such results, further work on both of these variables is needed before firm conclusions can be made. As a predictor of youthful social competence, for example, love withdrawal has produced inconclusive results (Hoffman, 1970; Peterson & Rollins, 1987; Rollins & Thomas, 1979). Finally, work on parental commands has been initiated only recently and additional research is needed (Smith, 1988) to produce a clear pattern of results.

Support

Parental support, whether conceptualized as general support, physical affection, acceptance, or companionship, is a diverse category of gestures or behaviors that communicate warmth, affection, and rapport and convey a feeling of worth (Barber & Thomas, 1986; Becker, 1964; Rollins & Thomas, 1979). Support has often been operationalized in a diversity of studies as hugging, touching, praising, approving, encouraging, helping, cooperating, expressing endearment, and spending positive time together (Barber & Thomas, 1986; Ellis, Thomas, & Rollins, 1976). An interesting paradox is that parental support seems to foster both connectedness within the parent-adolescent relationship and sufficient autonomy for the young to engage in successful interpersonal associations beyond family boundaries. Failure to receive sufficient levels of support hinders the development of social competence by contributing to feelings of separation, the expression of hostility and aggression, an absence of self-confidence, emotional unresponsiveness, and disturbed peer relations (Becker, 1964; Rollins & Thomas, 1979).

Several studies have reported that supportive child-rearing behavior predicts adolescent conformity to parents' expectations in a positive manner (Coopersmith, 1967; Gecas & Schwalbe, 1986; Openshaw, Thomas, & Rollins, 1983; Peterson, Southworth, & Peters, 1983; Rosenberg, 1965; Thomas, Gecas, Weigert & Rooney, 1974). Because parental support communicates that adolescents are valued and accepted, the young often seek to increase the frequency of this behavior by accommodating their actions to parental expectations (Aronfreed, 1969; Peterson, Rollins, & Thomas, 1985; Rollins & Thomas, 1979). Furthermore, nurturant or emotionally supportive relationships encourage the young to identify with parents and incorporate their attitudes, values, and role expectations. Parental support, therefore, often contributes to moral internalization and voluntary responsiveness to parental expectations (e.g., internalized conformity; Henry, Wilson, & Peterson, 1989; Hoffman, 1980; Peterson, Rollins, & Thomas, 1985; Staub, 1979).

In addition to this continued responsiveness to parents, parental support also provides the paradoxical feature of predicting a seemingly opposite development—the progress of adolescents toward autonomy. Specifically, parent-adolescent relationships characterized by considerable nurturance provide a secure base from which the young can explore and meet the many challenges that exist beyond family boundaries (Peterson & Stivers, 1986). For many adolescents, parental support is an important feature of the social environment that contributes to a balance between continued ties with parents and gradual progress toward independence.

Parental support may also play a key role in the development of self-esteem in adolescents. Because support conveys information to the young about the extent to which they have inherent worth, the self-esteem of adolescents is fostered by the use of this behavior. Supportive actions by parents also suggest that parents trust and consider the young to be responsible persons. The communication of such confidence and warmth by parents, in turn, often has favorable consequences for the self-esteem of adolescents (Bachman, 1970; Cooper, Holman, & Braithwaite, 1983; Openshaw, Thomas, & Rollins, 1983; Peterson, Southworth, & Peters, 1983; Rosenberg, 1965; Thomas, Gecas, Weigert, & Rooney, 1974).

An important point is that the cross-sectional and correlational designs that characterize much of the parental support research do not establish the direction of influence in the parent-child dyad (Bell & Harper, 1977; Peterson & Rollins, 1987). Consequently this "social mold" research on parental support can be reinterpreted as an "adolescent" rather than a "parent effect." For example, adolescents who exhibit such socially competent behavior as conformity to parent's expectations or prosocial behavior may receive favorable (or supportive) responses from parents because their actions are valued and meet their elders' expectations. Perhaps the most accurate interpretation of these "direction of influence issues," however, is that parental support and dimensions of adolescent social competence are mutually influential. Future investigators should also examine the extent to which supportive behavior by adolescents may have consequences for the social and personality characteristics of parents (Demo, Small, & Savin-Williams, 1987).

OBSERVATIONAL LEARNING

Another form of socialization is concerned with the possibility that adolescents may learn from behaviors that parents model unintentionally rather than from actions used deliberately by their elders to exercise influence. According to the perspective, socialization occurs on a moment-to-moment basis as parents serve as models who teach their offspring components of social competence or incompetence by example.

The imitation-modeling tradition, originated by Albert Bandura and associates (Bandura, 1976; Bandura & Walters, 1963), identifies a process through which the young learn and reproduce behavior through observations of behavior by parents (and other models). In this perspective adolescents are viewed as active mediators who observe the actions of others, acquire information, and develop expectancies that guide their behavior and internal standards in subsequent situations. Children and adolescents acquire these new characteristics (a) vicariously, by attending to reinforcements received by others (i.e., vicarious reinforcement); (b) by defining situations in a manner that provides them with their own rewards (i.e., self-reinforcement); and (c) by anticipating their own futures. Such capacities allow the young to represent the characteristics of models (i.e., parents) internally and reproduce a complicated array of behaviors (e.g., aggressive behavior) and internal qualities (e.g., self-esteem attributes) that models exhibit. Children and adolescents learn to copy the behavior of others by defining situations they observe as rewarding and especially by attending to the positive consequences befalling others during social interaction (e.g., vicarious reinforcement). Various aspects of social competence or incompetence such as aggression, social behavior, self-esteem, and prosocial behavior are reported to be products of observational learning in the young (Bandura, 1976; Smith, 1986).

Specific attributes of models (e.g., parents), such as being perceived to be both nurturant and powerful, are most effective in prompting others to imitate their behavior (Bandura, 1976; Bandura & Huston, 1961). Any modeling of a parent's behavior, of course, is filtered through a young person's existing social and personality characteristics and is largely a product of the adolescent's cumulative history of experiences.

PARENTAL POWER

Although parental behavior and observational learning deal with influence that is *actualized* through overt behavior, another means of influence, referred to as *parental power*, is concerned with the *potential ability* of parents to influence the young. Parental power is the subjective assessment by adolescents of their elder's attributes that does not have to be used for the behavior and internal states of the young to be affected. Conceptualized as interpersonal resources that a person is perceived as *capable* of using in a relationship, power refers to distinctive social bases of influence that one person attributes to another (French & Raven, 1959). As such, parental power is the *perception* by adolescents that mothers and fathers are competent in specific ways that have considerable importance within the parent-youth relationship (Peterson, 1986; Peterson & Rollins, 1987).

The power of a parent in relation to an adolescent is a product of the young person's perception of their elder's interpersonal resources. That is, the power of a parent resides in the "eyes of the beholder"—or in the adolescent's subjective assessment of the parent's ability to exercise influence within their relationship. Because power is based on subjective interpretations, therefore, a very different assessment of a parent's interpersonal resources may be held by a third party outside a specific parent-adolescent relationship. Thus the perceived power of a parent may differ from one relationship to another.

In addition to its subjective nature, power is also a multidimensional concept (Cromwell & Olson, 1975; French & Raven, 1959) with several dimensions or forms of power, identified as follows: (a) *reward power,* or the ability to supply gratifications; (b) *coercive power,* or the ability to administer punishments or adverse consequences; (c) *legitimate power,* or the perceived right to exercise influence based on social norms; (d) *expert power,* or the potential to provide useful information; and (e) *referent power,* or the potential to function as an identification object or significant other (French & Raven, 1959; Henry, Wilson, & Peterson, 1989; Peterson, Rollins, & Thomas, 1985; Smith, 1970, 1983, 1986).

These dimensions of parental power have been reported to predict such dimensions of social competence as conformity to parents, identification with parents, and autonomy in reference to parents (Henry, Wilson, & Peterson, 1989; McDonald, 1977, 1979, 1980; Peterson, Rollins, & Thomas, 1985; Smith, 1970, 1983, 1986). Adolescents are likely to be responsive and conform to parents who are perceived as having the potential to function as referents (referent power), provide useful information (expert power), offer gratifications (reward power), inflict adverse consequences (coercive power), and exercise authority based on social norms (legitimate power) (Wilson, & Peterson, 1989; Peterson, Rollins, & Thomas, 1985; Smith, 1970, 1983, 1986).

Although appearing contradictory, the same dimensions of perceived parental power may contribute to the development of autonomy in adolescents as well as continued responsiveness to parents. Specifically, adolescents are likely to become autonomous within the context of continued ties with parents (i.e., not "separate" from parents) when they perceive their elders as having expert, legitimate, referent, and reward power. Coercive power, on the other hand, is the only dimension of potential influence that either inhibits youthful autonomy or contributes to a process of separation (Peterson, 1986).

Recent research and scholarship also has indicated that power may be examined bidirectionally as a "child effect" as well as a "parent effect" within the parent-youth relationship (Peterson & Rollins, 1987; Smith, 1983, 1986). Specifically, a recent study has indicated that parents viewed their adolescents as having reward, coercive, expert, legitimate, and referent power. Such results indicated, in turn, that potential influence is a "two-way street," with both adolescents *and* parents viewing each other as having interpersonal resources (Peterson, 1986). Other results from the same research indicated that adolescents who were perceived by parents as high in expert, legitimate, reward, and referent power also were viewed by their elders as functioning in an autonomous manner from parents (Peterson, 1986). Thus autonomy may be earned by adolescents and granted by parents to the extent that adolescents are perceived as possessing interpersonal resources (i.e., power) within the parent-youth relationship.

FAMILY SYSTEMS DYNAMICS

Although much of the research on adolescent social competence has been focused on the parent-youth dyad, other scholarship has addressed the processes and patterns that are part of the larger family system. Research and theory from the family systems perspective has concentrated on the interaction patterns and interrelationships of adolescents, parents, and other family members on a wide range of systemic variables, including family cohesion, adaptability, conflict resolution, family hierarchies, and communication patterns. Generally, research on these topics indicates that family processes influence adolescent social competence in varying degrees, depending upon the specific dimension that is studied (Amato & Ochiltree, 1986). This section reviews the current scholarship on dimensions of family systems that are associated with aspects of adolescent social competence.

Family Cohesion

The work on family cohesion has developed from many sources. Generally, *cohesion* refers to the emotional bonding (closeness or distance) that family members experience in reference to each other (Olson, Russell, & Sprenkle, 1983). Several bipolar terms often have been used to convey similar concepts: *separateness* versus *connectedness* (Hess & Handel, 1959), emotional *divorce* versus emotional *fusion* (Bowen, 1960), *centrifugal* effects versus *centripetal* effects (Stierlin, 1974), and *disengagement* versus *enmeshment* (Minuchin, 1974).

Olson (1986) and colleagues have developed both a conceptual and a measurement model for a cohesion dimension that varies in terms of the categories: disengagement, separateness, connectedness, and enmeshment. A major result of this research indicates that a moderate level of cohesion seems to provide the most conducive environment for the development of adolescent social competence (Grotevant & Cooper, 1986). Families that balance these processes often create environments in which adolescents demonstrate social competence through negotiation, effective communication, responsibility for self, cooperation, identity formation, role-taking skills, and positive goals (Grotevant & Cooper, 1986; Olson, 1986).

In addition to Olson's work, Minuchin, Rosman, and Baker (1978) report that adolescents who demonstrated problematic behavior, including anorexia nervosa and uncontrolled diabetic attacks, often were from families who were enmeshed. Processes within these families inhibited social competence by providing little room for individuality or separateness as family members engaged in conversations, assumed they felt what others were experiencing, and attempted to function as single units (Minuchin,

1974). Such family environments make it difficult for adolescents to make progress toward autonomy (Grotevant, Cooper, & Condon, 1983).

In contrast, adolescents find it easier to explore worlds outside the family, develop close relationships, exhibit less depressive affect (Feldman, Rubenstein, & Rubin, 1988), and develop more mature adult relationships after leaving home (White, Spiesman, & Costos, 1983) when a balance between separateness and connectedness is developed within the family system. The development of autonomy also is related to friendship and dating identity, both of which are influenced by family processes. Girls, for example, seem to explore friendship identities as they develop greater separateness, but boys tend to explore both friendship and dating identities within the context of connectedness (Cooper & Grotevant, 1987). Given that autonomy is viewed as occurring much later by parents than adolescents (Feldman & Quatman, 1988), it becomes even more difficult when families manifest other obstacles such as interaction patterns that inhibit the development of autonomy.

Family Change or Adaptability

Another important variable in Olson's Circumplex Model (Olson, Sprenkle, & Russell, 1979) is the dimension of family change or adaptability (Olson, 1986), which varies in terms of the categories: rigid, structured, flexible, and chaotic. This concept describes the diverse means through which families deal with rules, roles, negotiation, discipline, and leadership. Olson and colleagues conclude that moderate levels of adaptability, or a balance between rigid styles (i.e., overly structured, little change) and chaotic styles (i.e., little structure, possibly constant change), provides the best environment for adolescent development (Olson, 1986). This moderately structured environment also seems consistent with child-rearing approaches in which parents outline rules, provide rationales, and allow adolescents significant freedom to make their own choices. Such findings also correspond with those from a study by Minuchin, Rosman, and Baker (1978) on problem adolescents from families that were rigid and resistant to change in which the adolescents were allowed few choices and were not encouraged to be independent. Parents from these families often relied on forms of verbal persuasion, including appeals to their teenager's sense of morality, altruism, and esteem.

Conflict Resolution

The manner in which conflict is handled in families seems to have important implications for the development of adolescent competence. The study by Minuchin, Rosman, and Baker (1978) also examined conflict resolution strategies in families with problem adolescents and reported that overt conflict tended to be avoided in these families, while covert conflict was rampant, which made it difficult to resolve such issues. These adolescents also tended to be poorer at problem-solving and often would interrupt interaction through acting out or humor to lower the intensity and take the focus off potential conflicts. Specific sequences of this kind served to "entrap" the very adolescent behavior that families had wished to decrease.

Although parent-youth conflict occurs to some extent in almost all families, it is of particular significance in families in which conflict occurs either at high levels (Montemayor, 1986) or is avoided and not resolved (Minuchin, Rosman, & Baker, 1978). In both situations there is a tendency for the young not to develop methods or problem-solving strategies that prove useful during adolescence and later in life. In particular, negative emotional patterns, often associated with family conflict, were reported to be associated inversely with good problem-solving skills and other components of adolescent competence (Forgatch, 1989). It is apparent, therefore, that adolescents often fail to learn useful problem-solving skills when families are characterized by negative emotional patterns and use extreme measures to avoid conflict. Furthermore, negative emotional patterns and ineffective problem solving were associated with higher levels of aggression in younger adolescents (Forgatch, 1989).

Family Hierarchy

Family hierarchies are another dimension of the adolescent's immediate social context that may provide insight into the development of social competence. Specifically, this concept refers to the position and status of each member relative to others within the structure of the family system (Madanes, 1981). Minuchin, Rosman, and Baker (1978), for example, have argued that anorexic adolescents are more likely to have families in which boundaries are unclear and the young are involved as part of parental coalitions. These adolescents often become involved in parental conflicts that do not directly involve the young but through which the young often were pulled from one side to the other into coalitions with family members (e.g., parents). Again, adolescent involvement in such cross-generational coalitions or reversed hierarchies appears to inhibit the development of youthful social competence by making it difficult for adolescents to become autonomous and develop separate ego identities (Wood, 1985). In such cases, adolescents tend to be assaultive, have lower individuation from families, report feelings of less control in their lives, achieve less well in college, and become less well adjusted (Kleiman, 1981; Madden & Harbin, 1983; Oltmanns, Broderick, & O'Leary, 1977; Teyber, 1983a, 1983b). In addition, both proximity (interpersonal boundaries) and generational hierarchies (subsystem boundaries) appear to be related to competent behavior in target adolescents and their siblings (Wood, 1985).

Communication

The specific ways that family members communicate with one another is a final process that is associated with the development of adolescent social competence. Parents and adolescents develop their own sets of meanings, styles, and patterns that are communicated when they interact, respectively, in the same way (Leigh, 1986). These meanings and patterns convey information but also define relationships, boundaries, and networks; set rules about interactions; and establish the pace of change within families (Galvin & Brommel, 1982; Leigh, 1986). Particular styles and patterns can be helpful for the development of adolescent competence, while others tend not to facilitate or even to hinder development. In Olson's Circumplex Model, for example, communication is described as the mediating factor contributing to levels of cohesion and adaptability within families (Olson, 1986).

Specific communication styles used by families have been characterized as "positive," or supportive communication and "negative," or defensive communication (Alexander, 1973). Supportive communications tend to facilitate spontaneous problem solving, genuine information giving and seeking, empathic understanding, and equity between family members. Defensive communications, on the other hand, tend to involve judgments, dogmatism, name calling, blaming, or the acquisition of control or superiority (Gibb, 1961). In families in which defensive communication runs high, parents and adolescents also tend to have fewer conflict resolution skills and problem-solving capabilities and more threatening and punishing experiences as well as nonproductive family systems (Alexander & Barton, 1976). Alexander (1973) also found that, within families in which adolescents had run away previously, both parents and adolescents were more likely to use defensive communications and less likely to use supportive communications. Family members also were more likely to reciprocate with defensive rather than supportive communications, and such styles were difficult to alter (Alexander & Barton, 1976). Furthermore, these styles appeared to be continued from one generation to the next (Buerkel-Rothfuss & Yerby, 1981).

SUMMARY AND IMPLICATIONS

This chapter has reviewed the main issues and variables related to family influences on the development of adolescent social competence. We have examined research on family structural variables, parental characteristics, and parenting styles including support, control, modeling, and power as well as family systems variables. Such bodies of literature, although dealing with many different elements, also share common issues that suggest broad directions for intervention. In concluding this chapter, therefore, the following principles are provided for interventionists to change family environments so that adolescent social competence might be enhanced.

(1) Parenting programs and family therapy strategies that encourage at least moderate levels of nurturance in the parent-youth relationship and supportive rather than defensive communication in families may contribute to moderate levels of family cohesion and adaptability and, in turn, enhance social competence in adolescents (Alexander & Barton, 1976; Guerney, Guerney, & Cooney, 1985). Furthermore, parental support is a key predictor of such

dimensions of social competence as continued responsiveness to parents, autonomy, moral internalization, prosocial behavior, and self-esteem.

(2) Intervention programs that encourage firm control that is inductive, which is an important aspect of authoritative parenting, as well as moderate levels of cohesion and change, seem to foster adolescent social competence. All of these concepts share the ideas that social competence is most likely to result when forms of control are used that maintain ties with parents while being flexible enough so that individuality exists and change can proceed in families. Adolescents from such environments seem to maintain an effective balance between autonomy and connectedness in reference to parents. Firm control also seems to have implications for such dimensions of social competence as self-esteem, prosocial behavior, social perspective taking, problem-solving abilities, and interpersonal skills.

(3) Useful interventions may include family therapy and educational strategies that seek to enhance awareness of feelings, problem-solving skills, effective communication styles, negotiation, and conflict resolution strategies. Such processes may provide direct training to adolescents and other family members in skills that are components of social competence and maintain the important balance between moderate levels of family cohesiveness and adaptability.

In conclusion, therefore, it is clear that families have strong influences on many of the indicators of adaptive qualities in adolescence. Additional research is needed to determine more specifically how families and adolescents influence each other and how such influences relate to other significant influences such as friends, close relationships, and school environments.

REFERENCES

Adams, B. N. (1974). Birth-order: A critical review. *Sociometry, 35,* 411-439.

Adams, G. R. (1983). Social competence during adolescence: Social sensitivity, locus of control, empathy, and peer popularity. *Journal of Youth and Adolescence, 12*(3), 203-211.

Adler, A. (1928). Characteristics of the first, second, and third child. *Children, 3,* 14-52.

Alexander, J. F. (1973). Defensive and supportive communication in normal and deviant families. *Journal of Consulting and Clinical Psychology, 40*, 223-231.

Alexander, J. F., & Barton, C. (1976). Behavioral systems therapy for families. In D. H. Olson (Ed.), *Treating relationships*. Lake Mills, IA: Graphic.

Amato, P. R., & Ochiltree, G. (1986). Family resources and the development of child competence. *Journal of Marriage and the Family, 48*, 47-56.

Aronfreed, J. (1969). The concept of internalization. In D. A. Goslin (Ed.), *Handbook of socialization theory and research*. Chicago: Rand McNally.

Bachman, J. G. (1970). *Youth in transition: Vol. 2. The impact of family background and intelligence on tenth grade boys*. Ann Arbor, MI: Institute for Social Research.

Bandura, A. (1976). *Social learning theory*. Englewood Cliffs, NJ: Prentice-Hall.

Bandura, A., & Huston, A. (1961). Identification as a process of incidental learning. *Journal of Abnormal and Social Psychology, 63*, 311-318.

Bandura, A., & Walters, L. H. (1959). *Adolescent aggression: A study of the influences of child-training practices and family interrelation*. New York: Ronald.

Bandura, A., & Walters, R. H. (1963). *Social learning and personality development*. New York: Holt, Rinehart & Winston.

Barber, B. K., & Thomas, D. L. (1986). Dimensions of fathers' and mothers' supportive behavior: The case for physical affection. *Journal of Marriage and the Family, 48*, 783-794.

Baumrind, D. (1971). Current patterns of parental authority. *Developmental Psychology Monograph, 4*(1, Pt. 2), 1-103.

Baumrind, D. (1972). Socialization and instrumental competence in young children. In E. Hartup (Ed.), *The young child: Reviews of research* (pp. 202-224). Washington, DC: National Association for the Education of Young Children.

Baumrind, D. (1975). Early socialization and adolescent competence. In S. E. Dragastin & G. Elder, Jr. (Eds.), *Adolescence in the life cycle* (pp. 117-143). Washington, DC: Hemisphere.

Baumrind, D. (1978). Parental disciplinary patterns and social competence in children. *Youth and Society, 9*(3), 239-276.

Baumrind, D. (1980). New directions in socialization research. *American Psychologist, 35*, 639-652.

Baumrind, D. (1983). Rejoinder to Lewis's reinterpretation of parental firm control effects: Are authoritative families really harmonious? *Psychological Bulletin, 94*(1), 132-144.

Baumrind, D. (1987). A developmental perspective on adolescent risk taking in contemporary America. In C. Irwin (Ed.), *Adolescent social behavior and health: New directions for child development* (pp. 93-125). San Francisco: Jossey-Bass.

Baumrind, D., & Black, A. E. (1967). Socialization practices associated with dimensions of competence in preschool boys and girls. *Child Development, 38*, 291-327.

Becker, W. C. (1964). Consequences of different kinds of parental discipline. In M. L. Hoffman & L. Hoffman (Eds.), *Review of child development research* (Vol. 1, pp. 169-208). Chicago: University of Chicago Press.

Bell, R. Q., & Harper, L. V. (1977). *Child effects on adults*. Hillsdale, NJ: Lawrence Erlbaum.

Blechman, E. A. (1982). Are children with one parent at psychological risk? A methodological review. *Journal of Marriage and the Family, 44*, 179-195.

Block, J. H. (1973). Conceptions of sex roles: Some cross-cultural and longitudinal perspectives. *American Psychologist, 28*, 512-526.

Block, J. H. (1980). Another look at sex differentiation in the socialization behaviors of mothers and fathers. In F. Denmark & J. Sherman (Eds.), *Psychology of women: Future directions of research.* New York: Psychological Dimensions.

Bios, P. (1962). *On adolescence: A psychoanalytic interpretation.* New York: Free Press.

Bossard, J. H. S., & Boll, E. S. (1956). *The large family system: An original study in the sociology of family behavior.* Philadelphia: University of Pennsylvania Press.

Bowen, M. (1960). A family concept of schizophrenia. In D. Jackson (Ed.), *The etiology of schizophrenia.* New York: Basic Books.

Bronfenbrenner, U. (1970). *Two worlds of childhood: U.S. and U.S.S.R.* New York: Russell Sage.

Buerkel-Rothfuss, N. L., & Yerby, J. (1981, November). *Two studies in member perception of family communication.* Paper presented at the annual meeting of the National Council on Family Relations, Milwaukee.

Burns, G. L., & Farina, A. (1984). Social competence and adjustment. *Journal of Social and Personal Relationships, 1*, 99-113.

Burr, W. R., & Lowe, T. A. (1987). Olson's circumplex model: A review and extension. *Family Science Review, 1*, 5-22.

Cartwright, D. (1959). A field theoretical conception of power. In D. Cartwright (Ed.), *Studies in social power* (pp. 183-200). Ann Arbor: University of Michigan Press.

Condry, J. C. (1984). Gender identity and social competence. *Sex Roles, 11*, 485-511.

Cooper, C. R., & Grotevant, H. D. (1987). Gender issues in the interface of family experience and adolescents' friendship and dating identity. *Journal of Youth and Adolescence, 16*, 247-264.

Cooper, J. F., Holman, J., & Braithwaite, S. (1983). Self-esteem and family cohesion: The child's perspective and adjustment. *Journal of Marriage and the Family, 45*, 153-159.

Coopersmith, S. (1967). *The antecedents of self-esteem.* San Francisco: Freeman.

Cromwell, R. E., & Olson, D. H. (1975). Multi-disciplinary perspectives of power. In D. H. Olson & R. E. Cromwell (Eds.), *Power in families* (pp. 15-37). New York: Russell Sage.

Crouter, A. C., Belsky, J., & Spanier, G. B. (1984). The family context of child development: Divorce and maternal employment. *Annals of Child Development, 1*, 201-238.

Demo, D. H., Small, S. A., & Savin-Williams, L. C. (1987). Family relations and the self-esteem of adolescents and their parents. *Journal of Marriage and the Family, 49*, 705-715.

DeTurk, M. A., & Miller, G. R. (1983). Adolescent perception of parental persuasive message strategies. *Journal of Marriage and the Family, 45*, 543-552.

Dodge, K. A., Pettit, G. L., McClaskey, C. L., & Brown, M. M. (1986). Social competence in children. *Monographs of the Society for Research in Child Development, 51*(2), 1-85.

Dornbusch, S. M., Carlsmith, J. M., Bushwall, S. J., Ritter, P. L., Leiderman, H., Hastorf, A. H., & Gross, R. T. (1985). Single parents, extended households, and the control of adolescents. *Child Development, 56*, 326-341.

Douvan, E., & Adelson, J. (1966). *The adolescent experience.* New York: John Wiley.

Dyk, P. A. H., & Adams, G. R. (1987). The association between identity development and intimacy during adolescence: A theoretical treatise. *Journal of Adolescent Research, 2*(3), 223-235.

Elder, G. H. (1963). Parental power legitimation and its effect on the adolescent. *Sociometry, 26,* 50-65.

Elder, G. H., & Bowerman, C. W. (1963). Family structure and childrearing patterns: The effect of family size and sex composition. *American Sociological Review, 28,* 891-905.

Ellis, G. J., Thomas, D. L., & Rollins, B. C. (1976). Measuring parental support: The interrelationship of three measures. *Journal of Marriage and the Family, 38,* 713-722.

Ernst, C., & Angst, J. (1983). *Birth order: Its influence on personality.* New York: Springer-Verlag.

Feldman, S. S., & Quatman, T. (1988). Factors influencing age expectations for adolescent autonomy: A study of early adolescents and parents. *Journal of Early Adolescence, 8,* 325-344.

Feldman, S. S., Rubenstein, J. L., & Rubin, C. (1988). Depressive affect and restraint in early adolescents: Relationships with family process, and friendship support. *Journal of Early Adolescence, 8,* 279-298.

Foote, N., & Cottrell, B. (1955). *Identity and interpersonal competence.* Chicago: University of Chicago Press.

Forgatch, M. S. (1989). Patterns and outcome in family problem solving: The disrupting effect of negative emotion. *Journal of Marriage and the Family, 51,* 115-124.

French, J. R. P., & Raven, B. H. (1959). The bases of social power. In D. Cartwright (Ed.), *Studies in social power* (pp. 118-149). Ann Arbor: University of Michigan Press.

Freud, A. (1965). *Normality and pathology in childhood.* New York: International Universities Press.

Galvin, K. M., & Brommel, B. J. (1982). *Family communication.* Glenview, IL: Scott, Foresman.

Gecas, V. (1971). Parental behavior and dimensions of adolescent self-evaluation. *Sociometry, 34,* 466-482.

Gecas, V. (1976). The socialization and child care roles. In F. I. Nye (Ed.), *Role structure and the analysis of the family.* Beverly Hills, CA: Sage.

Gecas, V. (1979). The influence of social class on socialization. In W. R. Burr, R. Hill, F. I. Nye, & I. L. Reiss (Eds.), *Contemporary theories about the family* (Vol. 1). New York: Free Press.

Gecas, V. (1981). Contexts of socialization. In M. Rosenberg & R. Turner (Eds.), *Sociological perspectives in social psychology.* New York: Basic Books.

Gecas, V. (1982). The self-concept. In R. H. Turner & I. F. Short (Eds.), *Annual review of sociology* (Vol. 8, pp. 1-33). Palo Alto, CA: Annual Reviews.

Gecas, V., & Pasley, K. (1984). Birth order and self-concept in adolescence. *Journal of Youth and Adolescence, 12,* 521-537.

Gecas, V., & Schwalbe, M. L. (1986). Parental behavior and adolescent self-esteem. *Journal of Marriage and the Family, 48,* 37-46.

Gibb, J. R. (1961). Defensive communications. *Journal of Communication, 3,* 141-148.

Gilligan, C. (1982). *In a different voice: Psychological theory and women's development.* Cambridge, MA: Harvard University Press.

Gilligan, C. (1987). Adolescent development reconsidered. In C. Irwin (Ed.), *Adolescent social behavior and health: New directions for child development* (pp. 63-92). San Francisco: Jossey-Bass.

Goldfried, M. R., & d'Zurilla, T. J. (1969). A behavioral-analytic method for assessing competence. In C. D. Spielberger (Ed.), *Current topics in clinical and community psychology* (Vol. 1, pp. 151-219). New York: Academic Press.

Greenberger, E., & Sorensen, A. B. (1974). Toward a concept of psychosocial maturity. *Journal of Youth and Adolescence, 3,* 329-358.

Gresham, F. M., & Reschly, D. J. (1987). Dimensions of social competence: Method factors in the reassessment of adaptive behavior, social skills, and peer acceptance. *Journal of School Psychology, 23,* 367-381.

Grotevant, H. D. (1983). The contribution of the family to the facilitation of identity formation in early adolescence. *Journal of Early Adolescence, 3,* 225-237.

Grotevant, H. D., & Cooper, C. R. (1986). Individuation in family relationships: A perspective on individual differences in the development of identity and role-taking skill in adolescence. *Human Development, 29,* 82-100.

Grotevant, H. D., Cooper, C. R., & Condon, S. M. (1983). Individuality and connectedness in the family as a context for adolescent identity formation and role-taking skill. In H. D. Grotevant & C. R. Cooper (Eds.), *Adolescent development in the family* (pp. 43-59). San Francisco: Jossey-Bass.

Guerney, B. G., Jr., Guerney, L., & Cooney, T. (1985). Marital and family problem prevention and enrichment programs. In L. L'Abate (Ed.), *The handbook of family psychology and therapy* (Vol. 2, pp. 1179-1217). Homewood, IL: Dorsey.

Gurman, A. S., Kniskern, D. P., & Pinsof, W. M. (1986). Research on the process and outcome of marital and family therapy. In S. L. Garfield & A. E. Bergin (Eds.), *Handbook of psychotherapy and behavior change* (pp. 565-624). New York: John Wiley.

Hall, G. S. (1904). *Adolescence.* New York: Appleton.

Hauser, S. T., Powers, S. I., Noam, G., & Bowlds, M. K. (1987). Family interiors or adolescent ego development trajectories. *Family Perspective, 21*(4), 263-282.

Hauser, S. T., Powers, S. I., Noam, G. G., & Jacobson, A. M. (1984). Familial contexts of adolescent ego development. *Child Development, 55,* 195-213.

Hayley, J. (1980). *Leaving home.* New York: McGraw-Hill.

Hazelrigg, M. D., Cooper, H. M., & Borduin, C. M. (1987). Evaluating the effectiveness of family therapies: An integrative review and analysis. *Psychological Bulletin, 101,* 428-442.

Healy, J. M., & Stewart, A. J. (1984). Adaptation to life changes in adolescence. In P. Karoly & J. J. Steffen (Eds.), *Adolescent behavior disorders: Foundations and contemporary concerns* (Vol. 3, pp. 39-60). Lexington, MA: D. C. Heath.

Henry, C. L., Wilson, L. M., & Peterson, G. W. (1989). Parental power bases and processes as predictors of adolescent conformity. *Journal of Adolescent Research, 4,* 15-32.

Hess, R. D., & Handel, G. (1959). *Family worlds: The psychosocial interior of the family.* Chicago: University of Chicago Press.

Hetherington, E. M. (1965). A developmental study of the effects of sex of the dominant parent on sex-role preference, identification and imitation on children. *Journal of Personality and Social Psychology, 2,* 188-194.

Hetherington, E. M. (1972). Effects of father absence on personality development in adolescent daughters. *Developmental Psychology, 7,* 313-326.

Hetherington, E. M. (1981). Children and divorce. In R. Henderson (Ed.), *Parent-child interaction: Theory, research, and prospects* (pp. 33-58). New York: Academic Press.

Hetherington, E. M. (1984). Stress and coping in children and families. In A. Doyle, D. Gold, & D. S. Moskowitz (Eds.), *Children in families under stress: No. 24. New directions in child development* (pp. 7-33). San Francisco: Jossey-Bass.

Hetherington, E. M., Cox, M., & Cox, R. (1985). Long-term effects of divorce and remarriage on the adjustment of children. *Journal of the American Academy of Child Psychiatry, 24,* 518-530.

Hoffman, M. L. (1970). Moral development. In P. H. Mussen (Ed.), *Carmichael's manual of child psychology* (Vol. 2, pp. 261-359). New York: John Wiley.

Hoffman, M. L. (1977a). Empathy, its development and prosocial implications. *Nebraska Symposium on Motivation* (Vol. 25, pp. 169-218). Lincoln: University of Nebraska.

Hoffman, M. L. (1977b). Moral internalization: Current theory and research. In L. Berkowitz (Ed.), *Advances in experimental social psychology* (Vol. 10, pp. 85-133). New York: Academic Press.

Hoffman, M. L. (1980). Moral development in adolescence. In J. Adelson (Ed.), *Handbook of adolescent psychology.* New York: John Wiley.

Hoffman, M. L. (1982). Development of prosocial motivation: Empathy and guilt. In N. Eisenberg (Ed.), *The development of prosocial behavior* (pp. 281-313). New York: Academic Press.

Hogan, R. (1975). Theoretical egocentrism and the problem of compliance. *American Psychologist, 30,* 533-540.

Hollander, E. P. (1975). Independence, conformity, and civil liberties: Some implications from social psychological research. *Journal of Social Issues, 31,* 55-67.

Jacobson, D., & Ryder, R. (1978). The impact of marital separation/divorce on children: Parent-child separation and child adjustment. *Journal of Divorce, 4,* 341.

Jurich, A. J., & Jones, W. C. (1986). Divorce and the experience of adolescents. In G. K. Leigh & G. W. Peterson (Eds.), *Adolescents in families* (pp. 308-336). Cincinnati, OH: South-Western.

Kammeyer, K. (1967). Birth order as a research variable. *Social Forces, 46,* 71-80.

Kandel, D., & Lesser, G. S. (1972). *Youth in two worlds.* San Francisco: Jossey-Bass.

Kelman, H. C. (1961). Processes of opinion change. *Public Opinion Quarterly, 25,* 57-78.

Kidwell, J. S. (1981). Number of siblings, sibling spacing, sex, and birth order: Their effects on perceived parent-adolescent relationships. *Journal of Marriage and the Family, 44,* 315-332.

Kidwell, J. S. (1982). The neglected birth order: Middleborns. *Journal of Marriage and the Family, 44,* 225-235.

Kleiman, J. J. (1981). Optimal and normal family functioning. *American Journal of Family Therapy, 9,* 37-44.

Kohn, M. L. (1977). *Class and conformity: A study in values* (2nd ed.). Chicago: University of Chicago Press.

Kohn, M. L. (1983). On the transmission of values in the family: A preliminary formulation: In A. C. Kerckhoff (Ed.), *Research in sociology of education and socialization: A research annual.* Greenwich, CT: JAI.

Kohn, M. L., & Schooler, C. (1983). *Work and personality: An inquiry into the impact of social stratification.* Norwood, NJ: Ablex.

Leigh, G. K. (1986). Adolescent involvement in family systems. In G. K. Leigh & G. W. Peterson (Eds.), *Adolescents in families.* Cincinnati, OH: South-Western.

Leigh, G. K., & Peterson, G. W. (1986). *Adolescents in families.* Cincinnati, OH: South-Western.

Lepper, M. R. (1981). Social control processes, attributions of motivation, and the internalization of social values. In E. T. Higgins (Ed.), *Social cognition and social behavior: Developmental perspectives.* Cambridge: Cambridge University Press.

Lerner, R. M. (1987). A life-span perspective for early adolescence. In R. M. Lerner & T. T. Foch (Eds.), *Biological-psychosocial interactions in early adolescence* (pp. 9-34). Hillsdale, NJ: Lawrence Erlbaum.

Lerner, R. M., & Foch, T. T. (1987). Biological-psychological interactions in early adolescence: An overview of the issues. In R. M. Lerner & T. L. Foch (Eds.), *Biological and psychosocial interactions in early adolescence.* Hillsdale, NJ: Lawrence Erlbaum.

Lewis, C. C. (1981). The effects of firm control: A reinterpretation of findings. *Psychological Bulletin, 90,* 547-563.

Longfellow, C. (1979). Divorce in context: Its impact on children. In G. Levinger & O. C. Moles (Eds.), *Divorce and separation: Context, causes and consequences* (pp. 287-306). New York: Basic Books.

Maccoby, E. E. (1980). *Social development: Psychological growth and the parent-child relationship.* New York: Harcourt Brace Jovanovich.

Maccoby, E. E., & Martin, J. A. (1983). Socialization in the context of the family: Parent-child interaction. In E. M. Hetherington (Ed.), *Handbook of child psychology: Vol. 4. Socialization, personality, and social development.* New York: John Wiley.

Madanes, C. (1981). *Strategic family therapy.* San Francisco: Jossey-Bass.

Madden, D. J., & Harbin, H. T. (1983). Family structures of assaultive adolescents. *Journal of Marital and Family Therapy, 9,* 311-316.

Martin, B. (1975). Parent-child relations. In R. D. Horowitz (Ed.), *Review of child development research* (pp. 463-540). Chicago: University of Chicago Press.

McDonald, G. W. (1977). Parental identification by the adolescent: A social power approach. *Journal of Marriage and the Family, 39,* 705-718.

McDonald, G. W. (1979). Determinants of adolescent perceptions of maternal and paternal power in the family. *Journal of Marriage and the Family, 41,* 757-770.

McDonald, G. W. (1980). Parental power and adolescents' parental identification: A reexamination. *Journal of Marriage and the Family, 42,* 289-296.

Minuchin, S. (1974). *Families and family therapy.* Cambridge, MA: Harvard University Press.

Minuchin, S., Rosman, B. L., & Baker, L. (1978). *Psychosomatic families.* Cambridge, MA: Harvard University Press.

Mirkin, M. P., & Koman, S. L. (1985). *Handbook of adolescents and family therapy.* New York: Gardner.

Montemayor, R. (1984). Picking up the pieces: The effects of parental divorce on adolescents with some suggestions for school-based intervention programs. *Journal of Early Adolescents, 4,* 289-314.

Montemayor, R. (1986). Family variation in parent-adolescent storm and stress. *Journal of Adolescent Research, 1,* 15-31.

Moore, B. S., & Eisenberg, N. (1984). The development of altruism. In G. Whitehurst (Ed.), *Annals of child development* (pp. 107-174). Greenwich: JAI.

Mussen, P. H., Conger, J. J., & Kagan, J. (1974). *Child development and personality.* New York: Harper & Row.

Offer, D., & Offer, J. B. (1975). *From teenage to young manhood.* New York: Basic Books.

Olson, D. H. (1986). Circumplex model VII: Validation studies and FACES III. *Family Process, 25,* 337-352.

Olson, D. H., Russell, C. S., & Sprenkle, D. H. (1983). Circumplex model of marital and family systems: VI. Theoretical update. *Family Process, 22,* 69-83.

Olson, D. H., Sprenkle, D. H., & Russell, C. S. (1979). Circumplex model of marital and family systems: I. Cohesion and adaptability dimensions, family types, and clinical applications. *Family Process, 18,* 3-29.

Oltmanns, R. F., Broderick, J. E., & O'Leary, K. D. (1977). Marital adjustment and the efficacy of behavior therapy with children. *Journal of Consulting and Clinical Psychology, 45,* 724-729.

Openshaw, D. K., & Thomas, D. L. (1986). The adolescent self and the family. In G. K. Leigh & G. W. Peterson (Eds.), *Adolescents in families* (pp. 104-129). Cincinnati, OH: South-Western.

Openshaw, D. K., Thomas, D. L., & Rollins, B. C. (1983). Socialization and adolescent self-esteem: Symbolic interaction and social learning explanations. *Adolescence, 18,* 317-329.

Patterson, G. R. (1976). The aggressive child: Victim and architect of a coercive system. In L. A. Hamerlynck, L. C. Handy, & E. J. Mash (Eds.), *Behavior modification and families: Vol. 1. Theory and research.* New York: Brunner/Mazel.

Patterson, G. R. (1979). A performance theory for coercive family interactions. In R. B. Cairns (Ed.), *The analysis of social interactions: Methods, issues and illustrations.* Hillsdale, NJ: Lawrence Erlbaum.

Patterson, G. R. (1980). Mothers: The unacknowledged victims. *Monographs of the Society for Research in Child Development, 45*(5, Serial No. 186).

Patterson, G. R. (1982). *Coercive family process.* Eugene, OR: Castalia.

Patterson, G. R. (1986). Performance models for antisocial boys. *American Psychologist, 41,* 432-444.

Patterson, G. R., & Cobb, J. S. (1971). A dyadic analysis of "aggressive" behavior. In J. P. Hill (Ed.), *Minnesota Symposium on Child Psychology* (Vol. 5). Minneapolis: University of Minnesota Press.

Patterson, G. R., & Cobb, J. A. (1973). Stimulus control for classes of various behaviors. In J. F. Knutson (Ed.), *The control of aggression: Implications from basic research.* Chicago: Aldine.

Peterson, E. T., & Kunz, P. R. (1975). Parental control over adolescents according to family size. *Adolescence, 10,* 419-427.

Peterson, G. W. (1986a). Family conceptual frameworks and adolescent development. In G. K. Leigh & G. W. Peterson (Eds.), *Adolescents in families* (pp. 12-35). Cincinnati, OH: South-Western.

Peterson, G. W. (1986b). Parent-youth power dimensions and the behavioral auton-omy of adolescents. *Journal of Adolescent Research, 1,* 231-249.

Peterson, G. W. (1987). Role transitions and role identities during adolescence: A symbolic interactionist view. *Journal of Adolescent Research, 2,* 237-254.

Peterson, G. W., Leigh, G. K., & Day, R. (1984). Family stress theory and the impact of divorce on children. *Journal of Divorce, 7,* 1-20.

Peterson, G. W., & Rollins, B. C. (1987). Parent-child socialization. In M. B. Sussman & S. K. Steinmetz (Eds.), *Handbook of marriage and the family.* New York: Plenum.

Peterson, G. W., Rollins, B. C., & Thomas, D. L. (1985). Parental influence and adolescent conformity: Compliance and internalization. *Youth and Society 16,* 397-420.

Peterson, G. W., Rollins, B. C., Thomas, D. L., & Ellis, G. (1980, October). *Multiple dimensions of parental control and support.* Paper presented at the Annual Meeting of the National Council on Family Relations, Portland, OR.

Peterson, G. W., Southworth, L. E., & Peters, D. F. (1983). Children's self-esteem and maternal behavior in three low-income samples. *Psychological Reports, 52,* 79-86.

Peterson, G. W., & Stivers, M. E. (1986). Adolescent behavioral autonomy and family connectedness in rural Appalachia. *Family Perspective, 20,* 07-322.

Powers, S. I., Hauser, S. T., Schwartz, J. M., Noam, G. G., & Jacobson, A. M. (1983). Adolescent ego development and family interaction: A structural-developmen-tal perspective. In H. D. Grotevant & C. R. Cooper (Eds.), *Adolescent development in the family.* San Francisco: Jossey-Bass.

Raschke, H. J. (1987). Divorce. In M. B. Sussman & S. K. Steinmetz (Eds.), *Handbook of marriage and the family* (pp. 597-624). New York: Plenum.

Rohner, R. P. (1986). *The warmth dimension: Foundations of parental acceptance-rejection theory.* Beverly Hills, CA: Sage.

Rollins, B. C., & Thomas, D. L. (1979). Parental support, power, and control tech-niques in the socialization of children. In W. R. Burr, R. Hill, F. I. Nye, & I. R. Reiss (Eds.), *Contemporary theories about the family* (Vol. 1). (pp. 317-364). New York: Free Press.

Rosenberg, M. (1965). *Society and the adolescent self-image.* Princeton, NJ: Princeton University Press.

Rosenthal, D., Nelson, T., & Drake, N. (1986). Adolescent substance use and abuse: A family context. In G. K. Leigh & G. W. Peterson (Eds.), *Adolescents in families* (pp. 337-357). Cincinnati, OH: South-Western.

Schaefer, E. S. (1965). Children's reports of parental behavior. *Child Development, 36,* 413-424.

Scheck, D. C., & Emerick, R. (1976). The young male adolescent's perception of early childrearing behavior: The differential effects of socioeconomic status and fam-ily size. *Sociometry, 39,* 39-52.

Schiamberg, L. (1986). A family systems perspective on adolescent alienation. In G. K. Leigh & G. W. Peterson (Eds.), *Adolescents in families* (pp. 277-307). Cincin-nati, OH: South-Western.

Schooler, C. (1972). Birth order studies: Not here, not now! *Psychological Bulletin 78,* 161-175.

Schvaneveldt, J. D., & Ihinger, M. (1979). Sibling relationships in the family. In W. R. Burr, R. Hill, F. I. Nye, & I. L. Reiss (Eds.), *Contemporary theories about the family.* New York: Free Press.

Schwartz, R., & Gottman, J. M. (1976). Toward a task analysis of assertive behavior. *Journal of Consulting and Clinical Psychology, 44,* 910-920.

Shure, M. B. (1981). Social competence as a problem-solving skill. In J. D. Wine & M. D. Smye (Eds.), *Social competence* (pp. 158-185). New York: Guilford.

Smith, T. E. (1970). Foundations of parental influence upon adolescents: An application of social power theory. *American Sociological Review, 35,* 860-873.

Smith, T. E. (1983). Parental influence: A review of the evidence of influence and a theoretical model of the parental-influence process. In A. Kerckhoff (Ed.), *Research in the sociology of education and socialization, an annual compilation* (Vol. 4).

Smith, T. E. (1986). Influence in parent-adolescent relationships. In G. K. Leigh & G. W. Peterson (Eds.), *Adolescents in families* (pp. 130-154). Cincinnati, OH: South-Western.

Smith, T. E. (1988). Parental control techniques: Relative frequencies and relationships with situational factors. *Journal of Family Issues, 9,* 155-176.

Sorosky, A. D. (1977). The psychological effects of divorce on adolescents. *Adolescence, 12,* 123-135.

Staub, E. (1979). *Positive social behavior and morality: Socialization and development* (Vol. 2). New York: Academic Press.

Steinberg, L. (1987). Familial factors in delinquency: A developmental perspective. *Journal of Adolescent Research, 2,* 255-268.

Steinberg, L., & Silverberg, S. B. (1986). The vicissitudes of autonomy in early adolescence. *Child Development, 57,* 841-851.

Steinmetz, L. (1987). Family violence, past, present, and future. In M. Sussman & L. Steinmetz (Eds.), *Handbook of marriage and the family* (pp. 725-765). New York: Plenum.

Stierlin, H. (1974). *Separating parents and adolescents: A perspective on running away, schizophrenia, and waywardness.* New York: Quadrangle.

Teyber, E. (1983a). Effects of the parental coalition on adolescent emancipation from the family. *Journal of Marital and Family Therapy, 9,* 305-310.

Teyber, E. (1983b). Structural family relations: Primary dyadic alliances and adolescent adjustment. *Journal of Marital and Family Therapy, 9,* 89-99.

Thomas, D. L., Gecas, V., Weigert, A., & Rooney, E. (1974). *Family socialization and the adolescent.* Lexington, MA: Lexington.

Thornburg, H. (1986). Adolescent delinquency and families. In G. K. Leigh & G. W. Peterson (Eds.), *Adolescents in families* (pp. 358-380). Cincinnati, OH: South-Western.

Wallerstein, J. S., & Kelly, J. (1980). *Surviving the breakup: How children and parents cope with divorce.* New York: Basic Books.

Waterman, A. S. (1984). *The psychology of individualism.* New York: Praeger.

Waters, E., & Sroufe, L. A. (1983). Social competence as a developmental construct. *Developmental Review, 3,* 79-97.

White, K. M., Speisman, J. C., & Costos, D. (1983). Young adults and their parents: Individuation to mutuality. In H. D. Grotevant & C. R. Cooper (Eds.), *Adolescent development in the family* (pp. 61-76). San Francisco: Jossey-Bass.

White, R. W. (1959). Motivation reconsidered: The concept of competence. *Psychological Review, 66,* 297-323.

Wine, J. D. (1981). From defect to competence models. In J. D. Wine & M. D. Smye (Eds.), *Social competence* (pp. 3-35). New York: Guilford.

Wood, B. (1985). Proximity and hierarchy: Orthogonal dimensions of family inter-connectedness. *Family Process, 24,* 487-507.

York, P., York, D., & Wachtel, T. (1982). *Toughlove.* Garden City, NY: Doubleday.

Youniss, J., & Smollar, J. (1985). *Adolescent relations with mothers, fathers, and friends.* Chicago: University of Chicago Press.

Zigler, E., & Trickett, P. K. (1978). IQ, social competence, and evaluation of early childhood intervention programs. *American Psychologist, 33,* 789-798.

Zill, N., & Peterson, J. (1983). *Marital disruption and children's need for psychological help* (NIMH Paper No. 6). Washington, DC: Child Trends.

5. Promoting Social Competencies Through Educational Efforts

Joseph H. Johnson
Leonard A. Jason
David M. Betts
De Paul University

Preventive academic interventions have the ability to enhance personal competencies among school-age children. The actual and potential contributions of such interventions will be reviewed. Those programs affecting the broader ecological niches in which youngsters are situated will be highlighted, as they represent the most promising approaches for bringing about stable and enduring change.

Schools are increasingly being called upon to provide adolescents not only with traditional academic resources but also with direction and guidance in their socialization (Durlak & Jason, 1984; Elias & Clabby, 1988; Hawkins & Weis, 1985). Discussing interventions for dropouts, Ginzberg, Berliner, and Ostow (1988) allude to the complex multidimensional problems associated with promoting adolescents' social competence, especially in many faltering inner-city school systems. Educators and mental health experts face considerable obstacles, such as deteriorating morale among school staff and the pervasive problems seen in adolescence including drug abuse, teenage pregnancy, and academic failure (Glenwick & Jason, 1984). In this challenging and compelling climate, U.S. schools must introduce creative, effective, and cost-efficient programs to facilitate the academic and social development of high school students.

Preventive educational interventions can enhance personal competencies among school-age children (Jason, Durlak, & Holton-Walker, 1984). Considering the social problems that adolescents must confront as well as their cognitive developmental level, adolescence may be the ideal time for preventive interventions (LeCroy & Rose, 1986). The purpose of this chapter is to

139

review actual and potential contributions of interventions that can be implemented in schools. We will present examples of academic and social skills assessments and interventions as well as broader environmental approaches aimed at increasing social competency. Those programs affecting youngster's ecological environs will be highlighted, as they represent the most promising approaches for initiating stable and enduring change.

SOCIAL COMPETENCY IN SCHOOLS

There is evidence that students' academic achievement and social performance are related when considering overall social competence in the classroom (Gresham, 1988; Zigler & Trickett, 1978). In addition, there appears to be some general overlap between cognitive and social domains of functioning (Cauce, 1987; Ford, 1982). From this perspective, social competence can be viewed as a composite of adolescents' adaptive behavior and social skills. Some research findings suggest that children maintaining high academic achievement tend to be liked by and interact positively with peers (Green, Forehand, Beck, & Vosk, 1980). Poor academic performance is often related to problems in successful adaptation to school social settings. For example, the presence of learning disabilities may be associated with social behavior problems, particularly in male adolescents (McConaughy, 1986). Also, researchers have associated self-reported delinquency with academic skill deficits in such areas as reading achievement, verbal intelligence, and homework completion as well as poor interpersonal problem-solving (Dishion, Loeber, Stouthamer-Loeber, & Patterson, 1984).

Investigators have argued that adolescents' school and peer competence can be distinguished (Cauce, 1987; Harter, 1988). Harter (1988) identifies eight domains of teenagers' self-concept; those relevant to this discussion are (a) scholastic competence, (b) behavioral conduct, (c) peer social acceptance, (d) close friendship, and (e) romantic appeal. Collectively, these five self-concept domains point to potential areas for school-based interventions aimed at enhancing adolescents' social competence. For example, one study demonstrated that young adolescents may experience considerable anxiety concerning anticipated transitions to junior high school as well as dissatisfaction with themselves and peer relationships (Gilchrist, Schinke, Snow, Schilling, & Senechal, 1988); it is not surprising that students were more worried about social than academic difficulties. These findings reveal that many youth find it difficult to manage the stress associated with the demanding social and academic tasks confronted in secondary school. In this case, educators' rigid emphasis on basic academic skills would narrow the educational process and dismiss opportunities for school-based efforts to promote students' socialization and sense of connectedness (Bickel & Bickel, 1986; Elias & Clabby, 1988). Indeed, social competence indices, rather than intellectual measures, might be the best primary measure of the success of an intervention program for high school students (Zigler & Trickett, 1978).

Weissberg and Allen (1986) submit convincing reasons for choosing schools to implement strategies that promote social competencies. School settings can potentially offer students numerous opportunities to discuss social skills, practice using them, and receive feedback on their performance. Gilchrist, Schinke, Snow, Schilling, and Senechal (1988) call for broad-based preventive interventions to support adolescents during developmental transitions, such as entrance to high school. They recommend strengthening not only independent study skills but also a range of cognitive and behavioral skills to promote adolescent students' ongoing social, emotional, and academic adaptation. Teenage students served by school-based academic and social skills training programs may be "average" students; adolescents being mainstreamed back into regular classes from special education, residential, or hospital settings (Leone, 1984); or perhaps those youth experiencing planned or unplanned transitions to new high schools (Felner, Ginter, & Primavera, 1982). With this in mind, some researchers' goal of reorganizing school priorities and resources would be to match specific student academic and social skill deficits with powerful instructional environments and interventions (Bickel & Bickel, 1986).

ACADEMIC INTERVENTIONS

Adaptive classroom behaviors, particularly in high school, include self-direction, personal responsibility, and functional academic skills (Gresham, 1988). It is likely that most secondary school classes contain students who demonstrate varying degrees of such adaptive behaviors. The concept of academic engaged time, as it relates to school achievement, is an example of the inherent problems that teachers encounter in structuring classes to ensure optimal performance from each student. As Gettinger (1984) acknowledges that students' academic achievement is related to time spent learning, she also proposes that time provided for learning may be an equally important consideration for planning optimal lessons. High school classes typically allot uniform periods of time for instruction in different subjects, assuming the "time spent learning" is adequate for the majority of students; however, classes often do not accommodate well those students who might require longer or more elaborate presentations and practice. For these latter students, spending less time than needed in learning probably hurts their achievement. Considering the extent of many students' experience of frustration and sense of incompetence in high school classrooms, it is no surprise that maladaptive and compensatory behaviors develop.

Bickel and Bickel (1986) critique reviews on effective schools and summarize the prominent characteristics, which include (a) educational leadership, (b) orderly school climate, (c) high achievement expectations, (d) systematic monitoring of student progress, and (e) an emphasis on basic skills. Schools that implement administrative and instructional practices embodying these principles can potentially promote social competencies in adolescent students. A continuing objective for educators should be to indirectly manage social problems and disruptive behaviors in the classroom by refocusing students on the successful performance of academic tasks (Coie & Krehbiel, 1984). In this regard, academic interventions discussed in this section can potentially be used with students who possess a wide range of educational abilities. Particular emphasis will be placed on remedial approaches for nonretarded students who need and want to improve their basic skills to facilitate their academic competence (Halpern, 1979).

Teacher Instruction

In his review of programs aimed at preventing school failure, Shapiro (1988) highlighted several qualities of successful instructional interventions. Students should have opportunities to make frequent, correct responses to lessons at their instructional levels as well as receive frequent feedback and structured correction procedures. Also, it is important for teachers to set goals and monitor students' academic progress. Contingencies for performance need to be clearly delineated and consistently applied. Deshler and Schumaker (1986) suggest a number of additional teaching behaviors that enhance the quality of instruction. Using organizers throughout a lesson, including student discussions, giving regular reviews of key points and checks of comprehension, requiring mastery learning, communicating high expectations, and promoting independence are all important components of successful lessons.

Hawkins and Weis (1985) review two instructional methods that represent similar effective teaching principles. First, interactive teaching requires teachers to specify goals and objectives with students in order to clarify expectations for mastery. Students' grades are determined by skill mastery rather than by comparison with peers' academic performance. Halpern (1979) asserts that instructionally relevant data usually are complex, individualized, and targeted at specific instructional objectives; hence useful student assessments are ideally a profile of functional assets and limitations rather than merely global administrative records. Second, proactive classroom management strategies comprise establishing clear behavioral rules, giving students responsibilities, voicing clear directions and using praise effectively.

Shapiro cites several examples of instructional programs that demonstrate these effective teaching practices. For example, direct instruction technology, as practiced in the formal Direct Instruction curricula, has proved to be a successful educational approach for elementary-age children (Becker, Engelmann, Carnine, & Maggs, 1982). The systematic, mastery-oriented coverage of basic subjects might be equally efficacious for remedial education at the high school level. Emphasis on high rates of student responding, immediate corrective feedback, and frequent reinforcement are applicable in large group formats. The approach promotes student motivation, on-task behavior, and a reduction of disruptive problem behaviors. Overall, active student involvement with learning tasks, guided practice sessions, and systematic error correction are commonalities seen in successful academic interventions for low-achieving students (Algozzine & Maheady, 1986).

A recent instructional intervention has been developed to teach low-achieving adolescents "learning strategies" as opposed to simple remedial work in basic subject areas (Deshler & Schumaker, 1986). The authors define *learning strategies* as the techniques, principles, or rules that enable students to learn, to solve problems, and to complete schoolwork independently. Deshler and Schumaker describe the Learning Strategies Curriculum as being composed of three major strands that correspond to the major demands of secondary education and can be incorporated into classroom instruction by teachers. The first strand consists of strategies that aid students' acquisition of information from written material (e.g., decoding, reading comprehension, and self-questioning). The second strand helps students identify and store important information (e.g., memorizing key information). The third strand enhances written expression and demonstration of academic competence (e.g., sentence and paragraph writing strategies). The authors predict that teens who "learn how to learn" will be better able to learn new skills over time, and the learning strategies approach compels students to take responsibility for their own education.

Peer Tutoring

Cauce and Shrebnik (in press) emphasize the prominence of peer groups in adolescents' school lives. The authors cite findings that indicate that peer support is positively related to school competence; hence they encourage administrators of school-based prevention programs to consider ways to channel supportive activities within peer groups. Peer tutoring presents one promising approach to allow teachers to program for academic and social benefits simultaneously (Algozzine & Maheady, 1986). For example, Greenwood et al. (1984) found that classwide peer tutoring in basic subject areas, as opposed to teacher instruction, can actually produce more student academic response and higher achievement. A variant of paired peer tutoring, student team learning is another educational approach that groups students together (e.g., in groups of four or five) to complete class assignments; using this strategy, individual student achievement depends on the cooperation and success of the group (Hawkins & Weis, 1985).

One successful peer instruction approach established classwide student tutoring teams during math period, matching mainstreamed learning disabled or behavior disordered high school students with nonhandicapped classmates (Maheady, Sacca, & Harper, 1987). Regular classroom practice material and texts were used. During regularly scheduled instructional periods, heterogeneous three- to five-member student teams practiced their weekly course content for approximately 30 minutes. At the same time, teachers moved around the room awarding points to team members who displayed the designated behaviors such as cooperative work habits and good tutoring. After weekly quizzes, team point totals were summed and the winning team was announced; also, team and individual performances were published in the school's weekly bulletin. Considerable academic gains were achieved in math for both handicapped and nonhandicapped students; the percentage of students earning As rose sharply and failing grades were nearly eliminated. The investigators note several important implications for this peer tutoring intervention. Regular teachers were the primary implementors of the programs as opposed to special education staff. Also, regular curricular materials were used and time allocations were followed. It is notable that both disabled and regular students benefited from the program.

A word of caution is in order concerning peer tutoring at the high school level. Miller and Gibbs (1984) examined high school students' attitudes and willingness to tutor "slow learning" peers. In this study, students who volunteered to peer tutor were advised to meet with their tutees at least one to two hours each week outside of regular class time. Overall, tutors expressed relatively negative attitudes toward slow learners; nevertheless, perceptions of their own tutees were more positive. Differences were found in the attitudes of students who tutored regularly versus those who did not. Those tutors who met sporadically or not at all tended to think that tutoring was not likely to help the tutee, was less likely to leave them time to do their own work, and would decrease their chances to socialize.

This study points to the importance of addressing participating students' attitudes and motivation when implementing peer tutoring with adolescents. It should be noted that, in the Miller and Gibbs's study, peer tutoring occurred outside of class in a largely unprogrammed and unsupervised fashion. Well-organized peer tutoring would be likely to increase most students' motivation and engender positive interactions among students with varying educational abilities.

Jason, Ferone, and Soucy (1979) developed a peer tutoring project for children as early as the first and third grades, and then eighth graders were taught to supervise the project (Jason, Frasure, & Ferone, 1981). In addition to achieving academic and social gains, 50% of the children indicated that they practiced the tutoring skills at home with a friend or sibling. Another tutoring project focused on teaching computer skills and tutoring skills to adolescents who were having academic problems as well as some who were performing well in school but needed the challenge this program provided (Jason, Olson, & Pillen, 1987). Transfer students in grades one through four were given twice-weekly tutoring by the older students. The tutors learned to program microcomputers and developed individual programs for their tutees. This study provided a competency-enhancing experience for at-risk children—the type of experience frequently reserved for honor students and high achievers. Rather than being perceived as remedial in nature, the intervention was viewed both by project participants and by others in the school as an important experience in building skills, and many nonparticipants asked if they could be part of the project. These types of projects indicate that adolescents can play meaningful roles in helping other children with academic problems.

SOCIAL SKILLS EDUCATION

Investigators in the field of social skills training continue to debate the criteria for competent social behavior (e.g., Curran, Farrell, & Grunberger, 1984), and no broad consensus has been reached. Numerous definitions and heuristic models have been proposed. LeCroy (1982, p. 92) defines *social skills* as "a complex set of skills which allow the adolescent the ability to successfully mediate interactions between peers, parents, teachers, and other adults." Gresham (1988, p. 525) suggests that social skills seen in school settings encompass academic performance, cooperative behaviors, social initiation behaviors, assertive behaviors, peer reinforcement behaviors, communication skills, problem-solving skills, and social self-efficacy. Additionally, he identifies four types of social skill deficiencies: social skills deficits, self-control deficits, social performance deficits, and self-control performance deficits. Dishion, Loeber, Stouthamer-Loeber, and Patterson (1984) conceptualized adolescents' interpersonal skills deficits into only two categories: (a) the interpersonal style of the individual, which may precipitate social rejection or isolation, and (b) the style of interpersonal problem-solving, which may result in poor resolutions of social dilemmas.

Ford (1982) presents evidence that social competence is at least partially distinguishable from cognitive or general competence. He concludes that social cognition is related to effective social behavior. The author proposes a process-oriented model of social competence emphasizing cognition that directs, controls, and regulates behavior as well as collects, stores, and retrieves social information. Ford's "open systems" approach provides one heuristic for designing cognitive-behavioral social skills enhancement programs. He cited replicated findings demonstrating that socially competent adolescents are more cognitively resourceful and empathic and perceive themselves as having a broad social support network. Ford and Tisak (1983) advocate educational programs that focus on the development of social competence, which may not be addressed by regular academic curricula. Social-cognitive skill training is viewed as a promising strategy to address adolescent social skills deficits. However, the researchers caution that adolescents' acquisition of social-cognitive skills does not ensure socially intelligent behavior; for example, information processing and cognitive organization skills are not strongly associated with effective social behavior. In contrast, the social-cognitive abilities demonstrated in interpersonal goal-setting, planning, and evaluation skills appear to be more closely linked with competent social interaction.

Argyle (1985) suggests that rules are a major feature of social interactions. Social rules concern what behaviors group members believe should or should not be performed in various situations.

The author stresses nonverbal and verbal communication, empathy, and self-presentation of adolescents. Nonverbal communication and self-presentation consist of facial expressions, tone of voice, gestures, posture, and appearance. Verbal communication concerns conversational skills. Argyle notes that less socially skilled adolescents may lack fluency in identifying and participating in conversational sequences. Moreover, adolescents differ in their ability to perceive another person's point of view.

Dodge (1985) presents a five-faceted scheme of children's social interaction that elucidates different levels of assessment and intervention. In brief, Dodge's model includes (a) the judgments of social competence by peers and authority figures, (b) observable social behaviors, (c) social tasks or domains of interaction (d) unconscious influences, and (e) social information processing. This framework succeeds in delineating the major domains of social skills training programs to date. The task for researchers is to integrate these distinct components into effective multimodal programs that affect not only individual students but also the environments (e.g., school settings) in which they are socialized.

Kendall (1984) cautioned against the "developmental level uniformity myth," which is the assumption that children at various ages, but with the same behavior problems, are alike. Social competency interventions need to address not only different categorizations of social status and skill deficits but also developmental changes across the adolescent period. As mentioned earlier, meeting the needs of special education students may require school professionals to do extra planning as well. Compared with "average" teenagers, learning disabled youth are often at a disadvantage in socialization because they may have fewer initial social skills, may learn new skills more slowly, and may be less sensitive to the many subtleties in social interaction (Hazel, Schumaker, Sherman, & Sheldon-Wildgen, 1982). Hence programs might do well to implement different formats for heterogeneous adolescent populations (Carpenter & Sugrue, 1984). There have recently been great improvements in these directions. The following discussion illustrates some promising school-based social competence assessments and interventions that might be widely adopted for use with adolescent populations.

Social Skills Assessment

In school settings, adolescents' social competence can be assessed from three perspectives: (a) by an adult such as the classroom teacher or independent observer, (b) by peers, and (c) from the individual student's point of view. In assessing social competence, teenagers' academic achievement is also important (Green, Forehand, Beck, & Vosk, 1980). Trower (1982) advises that social skills assessment should be aimed at social skill competence, which means both social knowledge and the ability to produce appropriate plans. He also suggests measuring individuals' outcome expectancies and the beliefs that generate them.

Numerous group observation schemes have been developed for coding student social interactions (e.g., Coie & Kupersmidt, 1983; Michelson, Sugai, Wood, & Kazdin, 1983), but the complexity of such strategies prevent economical use beyond research purposes. Perhaps teacher rating forms are less descriptive but more applicable for widespread use in classrooms. Probably the most recent validated teacher rating form is the Child Behavior Checklist: Teacher Rating Form (Achenbach & Edelbrock, 1986). This standardized assessment provides a differentiated description of student behavior and can be administered across classrooms and other school settings to identify problem behavior, to discriminate school settings that possibly elicit or support such behaviors, and to measure behavioral change.

Three popular methods of peer assessment are peer nominations, peer ratings, and peer rankings (Kane & Lawler, 1978). For example, Coie (1985) provides a sociometric assessment framework for more accurately targeting groups in need of social skills interventions. In the assessment, students are asked to nominate three students whom they most like and three classmates whom they least like. In addition to average students, Coie has identified four extreme types of social status: popular, rejected, controversial, and neglected. Asher and Wheeler (1985) also distinguish between rejected children and neglected children. The rejected group is composed of students who lack friends in school and are disliked by many peers; they are seen as disruptive, often aggressive, and lacking in social skills appropriate to academic settings. Neglected children lack friends but are not disliked; they tend to be shy and isolated in school. Findings indicate rejected children tend to be more isolated and lonely group than neglected children, which may place them at more risk than other social status groups (Asher & Wheeler, 1985). Such distinctions between social status groups appear to be critical in determining the content and strategies used for individual and classroom social skills interventions.

Asher and Dodge (1986) note that negative-nomination sociometric measures are often viewed by school personnel as having potentially harmful effects. Therefore, Asher and Dodge developed an alternative method of identifying neglected and rejected children that consisted of a positive-nomination measure. They report that the alternative procedure is less accurate in identifying some status groups, especially neglected students.

One problem with sociometric ratings by peers is that little information is gained about the specific behaviors and the origin of adolescents' social incompetence (Dodge, 1985). Dodge, Pettit, McClaskey, and Brown (1986) propose a five-stage model of social information processing that offers more precise cognitive social skills assessment and intervention aimed at promoting competent social responses. The five steps of processing are as follows: (a) encoding social cues, (b) mentally representing and interpreting cues, (c) accessing or generating one or more possible responses to cues, (d) evaluating potential consequences in choosing various responses and then selecting the most appropriate one, and (e) enacting the response and self-monitoring its effects. Using second- through fourth-grade girls and boys, the investigators replicated findings demonstrating that the five processing steps are related to competent social behavior. Dodge, Pettit, McClaskey, and Brown admit that their gross description will probably be supplanted by more elaborate cognitive models emerging from information processing research. In the meantime the model might be successfully applied to adolescents for use in social skills program development.

Another possible measure for assessing social problem-solving during role-plays is the Adolescent Problem Inventory (API), a composite of 44 common social problem situations (Freedman, Rosenthal, Donahoe, Schlundt, & McFall, 1978). More recently Dodge and his colleagues (1986) developed the Taxonomy of Problematic Social Situations for Children (TOPS), which also consists of 44 social situations that occur with younger children.

Both API and TOPS provide models for developing new interactive assessment instruments for adolescents.

In recent years several scales have been developed to measure the social networks of children (Cauce, Reid, & Landesmann, in press). These scales might provide us with a more comprehensive context in which to base our evaluations. In addition to developing measures to understand children's competencies and deficits, we also need to understand the effect of social networks on children's adjustment and development. For example, a child with adequate grades might be assessed as having a truncated social network with few friends. Network members might not provide physical assistance and the network might not be heterogeneous (Nair & Jason, 1985, found that these two variables predict adjustment in school-age children). If low levels of satisfaction with social network variables were also evident, this student might be appropriate for some type of social intervention.

Regarding measurement of self-concept, the recently developed Self-Perception Profile for Adolescents (Harter, 1988) appears to most accurately differentiate the separate self-concept domains. This new measure can be used to assess baselines and changes in students' perceptions of their social competency in different areas such as scholastic competence and peer social acceptance. The information gained might potentially predict attitudes and motivation during the course of social skills programs.

Dodge (1985) concludes that a "profile approach" might be best in assessing social competency in order to design multimodal treatment interventions. An individual profile might be based on his proposed five-dimensional scheme. In addition, a profile could incorporate the elements of social skills assessment briefly discussed, including peer networks and adolescents' social self-concepts. We believe that, beyond an individual profile, a group and ecological dimension should be added to social competency assessments for adolescents.

Social Skills Training Programs

The unique aspect of social skills training (SST) is that problem behaviors are viewed as deficits in social skills (Goldstein, Sprafkin, Gershaw, & Klein, 1983; LeCroy, 1982). Moreover, SST may serve a preventive as well as an ameliorative function for adolescents (LeCroy, 1982). This perspective has far reaching implications for the school's role in providing adolescents with educational resources to promote social competencies as opposed to, for example, acting as a punitive agency. Past research has demonstrated that SST can promote prosocial behavioral and cognitive change in youth (for critical reviews, see Gresham, 1985, 1988; Ladd, 1984; LeCroy, 1982; Michelson, Sugai, Wood, & Kazdin, 1983; Weissberg & Allen, 1986). In general, the objectives of most SST programs are to enhance students' skill knowledge or concepts, help them translate this knowledge into effective social behavior, and promote skill generalization and maintenance across social settings (Ladd, 1984). Hawkins and Weis (1985) mention a variant of SST, Life Skills Training, that focuses on basic communication, decision making, negotiation, and conflict resolution skills. These latter authors believe schools should teach these skills just as they instruct in academic subjects. Hawkins and Weis predict that, by teaching social and life skills, programs not only can improve students' peer relationships but may also contribute to their academic success and attachment to the school. Hence such programs should provide adolescents with appropriate skills and the motivation to use them (Hazel, Schumaker, Sherman, & Sheldon-Wildgen, 1982).

Several issues need to be addressed when tailoring SST to individual school systems; for example, how well will the program fit into different geographic regions, ethnic groups, and age ranges? Gresham (1988) recommends that administrators validate the social significance, social acceptability, and social importance of programs. Social significance of intervention goals addresses the question of whether or not targeted social skills deficits are critical to successful social adaptation within the school and peer environment. Social acceptability questions assess whether administrators, teachers, and students adopt the social intervention as viable and productive. For example, does the individual adolescent view the new social skills as more reinforcing than current behaviors (LeCroy, 1982)? By assessing the social importance of an intervention, professionals emphasize whether or not the changes make a significant difference in adolescents' functioning. Many social skills programs may not adequately meet Gresham's social validation criteria. The following brief review is limited to only a few of the more recent and promising SST programs that directly apply in school settings.

The Improving Social Awareness-Social Problem-Solving (ISA-SPS) Project is an innovative program being developed to enhance children's capacities to cope with stress and to manage interpersonal situations (Elias & Clabby, 1988). Using a framework of decision making and the strategy of problem-solving thinking skills, the investigators employ eight skill-building steps to promote social problem-solving. The ISA-SPS Project has five tenets. First, the authors recommend teaching an ordered sequence of skills to ensure the acquisition of a hierarchy of skills for competent decision making. Second, during instruction it is important to focus on decision-making situations that are relevant to adolescents (e.g., school failure, vandalism, and substance abuse). Third, by providing a cognitive strategy (i.e., focusing on process rather than content) educators can facilitate skill generalization across situations. Thus training emphasizes the process of generating social skills performance rather than merely teaching the elements of social skills (Trower, 1982). A fourth tenet of Elias and Clabby is making the program usable to educators and parents so that it can be implemented consistently across developmental levels (see also Glick & Goldstein, 1987). A fifth consideration is building in curriculum activities to aid maintenance and generalization.

Furman (1980) advocates teaching rationales for the use of new social skills. In addition, rules can be taught to govern social behavior. Furman believes that rules may be useful in correcting competence deficits; that is, in cases where responses are not in adolescents' repertoires, rules can facilitate learning new responses. In contrast, rules may not be effective in modifying performance deficits wherein adolescents have prerequisite skills but do not wish to enact them.

Small and Schinke (1983) believe that problem-solving training holds promise in teaching social competence skills that can be transferred to other milieus. Working with six-member groups of preadolescent males during six 60-minute sessions, the investigators implemented a three-step problem-solving technique (stop and think, generate alternatives, choose the best solution) combined with interpersonal communication skills training. For this latter component, leaders modeled the use of appropriate gestures, expressions, and verbal statements and group members acted as protagonists, antagonists, and coaches during role-plays. Findings demonstrated that interpersonal cognitive problem-solving (ICPS) plus social skills training was more effective than ICPS alone. ICPS training modified cognition associated with social problem-solving. These social skills were generalized to classroom settings. The researchers attribute this success to the inclusion of practice situations based on problems identified by pupils and teachers as relevant to everyday experience.

Structured learning training (SLT) is a psychoeducational approach to teaching social competencies (Goldstein, Sprafkin, Gershaw, & Klein, 1983). In SLT students are taught 50 prosocial skills ranging from beginning social skills (e.g., starting a conversation, giving a complaint) and alternatives to aggression (e.g., negotiation), to planning skills (e.g., goal-setting, decision-making). The four major components of the program are (a) modeling, (b) role-playing, (c) performance feedback, and (d) transfer of training. Skill deficiencies addressed include problems manifested in aggressiveness, withdrawal, immaturity, and other difficulties associated with adolescent development ranging from the upper elementary grades through senior high school. SLT successfully trained students in such prosocial skills as empathy, negotiation, assertiveness, following instructions, and self-control. Goldstein and his colleagues report that SLT has been adapted to regular-sized classes, and trainers have usually been regular and special education teachers. The behaviorally oriented program is based on procedures and outcomes that educators and researchers easily observe and assess, enabling teachers to accurately measure students' progress—a feature especially helpful in developing individual educational plans (IEPs). Regarding the efficacy of SLT, the investigators have found that skill acquisition occurs in well over 90% of SLT trainees. Across diverse populations, problems, and settings, trainees have demonstrated a 50% rate of skill transfer to new social environments.

Adolescents who demonstrate behavior problems due to poor impulse control might benefit from an integration of social skills training with self-talk and relaxation procedures, possibly enabling such students to control their anger and mediate their behaviors (Baum, Clark, McCarthey, Sandler, & Carpenter, 1986). Glick and Goldstein (1987) recently developed Aggression Replacement

Training (ART), a multimodal, psychoeducational intervention for assaultive, hostile, and disruptive adolescents. Over a minimum 10-week course, ART integrates three components into the curriculum: (a) structured learning training (SLT), (b) anger control training (ACT), and (c) moral education. ACT teaches adolescents to inhibit anger through identifying external triggers and internal cues and using reminders (e.g., self-statements), reducers (i.e., techniques to lower anger levels), and self-evaluation. Moral education is designed to increase a student's sense of fairness and justice and concern with the needs and rights of others. Pilot studies of ART with incarcerated teenage males indicate that it offers viable strategies for intervention that may be applicable in school and community settings. Carpenter and Sugrue (1984) conducted another social skills training program that included values and affective education; although these components are often lacking in other programs, the authors explain that emphasis on social values, feelings, and behavior is more representative of real-life circumstances.

McCullagh (1982) conducted an assertion-training program for shy, quiet junior high school males who lacked friends. The author notes that these students are typically overlooked by teachers because they do not present disruptive behavior problems. His program included (a) developing social skills; (b) expressing positive and negative feelings; (c) expressing one's needs, desires, and opinions; and (d) increasing physical assertiveness. For each component, difficult social situations were described to students, who then imagined their own response. The trainer modeled and coached assertive responses, and then students were asked to compare their imagined response with the modeled behavior. The results indicate that no differences were found between three groups receiving audio- and/or videotaped feedback about their performance or audiotape plus specific assertion problems for resolution. The program proved to be effective in enhancing and maintaining assertion skills and increasing participants' friendships.

Schloss, Schloss, and Harris (1984) present a social skills training package developed for three severely depressed adolescents. Twenty 30- to 40-minute sessions consisted of adult modeling, behavior rehearsal, feedback, and contingent social reinforcement. The social skills taught were relatively simple greeting and conversational behaviors. Although a separate trainer conducted the sessions, teachers were involved in monitoring and reinforcing targeted prosocial behaviors. The program yielded modest gains in students' interpersonal responses. The limited success of this treatment approach may have been partly due to exempting classmates from direct involvement in the intervention. When treatment is administered individually, students may continue to be strongly influenced by peers in the classroom setting, regrettably, often in an undesirable direction (Baum, Clark, McCarthey, Sandler, & Carpenter, 1986).

Peer leader involvement in social competence training may be especially helpful with adolescents in order to model more prosocial behavior (Small & Schinke, 1983). For example, Bierman (1986) successfully implemented a conversational skills training format with preadolescents whereby a competent peer was paired with a less socially skilled classmate for videotaped cooperative activities; some less competent students received coaching in conversational skills. Both coaching and positive peer responses were associated with successful outcomes. These findings suggest that inclusion of socially skilled peers in social competency interventions might enhance treatment outcomes.

Operation Snowball, a substance abuse prevention program that began in Illinois, is a good example of a community-level intervention incorporating school systems (Rhodes & Jason, 1988). Operation Snowball, which exists in over 70 communities throughout Illinois, sponsors three-day retreats at which high school students receive training in problem-solving and helping skills. The retreats are organized and implemented by a community task force, parents, teachers, and students. The workshops all involve the teaching of personal and social skills and provide problem-solving support to improve participants' general competence and reduce potential motivations for substance use. On returning to their respective schools, the program participants, along with parents, teachers, and community members, are encouraged to engage in follow-up activities, such as an ongoing skills training seminar, sports events, awareness campaigns, and workshops. The idea of actively involving change agents in the actual preventive interventions increases the possibilities of initiating longer-lasting change (Bogat & Jason, in press; Jason & Rhodes, in press). Involvement in planning and implementation gives participants positive opportunities to be responsible to themselves and others.

Hardwick, Pounds, and Brown (1985) summarize several advantages of holding social skills groups in school settings. First, discipline problems are usually reduced when teachers are coleaders of the class groups. Also, immediate feedback can be given to teachers regarding support of students' newly learned social behaviors. Having teachers involved may help disseminate ideas and techniques among staff and promote incorporation of techniques into daily activities. Nelson-Jones (1986) reports several problems that can occur in managing school social skills programs. The author cautions that programs can be too general, perhaps imparting a broad overview of knowledge but not adequately developing social skills uniquely relevant to each participant. Also, group size can be a problem in adapting programs to classrooms. Larger groups diminish opportunities to model, monitor, and coach individuals' skill practice. Moreover, a large group tends to inhibit intimate discussions and present possible discipline problems. Training failure with some adolescents can occur due to time limitations that impede skill acquisition for youth with more serious deficits, in which case consultation or outside referral may be warranted (Michelson, Sugai, Wood, & Kazdin, 1983).

Generalization of Social Competency in Schools

Merely teaching students, for example, social problem-solving strategies may not promote social skills in the school milieu (Patton, 1985). Studies (e.g., Dishion, Loeber, Stouthamer-Loeber, & Patterson, 1984) indicate that improving social skills of teenagers does not necessarily result in decreased antisocial behavior. For instance, one investigation of a social skills training program found that adolescents rapidly acquired appropriate responses to vocational supervisor's instructions following verbal training and role-playing; however, these gains were not sustained in the actual work setting (Kelly et al., 1983). Students were then taught self-monitoring skills in the form of self-ratings of job performance, which facilitated response generalization. Training adolescents to use self-reinforcement in the form of positive self-statements or tangible rewards may also enhance maintenance of skills in independent situations (Goldstein, Sprafkin, Gershaw, & Klein, 1983).

Nonetheless, such procedures may often need to be augmented by additional, perhaps more potent, generalization strategies to enhance and maintain social skills gains.

Programs focused on the needs of participants ensure skill development and problem-solving specific to the demands of their own social situations (McCullagh, 1982). Entrapment is one behavioral process that naturally reinforces newly acquired social skills largely through the social behaviors of peers (McConnell, 1987). McConnell states that entrapment should be an essential feature of social skills intervention, that is, a primary objective should be to teach behaviors that will be naturally reinforced. The author suggests that the concept of entrapment expands the assessment and intervention focus to include teacher and peer behavior that reinforces and maintains adaptive (or maladaptive) social responses in target students. The implication for this perspective is that treatment procedures must also focus on the peer group.

In classrooms and other school settings, continued teacher and staff modeling and reinforcement of learned social skills seem to be important (Friedman, Quick, Mayo, & Palmer, 1982). Baum, Clark, McCarthey, Sandler, & Carpenter (1986) recommend involvement of every student in the class in a group training format to ensure peer modeling and reinforcement. Moreover, teachers might directly reinforce group behavior to promote socially adaptive behaviors in individuals. Hazel, Schumaker, Sherman, and Sheldon-Wildgen (1982) required participants to practice newly learned skills after training sessions at least three times in settings outside the group; in such cases, teachers could monitor and reinforce socially appropriate responses. To increase participants' motivation, Carpenter and Sugrue (1984) employed several reinforcement strategies; for example, those who successfully completed the SST program received high school course credit, a diploma, and employment opportunities.

To ensure the success of social competence enhancement programs, researchers advise programmers to solicit school staff cooperation by assigning them major roles in program development, instruction, assessment, and evaluation (Michelson, Sugai, Wood, & Kazdin, 1983) and by making programs easy to use (Hazel, Schumaker, Sherman, & Sheldon-Wildgen, 1982). Teachers may need training to support students' use of problem-solving in the classroom and in peer interactions (Elias & Clabby, 1988; Goldstein, Sprafkin, Gershaw, & Klein, 1983). They also should collaborate more closely with school counselors and/or psychologists to design and implement programs targeted specifically at social skills (Halpern, 1979). To provide the best school services for developing student social competencies, Halpern (1979) recommends that teachers develop counseling skills themselves or participate in team teaching with personnel competent in this area. As might be expected, there is evidence that the level of students' social skill acquisition can be greatly affected by the skill level of the trainer (Rotheram, 1982).

INTEGRATION OF ACADEMIC AND SOCIAL SKILLS EDUCATION

Combining academic and social skills education efforts in high schools might be a powerful strategy for professionals to use to enhance adolescents' social competency. Programs designed for elementary-age students have demonstrated success. Working with socially rejected low-achieving fourth graders, Coie and Krehbiel (1984) examined the impact of academic skills (AS) training and social skills (SS) training separately and in combination (AS and SS). Students receiving AS training were tutored by undergraduates throughout the school year twice weekly for 45 minutes in math and reading. SS training consisted of six weekly sessions, wherein targeted children were paired with other children from the classroom and coached in prosocial behaviors. The investigators found AS training to significantly improve students' reading, math, and social standing. Additionally, the AS groups showed more on-task behavior, tended to become less disruptive, and experienced increases in positive teacher attention. Unlike the AS and combined groups, SS students showed initial improvement but did not maintain social status increases. Coie and Krehbiel's findings suggest that school-based interventions aimed at increasing teenagers' social competence might also be effective for low achievers when both academic and social skills are targeted.

One team of investigators described a school program for emotionally disturbed adolescents that scheduled a daily social skills class (Friedman, Quick, Mayo, & Palmer, 1982). Published formal curricula were sometimes used, but the low reading level of many enrolled secondary students necessitated the development of additional materials adapted to students' academic ability levels. The social and life skills content areas covered verbal and nonverbal communication skills, assertiveness, value clarification, careers and job interviewing, understanding principles of positive reinforcement, dealing with separation, and using community resources.

Two successful features of this program are time-in counseling and fair fighting. Time-in counseling is a primary intervention procedure for disruptive or minor aggressive behavior and peer conflict. Students are referred by staff or elect to refer themselves. This immediate attention provides counseling opportunities to capitalize on real situations to teach problem-solving and communication skills. Fair fighting involves time-in referrals for two students demonstrating peer conflict. The two students are first seen separately and allowed to voice complaints and feelings. Then the two students are brought together for a discussion of the problem with the counselor. The students are not allowed to speak directly during the discussion but must communicate through the counselor, who models clear communication. When agreement is reached the adolescents are permitted to negotiate further. Both procedures were designed to teach and reinforce social skills being formally taught in the program. Implementation of these procedures required substantial changes in school policy, classroom structure, and personnel resources.

ENVIRONMENTAL CHANGES IN SCHOOLS

Restructuring school environments can promote social competency in adolescents. For example, access to clear, appropriate contingencies (i.e., teacher/peer rewards for prosocial behavior) and the absence of aversive conditions (e.g., failure, impersonal teacher/student contacts) within a school environment can potentially decrease adolescent antisocial behavior such as drug abuse (Bry, Conboy, & Bisgay, 1986). Jennings and Kohlberg (1983) offer one model to enhance adolescent involvement in school through more democratic participation. The investigators describe a "just community" program in which juvenile delinquents in residential placement met weekly in community meetings to make and change rules and develop a "constitution." Meetings were used as a forum to discuss rule enforcement and interpersonal issues and conflicts. The authors report substantial increases in the amount of students' power and responsibility for rules and decisions as well as their concern about the fairness of rules and policies. Participants viewed themselves as making significant moral behavior changes. Certainly implementing the "just community" concept in large high schools would require creative restructuring of organizational systems.

The size of a school and student/teacher ratios may determine the opportunities for students' involvement in school activities such as class participation, clubs, and sports programs. There is evidence that smaller schools tend to have fewer conduct problems and that lower student/teacher ratios discourage school crime (Hawkins & Weis, 1985). Maheady, Sacca, and Harper (1987) describe an experimental school program (i.e., Project PASS— Pupils Achieving Scholastic Success) in which regular high school teachers were given smaller class sizes (15-20) and consultative services from special education experts while integrating three to six mildly handicapped students into their classes. Fostering cooperative learning in the smaller class enhanced most students' academic achievement.

Given the fiscal limitations of most school districts, Hawkins and Weis (1985) recommend a school-within-a-school organizational structure; this refers to the division of a school into smaller units. The authors suggest that subdivisions within a school provide the benefits of a smaller school while retaining the diversity of resources and courses seen in larger schools. The subdivisions can support decentralized academic, extracurricular, student government, and sports activities. It is predicted that this restructuring will promote more accountable student participation and more personal contact between students and teachers. Furthermore, Hawkins and Weis suggest that school staff should recruit a broad range of natural student leaders for participation in policymaking and disciplinary committees to ensure involvement of students not typically represented in traditional student leadership groups. By such democratic action, school personnel might foster greater commitment and belief in the system's moral order (Jennings & Kohlberg, 1983).

Felner, Ginter, and Primavera (1982) report success in enhancing peer and teacher support as well as students' adjustment during a planned transition into high school. The first component of the transition project redefined the role of homeroom teachers so that they assumed many administrative and guidance responsibilities, the intention being to (a) increase teacher support, (b) increase students' accountability, and (c) increase student access to important school-related information. The second component of the project involved restructuring the social environment by establishing a stable peer support system. All project students remained together throughout four major subject periods during the school day. This change was made to promote peer support, enhance students' sense of belonging, and increase students' perception of the school as a stable environment. At the end of their ninth-grade year, project students' showed significantly better grades and attendance and more stable self-concepts than controls. Moreover, project participants reported that they viewed the school as having greater clarity of organization and expectations and higher teacher support and involvement than did nonparticipants. This project demonstrates how changing the ecology of a school system can potentially affect students' social competency.

THE DePAUL SCHOOL TRANSITION PROGRAM

We believe that interventions should be implemented during milestone events in children's lives in order to promote long-term developmental adjustment. With this goal in mind, the DePaul School Transition Program is in its fourth year of researching the adjustment factors of preadolescent transfer students and developing educationally based interventions to assist their adjustment to new schools (Jason et al., in press). By providing these children with additional resources at this critical time, we aim to enhance students' academic and social adaptation. This project is thus different from most of the previously described social skills training programs in that its focus is more preventive.

The multimodal intervention included an orientation program, assignment of a "buddy," and yearlong tutoring. The orientation program was designed to teach new students about the schools' expectations. A nontransfer "buddy" was asked to be a friend of each new student and to help with the orientation program. Individual tutoring was provided by paraprofessionals for those students identified as being at risk for academic failure and social maladjustment. For those students needing more potent and comprehensive intervention, parents or family members were asked to become more involved in their child's education by reading with them several times a week. These "home tutors" were trained to use direct instruction techniques and SRA story cards. Work with parents in an educationally based program is a potential entry point for more social and behavioral family training. Overall the integration of these efforts are directed toward improving children's current and future academic and social competence.

SUMMARY

Schools have implicitly been given the charge of educating and supporting youth in the development of social competency. This evolving role requires educators and mental health professionals to experiment with creative approaches designed to meet the diverse social and academic needs of a heterogeneous student population. Educational strategies that address academic skill enhancement were presented as one necessary intervention component. Also, representative social skills training procedures were considered. Critics have claimed that social skills programs are often too global; however, given the promising advances in assessment of social competency, researchers and practitioners can look forward to more individualized interventions in the future (Dodge, 1985). In addition, we recommended methods to promote generalization of social skills gains. In the future, school personnel must challenge themselves to integrate academic and social interventions to promote social competency.

Researchers must seek alternatives to traditional academic interventions for adolescents, such as environmental and multimodal preventive efforts. Reviewing prevention programs for school-age children, Elias and Branden (1988) concluded that most programs are underresearched with regard to a variety of geographic areas, age groups, populations, and school organizational climates. To promote social competence among youth, a continuing task for program innovators will be to combine and test exemplary school-based approaches that retain the flexibility and specificity to affect not only individual children but also school and community systems. Although the intervention strategies that were discussed are often implemented separately, it is our bias that an ideal program promoting social competency is comprehensive, adheres to a long-term developmental focus, and is largely preventive in its orientation.

REFERENCES

Achenbach, T. M., & Edelbrock, C. (1986). *Manual for the teachers' form and teacher version of the Child Behavior Checklist.* Burlington: University of Vermont, Department of Psychiatry.

Algozzine, B., & Maheady, L. (1986). When all else fails, teach! *Exceptional Children, 52,* 487-488.

Argyle, M. (1985). Social behavior problems and social skills training in adolescence. In B. H. Scheider, K. H. Rubin, & J. E. Ledingham (Eds.), *Children's peer relations: Issues in assessment and intervention* (pp. 207-224). New York: Springer-Verlag.

Asher, S. R. (1983). Social competence and peer status: Recent advances and future directions. *Child Development, 54,* 1427-1434.

Asher, S. R., & Dodge, K. A. (1986). Identifying children who are rejected by their peers. *Developmental Psychology, 22,* 444-449.

Asher, S. R., & Wheeler, V. A. (1985). Children's loneliness: A comparison of rejected and neglected peer status. *Journal of Consulting and Clinical Psychology, 53,* 500-505.

Baum, J. G., Clark, H. B., McCarthey, W., Sandler, J., & Carpenter, R. (1986). An analysis of the acquisition and generalization of social skills in troubled youths: Combining social skills training, cognitive self-talk, and relaxation procedures. *Child and Family Behavior Therapy, 8*(4), 1-27.

Becker, W. C., Engelmann, S., Carnine, D. W., & Maggs, A. (1982). Direct instruction technology: Making learning happen. In P. Karoly & J. J. Steffen (Eds.), *Improving children's social competence: Vol. 1. Advances in child behavioral analysis* (pp. 151-206). Lexington, MA: D. C. Heath.

Bickel, W. E., & Bickel, D. D. (1986). Effective schools, classrooms, and instruction: Implications for special education. *Exceptional Children, 52,* 489-500.

Bierman, K. L. (1986). Process of change during social skills training with preadolescents and its relation to treatment outcome. *Child Development, 57,* 230-240.

Bogat, G. A., & Jason, L. A. (in press). Dogs bark at those they do not recognize: Towards an integration of behaviorism and community psychology. In E. Seidman & J. Rappaport (Eds.), *Handbook of community psychology.* New York: Plenum.

Bry, B. H., Conboy, C., & Bisgay, K. (1986). Decreasing adolescent drug use and school failure: Long-term effect of targeted family problem-solving training. *Child and Family Behavior Therapy, 8,* 43-59.

Carpenter, P., & Sugrue, D. P. (1984). Psychoeducation in an outpatient setting: Designing a heterogeneous format for a heterogeneous population of juvenile delinquents. *Adolescence, 19,* 113-122.

Cauce, A. M. (1987). School and peer competence in early adolescence: A test of domain-specific self-perceived competence. *Developmental Psychology, 23,* 287-291.

Cauce, A. M., Reid, M., & Landesmann, S. (in press). Social support in young children: Measurement, description, and behavioral impact. In I. G. Sarason, B. R. Sarason, & G. Pierce (Eds.), *Social support: An interactional perspective.* New York: John Wiley.

Cauce, A. M., & Srebnik, D. S. (in press). Peer networks in social support: A focus for preventive efforts with youths. In L. Bond, B. Compas, & C. Swift (Eds.), *Primary prevention of psychopathology: Prevention in the schools.* Hanover, NH: University Press of New England.

Coie, J. D. (1985). Fitting social skills intervention to the target group. In B. H. Schneider, K. H. Rubin, & J. E. Ledingham (Eds.), *Children's peer relations: Issues in assessment and intervention* (pp. 141-156). New York: Springer-Verlag.

Coie, J. D., & Krehbiel, G. (1984). Effects of academic tutoring on the social status of low-achieving socially rejected children. *Child Development, 55,* 1465-1478.

Coie, J. D., & Kupersmidt, J. B. (1983). A behavioral analysis of emerging social status in boy's groups. *Child Development, 54,* 1400-1416.

Curran, J. P., Farrell, A. B., & Grunberger, A. J. (1984). Social skills: A critique and rapprochement. In P. Trower (Ed.), *Radical approaches to social skills training* (pp. 47-88). New York: Methuen.

Deshler, D. D., & Schumaker, J. B. (1986). Learning strategies: An instructional alternative for low-achieving adolescents. *Exceptional Children, 52,* 583-590.

Dishion, T. J., Loeber, R., Stouthamer-Loeber, M., & Patterson, G. R. (1984). Skill deficits and male adolescent delinquency. *Journal of Abnormal Child Psychology, 12,* 37-54.

Dodge, K. A. (1985). Facets of social interaction and the assessment of social competence in children. In B. H. Sneider, K. H. Rubin, & J. E. Ledingham (Eds.), *Children's peer relations: Issues in assessment and intervention* (pp. 5-22). New York: Springer-Verlag.

Dodge, K. A., Pettit, G. L., McClaskey, C. L., & Brown, M. M. (1986). Social competence in children. *Monographs of the Society for Research in Child Development, 51*(2), 1-85.

Durlak, J. A., & Jason, L. A. (1984). Preventive programs for school-aged children and adolescents. In M. C. Roberts & L. Peterson (Eds.), *Prevention of problems in childhood: Psychological research and applications* (pp. 103-132). New York: John Wiley.

Elias, M. J., & Branden, L. R. (1988). Primary prevention of behavioral and emotional problems in school-aged populations. *School Psychology Review, 17,* 581-592.

Elias, M. J., & Clabby, J. F. (1988). Teaching social decision making. *Educational Leadership, 45,* 52-55.

Felner, R. D., Ginter, M. A., & Primavera, J. (1982). Primary prevention during school transitions: Social support and environmental structure. *American Journal of Community Psychology, 10,* 277-290.

Ford, M. E. (1982). Social cognition and social competence in adolescence. *Developmental Psychology, 18*, 323-340.

Ford, M. E., & Tisak, M. S. (1983). A further search for social intelligence. *Journal of Educational Psychology, 75*, 196-206.

Freedman, B. J., Rosenthal, L., Donahoe, C. P., Jr., Schlundt, D. G., & McFall, R. M. (1978). A social-behavioral analysis of skill deficits in delinquent and nondelinquent adolescent boys. *Journal of Consulting and Clinical Psychology, 46*, 1448-1462.

Friedman, R. M., Quick, J., Mayo, J., & Palmer, J. (1982). Social skills training within a day treatment program for emotionally disturbed adolescents. *Child and Youth Services, 5*, 139-152.

Furman, W. (1980). Promoting social development: Developmental implications for treatment. In B. H. Lahey & A. E. Kazdin (Eds.), *Advances in clinical child psychology* (Vol. 3, pp. 1-40). New York: Plenum.

Gettinger, M. (1984). Achievement as a function of time spent learning and time needed for learning. *American Educational Research Journal, 21*, 617-628.

Gilchrist, L. D., Schinke, S. P., Snow, W. H., Schilling, R. F., & Senechal, V. (1988). The transition to junior high school: Opportunities for primary prevention. *Journal of Primary Prevention, 8*, 99-108.

Ginzberg, E., Berliner, H. S., & Ostow, M. (1988). *Young people at risk: Is prevention possible?* Boulder, CO: Westview.

Glenwick, D. S., & Jason, L. A. (1984). Locus of intervention in child cognitive behavior therapy: Implications of a behavioral community psychology perspective. In A. Meyers & W. E. Craighead (Eds.), *Cognitive behavior therapy for children* (pp. 129-162). New York: Plenum.

Glick, B., & Goldstein, A. P. (1987). Aggresssion replacement training. *Journal of Counseling and Development, 65*, 356-362.

Goldstein, A. P., Sprafkin, R. P., Gershaw, J., & Klein, P. (1983). Structured learning: A psychoeducational approach for teaching social competencies. *Behavioral Disorders, 8*, 161-170.

Green, K. D., Forehand, R., Beck, S. J., & Vosk, B. (1980). An assessment of the relationship among measures of children's social competence and children's academic achievement. *Child Development, 51*, 1149-1156.

Greenwood, C. R., Granger, D., Terry, B., Wade, L., Stanley, S. O., Thibadeau, S., & Delquadri, J. C. (1984). Teacher- versus peer-mediated instruction: An eco-behavioral analysis of achievement outcomes. *Journal of Applied Behavior Analysis, 17*, 521-538.

Gresham, F. M. (1985). Utility of cognitive-behavioral procedures for social skills training with children: A critical review. *Journal of Abnormal Psychology, 13*, 411-423.

Gresham, F. M. (1988). Social skills: Conceptual and applied aspects of assessment, training, and social validation. In J. C. Witt, S. N. Elliott, & F. M. Gresham (Eds.), *Handbook of behavior therapy in education* (pp. 523-546). New York: Plenum.

Halpern, A. S. (1979). Adolescents and young adults. *Exceptional Children, 45*, 518-528.

Hardwick, P. J., Pounds, A. B., & Brown, M. (1985). Preventative adolescent psychiatry? Practical problems in running social skills groups for younger adolescents. *Journal of Adolescence, 8*, 357-367.

Harter, S. G. (1988). Causes, correlates and the functional role of global self-worth: A life-span perspective. In J. Kolligian & R. Sternberg (Eds.), *Perceptions of competence and incompetence across the life-span.* New Haven, CT: Yale University Press.

Hawkins, J. D., & Weis, J. G. (1985). The social development model: An integrated approach to delinquency prevention. *Journal of Primary Prevention, 6,* 73-97.

Hazel, J. S., Schumaker, J. B., Sherman, J. A., & Sheldon-Wildgen, J. (1982). Social skills training with court-adjudicated delinquents. *Child and Youth Services, 5,* 117-137.

Jason, L. A., Betts, D. M., Johnson, J. H., Smith, S., Krueckenberg, S., & Craddock, M. (in press). An evaluation of an orientation plus tutoring prevention project. *Professional School Psychology.*

Jason, L. A., Durlak, J. A., & Holton-Walker, E. (1984). Prevention of child problems in the schools. In M. Roberts & L. Peterson (Eds.), *Prevention of problems in childhood* (pp. 311-341). New York: John Wiley.

Jason, L. A., Ferone, L., & Soucy, G. (1979). Teaching peer-tutoring behaviors in first and third grade classrooms. *Psychology in the Schools, 16,* 261-269.

Jason, L. A., Frasure, S., & Ferone, L. (1981). Establishing supervising behaviors in eighth graders and peer-tutoring behaviors in first graders. *Child Study Journal, 11,* 201-219.

Jason, L. A., Olson, T., & Pillen, B. (1987). Comp-tutor: A computer-based preventive intervention. *School Counselor, 34,* 116-122.

Jason, L. A., & Rhodes, J. E. (in press). Children helping children: Implications for prevention. *Journal of Primary Prevention.*

Jennings, W. S., & Kohlberg, L. (1983). Effects of a just community programme on the moral development of youthful offenders. *Journal of Moral Education, 12,* 33-50.

Kane, J. S., & Lawler, E. E., III. (1978). Methods of peer assessment. *Psychological Bulletin, 85,* 555-586.

Kelly, W. J., Salzberg, C. L., Levy, S. M., Warrenteltz, T. W., Adams, Crouse, T. R., & Beegle, G. P. (1983). The effects of role-playing and self-monitoring on the generalization of vocational social skills by behaviorally disordered adolescents. *Behavioral Disorders, 9,* 27-35.

Kendall, P. C. (1984). Social cognition and problem solving: A developmental and child-clinical interface. In *Applications of cognitive-developmental theory.* New York: Academic Press.

Ladd, G. W. (1984). Social skill training with children: Issues in research and practice. *Clinical Psychology Review, 4,* 317-337.

LeCroy, C. W. (1982). Social skills training with adolescents: A review. *Child and Youth Services, 5,* 91-116.

LeCroy, C. W., & Rose, S. D. (1986). Evaluation of preventive interventions for enhancing social competence in adolescents. *Social Work Research and Abstracts, 22,* 8-16.

Leone, P. (1984). A descriptive follow-up of behaviorally disordered adolescents. *Behavioral Disorders, 9,* 207-214.

Maheady, L., Sacca, M. K., & Harper, G. F. (1987). Classwide student tutoring teams: The effects of peer-mediated instruction on the academic performance of secondary mainstreamed students. *Journal of Special Education, 21,* 107-121.

McConaughy, S. H. (1986). Social competence and behavioral problems of learning disabled boys aged 12-16. *Journal of Learning Disabilities, 19,* 101-106.

McConnell, S. R. (1987). Entrapment effects and the generalization and maintenance of social skills training for elementary school students with behavioral disorders. *Behavioral Disorders, 12,* 252-263.

McCullagh, J. G. (1982). Assertion training for boys in junior high school. *Social Work in Education, 5,* 41-51.

Michelson, L., Sugai, D. P., Wood, R. P., & Kazdin, A. E. (1983). *Social skills assessment and training with children.* New York: Plenum.

Miller, C. T., & Gibbs, E. D. (1984). High school students' attitudes and actions toward "slow learners." *American Journal of Mental Deficiency, 89,* 156-166.

Nair, D., & Jason, L. A. (1985). An investigation and analysis of social networks among children. *Special Sciences in the Schools, 14,* 43-52.

Nelson-Jones, R. (1986). Relationship skills training in schools: Some fieldwork observations. *British Journal of Guidance and Counseling, 14,* 295-305.

Patton, P. L. (1985). A model for teaching rational behavior skills to emotionally disturbed youth in a public school setting. *School Counselor, 32,* 381-387.

Rhodes, J. E., & Jason, L. A. (1988). *Preventing substance abuse among children and adolescents.* New York: Pergamon.

Rotheram, M. J. (1982). Variations in children's assertiveness due to trainer assertion level. *Journal of Community Psychology, 10,* 228-236.

Schloss, P. J., Schloss, C. N., & Harris, L. (1984). A multiple baseline analysis of an interpersonal skills training program for depressed youth. *Behavioral Disorders, 9,* 182-188.

Shapiro, R. D. (1988). Preventing academic failure. *School Psychology Review, 17,* 601-613.

Small, R. W., & Schinke, S. P. (1983). Teaching competence on residential group care: Cognitive problem solving and interpersonal skills training with emotionally disturbed preadolescents. *Journal of Social Service Research, 7,* 1-16.

Trower, P. (1982). Toward a generative model of social skills: A critique and synthesis. In J. P. Curran & P. Monti (Eds.), *Social skills training: A practical handbook for assessment and treatment* (pp. 399-427). New York: Guilford.

Weissberg, R. P., & Allen, J. P. (1986). Promoting children's social skills and adaptive interpersonal behavior. In B. A. Edelstein & L. Michelson (Eds.), *Handbook of prevention* (pp. 153-175). New York: Plenum.

Zigler, E., & Trickett, P. K. (1978). IQ, social competence, and evaluation of early childhood intervention programs. *American Psychologist, 33,* 789-798.

6. Sport as a Context for Developing Competence

Steven J. Danish
Virginia Commonwealth University

Albert J. Petitpas
Springfield College

Bruce D. Hale
Pennsylvania State University

For some adolescents sport can be an opportunity to prove themselves; for others it can be an environment where they begin to know themselves. Sport has such a potential because it provides us with immediate and specific feedback about our performance. It is an experience that is personal, concrete, time limited, and intense. The opportunity for such feedback in most life experiences is infrequent because the criteria for evaluation are not so readily available. In this chapter we will examine how, and under what conditions, sport can enhance the development of competence. Specific programs designed to promote competence will be described. Finally, we will discuss how the skills learned through sport participation can be applied in later life.

> Sport is such a pervasive activity in contemporary America that to ignore it is to overlook one of the most significant aspects of society. It is a social phenomenon which extends into education, politics, economics, art, the mass media, and even international diplomatic relations. Involvement in sport, either as a participant or in more indirect ways, is almost considered a public duty by many Americans. (Eitzen, 1984, p. 9)

American culture places high value on sports. It is a major source of entertainment and provides heroes for the young and old (Reppucci, 1987). More than 20 million children aged 6-15 participate in one or more extraschool sports yearly (Magill, Ash, & Smoll, 1978) at a cost of $17 billion (Martens, 1978). Only family, school, and television involve children's time more than sport (Institute for Social Research, 1985). Not only has sport become a

AUTHORS' NOTE: *Preparation of this chapter was supported in part by Office of Substance Abuse Prevention Grant 1-H84-AD00489-01. Its contents are solely the responsibility of the authors and do not necessarily represent the official views of OSAP.*

169

major influence on the development of children, it has become a cultural phenomenon that permeates all of society (Nelson, 1982). It is a social institution comparable to other social institutions such as religion, law, government, politics, education, and medicine.

The status sport has attained in our society enhances its importance to youth. But even before children understand sport as a cultural phenomenon, the development of their self-esteem is influenced by their participation in sport. Despite its immediate value to children, the importance of sport as a vehicle to enhance personal development is in question. Psychologists have lined up on both sides of the discussion. Some have argued that sport builds character; others say it promotes character disorders.

In this chapter, we will briefly review the empirical literature that examines the relationship between sport and competence. Following the review a framework will be developed for understanding how, if, and under what conditions sport contributes to personal competence. This framework is based on our belief that sport has the potential either to enhance or to inhibit development among adolescents. For sport to promote competence, the sport experience must be designed specifically with such a purpose in mind. Examples of sport programs that enhance personal and social competence will be described. Finally, we will consider how the skills learned through sport participation can be applied in later life.

THE CONCEPT OF COMPETENCE

One of the inherent problems in understanding competence has been the difficulty of developing a definition with which both theorists and researchers can agree and that has validity across the life span. The issue of whether experience in one period of life affects an individual's behavior at a later point in life is critical to the understanding of this concept. If it is possible to show continuity over time and across situations, we will have a better understanding of the roots of competence and the nature of human development. As such the work of stage theorists such as Erikson (1950) is important for understanding the development of competence. Competence viewed developmentally is not an end state but a process related to an individual's particular stage of life.

White (1959, 1963) has been credited by many with introducing the concept of competence. He considered competence to be an innate need of infants to master their environment that exists independent of the instinctual drives for food, sex, or avoidance of pain. Observations of infants and young children at play reveal that they will stay actively involved with objects on which they can have some effect (Piaget, 1954). The more possibilities for manipulation, the longer the infant will explore. White felt that infants develop feelings of satisfaction and enjoyment in being able to influence their world. This independent energy is referred to as "effectance" and the emotional satisfaction as "feelings of efficacy" (White, 1963).

These feelings of efficacy experienced at one stage of the life span have an impact on subsequent stages. As described by Havighurst (1953), developmental tasks are encountered at each stage. These tasks are a set of skills that are acquired as individuals gain mastery over different areas of intellectual development, social and interpersonal skills, and emotionality. The recognition that competence is not a unitary concept but refers to several areas of mastery has resulted in a stronger construct (Harter, 1978). The mastery of skills associated with later stages of development is enhanced by competence in skills acquired at earlier life stages. However, mastery in one area, for example motor skills, does not necessarily transfer to another area. The issue of transferability is a critical one in our discussion of whether competence in sport relates to personal competence; it will be considered in more detail later.

As one progresses through the stages, certain demands or social expectations are placed upon the individual by society. The effort to adjust to these demands produces a state of tension that provokes action. This action is the use of the set of developmental skills just recently acquired. Successful achievement or learning of a task promotes happiness and suggests that the individual is likely to be successful at mastering other developmental tasks. Failure to acquire the skills necessary for task mastery can lead to personal unhappiness, societal disapproval, and difficulty in achieving later developmental tasks. Thus with age individuals begin to adopt external assessments of their performance that then influence their perceptions of their competence.

For the purposes of this chapter, the definition of *competence* developed by Danish, D'Augelli, and Ginsberg (1984) will be used. This definition is based, in part, on White's (1974) perspective on coping, which involves the ability to (a) gain and process new information, (b) maintain control over one's emotional state, and (c) move freely in one's environment. Danish, D'Augelli, and Ginsberg (1984, p. 531) define "competence" as "the ability to do life planning, to be self reliant, and to seek the resources of others in coping." At different stages or levels of development, these skills relate to different behaviors.

SPORT AND THE DEVELOPMENT OF PERSONAL COMPETENCE

The process whereby individuals acquire attitudes, behaviors, values, and skills through sport participation has been a topic of increasing interest and debate. Almost every coach, athlete, and sport psychologist believes that participation in sports can have a beneficial effect on the psychosocial development of children and adolescents. Further, many supporters of youth sports programs believe that what is learned "on the playing field" is directly transferable to "the classroom" and "the boardroom."

In this section we will examine the literature from three perspectives: historical, empirical, and conceptual.

A Historical Perspective

The belief that sport provides "training for life" has its roots in the turn-of-the-century movement to legitimize athletics and physical education. It was assumed that through sports children learned good sportsmanship and other values and skills necessary in a competitive society. At the same time participation in sports was viewed as an important means of maintaining social control over children. Youth could be taught to accept the norms and rules of the existing culture, use their free time constructively, and conform to the status quo. For many decades this philosophy prevailed.

By the 1960s and 1970s the philosophy concerning the value of sport had changed. Professionals began to worry that sport participation, especially for youth, had the potential of limiting rather than enhancing individual development. Ogilivie and Tutko (1971) discussed the potential for sport to produce "characters" as opposed to character. They contended that the environment of competitive athletics is not conducive to the development of prosocial behavior. Orlick and Botterill (1975) questioned the overly competitive nature of organized athletics with its unhealthy atmosphere of overbearing parents and the continuing opportunity for repeated failure and resulting loss of self-esteem. Martens (1983) warned that the emphasis on performance rather than learning was potentially dangerous. He noted that youth were being pushed toward unrealistic goals and that playing for extrinsic rewards was reducing intrinsic motivation.

What is most striking about this brief review is that the positions adopted by the writers seem to parallel the prevailing social philosophies of the day. Thus it is not surprising that writers differ on the value of sport during these different periods. Expectations concerning what constitutes appropriate behavior for a child have varied dramatically during this century. During the first half of the century, children were viewed as miniature adults and the activities in which they engaged were expected to prepare them to be hardworking, competitive adults. In recent years child rearing has emphasized the development of prosocial behavior and "doing things for oneself rather than always being concerned with how others see us." The expectations for sport then have mirrored society's present definition of competence.

Therefore, defining competence is a critical first step. The definition we have proposed is developmentally based and process-oriented rather than related to a particular end state. As a result, our review of the empirical literature will focus on the process behaviors specific to various developmental stages. For example, the psychosocial stage theory of development developed by Newman and Newman (1979) seems especially relevant. This theory is based on five organizing concepts: stages of development, developmental tasks, the psychosocial crisis, the central processes for resolving the crisis, and coping behaviors. Such a theory applied to children, adolescents, and young adults aged 8 to 20 could serve as the orienting framework for examining the empirical literature on the value of sport for developing competence.

An Empirical Perspective

Unfortunately, there is little empirical evidence on the relationship between participation in sport and competence. Much of the literature that does exist seems to be more opinion, speculation, and subjective observation than empirical research (Burchard, 1979). Furthermore, researchers who have reviewed the empirical studies conducted to examine the effects of athletic participation on psychosocial development have concluded that the literature consists largely of correlational findings, little experimental manipulation, few longitudinal studies, and a high probability of biased self-selectional effects (Browne & Mahoney, 1984; Morgan, 1980). In other words, few, if any, causal relationships have been established.

The most comprehensive review to date has been conducted by Iso-Aloha and Hatfield (1986). In their examination of correlational studies concerning sport involvement and development, they conclude that self-concept is likely to improve through involvement in activities highly valued by the participants. The basis for this conclusion was drawn from several studies: Koocher (1971) reported that learning to swim (a new skill) enhanced self-concept; Kay, Felker, and Varoz (1972) reported that those with higher athletic competence had higher self-concept; Sonestroem (1982) concluded that fitness training can enhance self-esteem not just merely by participating but by interpreting the experience as personal success and growth in competence; and Duke, Johnson, and Nowicki (1977) noted that increased fitness was associated with a sense of increased personal control.

Not all of the findings are so positive. The "Robbers Cave" experiments (Sherif, Harvey, White, Hood, & Sherif, 1961; Sherif & Sherif, 1953; Sherif, White, & Harvey, 1955) are examples of how competitive sports can be either destructive or constructive depending on their purpose and management. Competitive failure led to impaired interpersonal behavior whereas winning tended to increase aggressive tendencies. However, the inclusion of superordinate goals did reduce conflict and increase cooperation. Burchard (1977) found that losing reduced the enjoyment and produced a less positive attitude toward oneself and others among 11- and 12-year-old hockey players. Finally, Landers and Landers (1978) found that participation in sport may hinder academic performance and that failure in sport may accelerate movement toward increased delinquent behavior.

Following an examination of the considerable empirical literature in the area, Iso-Aloha and Hatfield (1986) concluded that early athletic participation may contribute to later success through reinforcement of the critical behaviors necessary for success. One recent study provides support for this perspective. Seidel and Reppucci (1989) assessed changes in self-perception of various kinds of competence and global self-worth after a season of participation in organized youth sports. Results revealed that, across all groups, children's perceptions of their athletic and scholastic competence, physical appearance, and global self-worth increased from pre- to postseason. The authors concluded that the activities at best promoted the children's psychological development and, at worst, were not psychologically damaging.

All in all, however, the empirical literature does not support a cause-and-effect relationship between sport participation and competence. To address this question, specific experimental studies including the random assignment of participants must be designed. The effect of participating in different sports, the different skill levels of the participants, the different reasons for participating, and the different ages at which participants start must be assessed, as should the impact of different expectations by family, coaches, and teachers, and friends. Finally, it will be important to be sensitive to the individual differences of the participants. Serious participation in sport may have different payoffs for girls than for boys in terms of self-actualization and achievement (Crandell & Battle, 1970; Kleiber & Kane, 1984).

Thus it is not possible to conclude definitively that sport participation enhances competence, largely because of the lack of well-designed studies and an understanding of the different variables that must be considered. However, before we reject a causal relationship, let's examine the issue from a conceptual perspective.

A Conceptual Perspective

If we adopt White's (1963) framework as described earlier, feelings of efficacy should motivate effort in the neophyte athlete. A sense of competence originates from subjective feelings of confidence in one's ability to master the environment. Preschoolers who are more coordinated interact more quickly and in a more extended manner with their environment and gain a better sense of trust in their environment and themselves. Better developed physical abilities enhance the acquisition of a sense of autonomy, achievement, and initiative and promote stronger family and peer relationships. As children continue to explore and play, they learn what they can do. Their feelings of competence result from their successful experiences with the world.

Effectance prompts manipulation and exploratory behavior. It can be observed in the child who engages in solitary practice of a specific sport skill. He or she spends hour after hour working on a jump shot or a headstand. This solitary effect is motivated by the intrinsic satisfaction of mastering the environment.

Children who are more physically coordinated seem to have a head start at developing self-esteem and the potential to reach higher levels of physical skills. Equally important is the likelihood that they will also develop more effective interpersonal and intra-personal skills. Because of these accomplishments (achieving age-appropriate developmental tasks) by the age of 10, athletic children are often seen as leaders (Ambron & Brodzinsky, 1979). Participation in sports then is rewarded by peers and adults at very early ages.

If children are not impeded by the competency needs of over-involved parents or coaches, they will continue to explore, take risks, and learn strategies to affect their environment. Children who are taught to fear failure or mistakes may develop self-im-posed restrictions that can severely compromise further opportunities for the development of feelings of efficacy. Play then ceases to be meaningful and rewarding.

White (1963) felt that an initial sense of competence was necessary or children would not be able to benefit from the process of identification. Children identify with those individuals whose competence they admire. They imitate basketball players, such as Michael Jordan, or tennis stars, such as Steffi Graf, in the hope of developing their own levels of competence. Like simpler forms of imitation, identification requires that children feel confident that the skills they want to improve or refine are already part of their repertoire. Through trial and error children discover which identifications will work and which are doomed to failure. Without an initial foundation of feelings of efficacy, it is doubtful whether children would be able to gain maximum benefits from the process of identification. White (1963) contends that identification must be viewed in terms of "attempted action." Clearly people can dream of acquiring skills beyond their present range, but it is action and its consequences that provide children with feedback on which identifications might succeed and which might fall.

Sports become a logical testing ground for levels of personal competence once children move outside the home environment, in part because of its value in society. Moreover, the mastery of the intricacies of sport requires considerable mental and physical skill. The intrinsic rewards of being able to master one's environment are quickly matched by the external reinforcements that also accrue from being the strongest, fastest, or simply the best player. Even in the sandlots children quickly learn that the most competent in the sport will get to choose the other players to make up the teams for the pickup games. On the other hand, the least competent will be the last one selected, often with comments like, "I guess that leaves me with Jimmy." For some children being the last one picked can become so traumatic that they will avoid the athletic field and never participate in the sport again. Other children will take the initial rebuff as a challenge and practice on their own until their level of competency matches or surpasses that of their playmates. Subsequent action depends on the child's appraisal of the meaning of the situation. A situation perceived as a threat will often result in avoidance; an appraisal of a situation as challenging will more likely result in approach (Lazarus & Folkman, 1984).

As children progress through the early school years, they are introduced to the more formal sports structure. Youth sports and school teams provide more clearly defined rules and criteria for measuring personal competence. Although numerous reasons for sports participation have been cited in the literature, Gould and Horn (1984) have identified six motives that are the most consistently listed by young athletics between the ages of 8 and 19. These are improving skills, having fun, being with friends, experiencing thrills and excitement, achieving success, and developing fitness. Gould (1987) concludes that children will continue to participate in sport if their motives are being fulfilled but will discontinue participation if their interests change or if they feel they are having little success in the activity. At the youth sport and school levels of experience, children continue to compare their skills with those of their peers. The most skillful will become identified as the star athletes. In addition to intrinsic rewards from the mastery of increasingly more difficult skills and competitions, they also accrue considerable external reinforcement for their athletic accomplishments. With increased levels of competition, sport becomes one of the most important proving grounds for personal competence. Sport provides clear, immediate feedback. Elite performers continue to develop confidence in their abilities and a stronger identification with the sport. The less gifted athletes often become victims of the athletic system that tends to reward success rather than simply participation. In a "win at all costs" sports environment, athletes with lesser skills are unlikely to get opportunities to develop feelings of competence from the sport due to lack of playing time and limited reinforcement for their efforts.

As athletes move into adolescence, their developmental focus shifts from a need to maintain a sense of industry (Erikson, 1959) to a quest for personal identity. As outlined by Erikson, all adolescents must synthesize childhood identifications in such a manner that they can establish a reciprocal relationship with society while simultaneously maintaining a sense of continuity within themselves. What a person thinks he or she can be is a product of past experiences and the feedback of significant others.

Although research (Coleman, 1961; Eitzen, 1975) has shown that athletic success in high school accrues more status than academic achievement, to fully examine the impact of sport on the development of competence among adolescents, we must consider the influence of sports in later adolescence. It is during this period that the need to acquire a personal identity becomes critical. Ironically it is the same sport system that apparently provides so many benefits for the young athlete that may later interfere with opportunities for optimal identity development during this period and in early adulthood.

Chickering (1969) describes late adolescence and early adulthood as periods during which a number of developmental tasks must be confronted. These include achieving competence, managing emotions, becoming autonomous, establishing relationships, developing more mature interpersonal relationships, clarifying purpose, and developing integrity. The psychosocial crisis (Erikson, 1950) of these periods is individual identity versus role diffusion and the central process is role experimentation. As can be seen, this is a period in which the focus is on broadening one's horizons. If the individual continues to invest all his or her energies in sport, he or she may be impeded in engaging in a quest for personal identity (Petitpas & Champagne, 1988). The immediate result may be role strain and frustration (Chartrend & Lent, 1987); the long-term consequences may be foreclosure of the search for an identity (Marcia, 1966).

Stein and Hoffman (1978) delineate a number of role strains athletes experience that are related to their development. Among these conflicts are (a) the demands of simultaneously being a student, athlete, friend, and son or daughter and the concomitant role overloads associated with these demands; (b) the increasing need to compete to meet the expectations of others as opposed to the desire to adopt a more cooperative posture consistent with the appropriate developmental tasks for this period; (c) anxiety about being physically injured while at the same time needing to take risks to excel and to play in pain when necessary; and (d) the increasing external rewards associated with high-level performance at the same time that the need for a sense of internal satisfaction becomes paramount.

Marcia (1966) describes foreclosure as occurring when a commitment to an occupation is made prematurely and without sufficient exploration of one's needs or values. Foreclosure is often brought on by the demands of the environment. However, it may also be the result of the individual choosing to forgo engaging in exploratory behaviors and instead opting to commit to the activity in which he or she has previously been rewarded. In other words, adolescents rewarded for their athletic endeavors may choose not to commit to seeking success in academic activities or other career opportunities. By avoiding exploration a sense of security is gained at the expense of one's search for identity. It should be pointed out that identity foreclosure is not in itself harmful. In fact, many professions require early and relatively complete commitments. Foreclosure becomes problematic when individuals fail to develop adequate coping skills. It is through the process of exploration that individuals learn more about themselves. They acquire additional social competencies through their interactions with others. They receive feedback about their strengths and weaknesses by testing themselves in a variety of situations. Without such exploration it is likely that one's self-esteem can be too narrowly defined and subject to severe threat in the face of possible loss (Petitpas, 1978).

Two types of foreclosure have been identified: psychological and situational (Henry & Renaud, 1972). In psychological foreclosure individuals avoid change at all cost. They rigidly hold to original commitments and avoid all challenges to their views as a means of maintaining their security. Although in situational foreclosure individuals appear resistant to change, it is a result of a lack of exposure to new ideas, information, or life-styles rather than resistance to change. It is our belief that some adolescents become so involved in sport that identity foreclosure may result.

From this review several conclusions can be drawn: (a) It is not possible to determine empirically that participation in sport contributes to the development of competence because of a paucity of well-designed studies in this area; (b) although we cannot say that sport enhances competence, we can conclude that more interpersonal and intrapersonal youth are more likely to become involved in sport, especially during early adolescence; and (c) for sport to have a positive impact on the development of competence during adolescence and beyond, sport activities must be more developmental in nature. In the next section sport activities designed to enhance the development of the participants will be considered.

DESIGNING SPORT ACTIVITIES TO ENHANCE DEVELOPMENT

Two aspects seem critical in determining developmentally appropriate sport activities: understanding why an adolescent is participating in a sport and ensuring that the activity is intrinsically rewarding. As noted earlier, Gould and Horn (1984) identified improving skills, having fun, being with friends, experiencing thrills and excitement, achieving success, and developing fitness as motives for youth sport participation. Which of these six actually motivates a particular child or adolescent is partially dependent on the individual's age. Therefore, at a minimum, knowing why a child begins an activity and what he or she gains from continuing to participate is necessary for designing appropriate activities.

For an activity to be intrinsically rewarding, it must be enjoyable and challenging. Csikszentmihalyi (1975) posits that the experience of self-rewarding involvement in play and work is a key to optimal development. He has proposed an empirically derived model of enjoyment titled the Flow Model. In the Flow Model *enjoyment* is defined as a balance between the challenges of an activity and the skills of the participant. When the individual perceives the challenges to be greater than his or her skills, anxiety results. Boredom results when an individual appraises his or her skills as being greater than the perceived challenges. When the perceived challenges are equal to an individual's sense of skills, the experience is optimal and is labeled *flow.* Whether in work or play, feedback from activities wherein competence is extended to meet expanding challenges contributes significantly to self-concept and the sense of well-being. Moreover, because greater challenges are sought as abilities expand, the activity becomes growth producing (Danish, Kleiber, & Hall, 1987).

Csikszentmihalyi and his colleagues (Chalip, Csikszentmihalyi, Kleiber, & Larson, 1984; Csikszentmihalyi & Larson, 1984) used an approach called "experience sampling" to examine the subjective experiences associated with various activities of adolescents. The authors found that the combination of challenge, concentration, intrinsic motivation, and positive affect was best reflected in arts, hobbies, sports, and games. They called these activities "transitional" because they require discipline and concentration while still being enjoyable. For this reason they serve as a template for adult activities.

The advantage of tasks that are intrinsically rewarding is that attention to the task is given more readily and intensity is governed more naturally. The individual does not have to struggle to raise or lower arousal if his or her abilities are well matched with, and effectively employed in relation to, the demands of an activity. The challenge for a coach then is to arrange or control circumstances to provide and protect that match.

This is an ongoing process; as abilities improve, greater challenges are required to maintain the intensity. If greater challenges are not present, intensity drops and the individual becomes bored. Of course, the opposite can also occur; a mentor's zeal for providing greater challenges or the individual's own ambitiousness can result in a situation of excessive demand, which is anxiety producing and makes concentration and investment extremely difficult (Danish, Kleiber, & Hall, 1987).

For a coach to understand what motivates an athlete to participate in sport and/or to be able to match the athlete's level of ability with the appropriate task requires not only a knowledge of coaching techniques but the ability to understand and communicate effectively with the athlete. Although adult coaches usually know their sports quite well, the real issue is whether they understand and can relate to their athletes (Singer, 1972). Intervention with the coach, and secondarily with the parents, is likely to have an immediate and significant impact on the motivation and enjoyment level of the athlete.

One program developed to train coaches was designed by Smith and his colleagues (Smith, Smoll, & Curtis, 1978, 1979). First, the authors identified a number of coach and player measures. The coach measures included (a) a system of assessment of observed behaviors, (b) the recall of behaviors by the coaches, (c) the coaches' goals, and (d) their perception of the player's motives. Among the player measures were (a) the players' perception of the coaches, (b) their attitudes toward the coaches, (c) participation and teammates, and (d) both general and athletic self-esteem.

In designing the program the authors collected behavioral observations on 51 Little League coaches and 542 players. At different age levels players were found to be sensitive to punitive comments by coaches. Children who played for supportive, encouraging coaches had significantly higher self-esteem scores at the end of the season. Finally, the technical proficiency of the coaches was more important to older players than to younger ones.

As a result of their initial research, Smith and his colleagues developed a Coaching Effectiveness Training module for coaches. During the two-hour clinic coaches were taught techniques for interacting with players. They were also given feedback on how they behaved during the games in which they coached. Compared with control group coaches, trained coaches were rated as giving more reinforcement, more encouragement after a mistake, and more general technical instruction. Trained coaches were seen as engaging in less punishment, less punitive technical instruction, and less nonreinforcement. Finally, children who played for trained coaches liked their coaches more, felt they were better teachers of the game, and felt that their teams were more cooperative (Smith, Smoll, & Curtis, 1979).

Other researchers and practitioners have developed coaching programs. Perhaps the best known is the certification designed by Martens (1982). The American Coaching Effectiveness Program (ACEP) is a comprehensive educational program for coaches of youth aged 6 to 18. ACEP consists of two parts: (a) sport-specific information and (b) sport medicine and science information.

Each of the coaching training programs has a segment on player-coach communication. Smoll and Smith (1984) make the following recommendations: provide plenty of praise and encouragement and make sure it is sincere; develop realistic expectations; reward effort and correct technique as much as outcome; and provide effective feedback. From our perspective, what is missing from these recommendations as well as the other training programs is the teaching of listening skills that reflect an empathic understanding of the player and his or her concerns (Danish, D'Augelli, & Hauer, 1980). Without the development of these skills, the coach is less able to understand the unique needs and goals of each player.

Although the programs described increase the likelihood that sport activities will enhance development among adolescents, especially younger ones, a significant problem remains. As adolescents are exposed to other activities and experiences and recognize the need to become adept at new developmental tasks, the sport experience may hinder rather than promote development.

DESIGNING SPORT-RELATED
LIFE SKILLS TRAINING PROGRAMS

Each year 35% of youth sport participants drop out (Gould, 1987). Some may drop out because the experience is not a positive one. Others stop participating because it no longer meets their needs. For example, for some youth what was once a pleasurable activity may have become a source of stress as performance demands outweigh perceived capabilities. Yet others have identified alternative means that are more rewarding and intrinsically motivating to reach the developmental tasks on which they are working. For still other youth their participation in sports remains positive and they have identified that much of their self-esteem is based on their level of athletic performance. Consequently they may be unable to develop alternative sources of satisfaction because they fear that they will not be successful in other areas. For this last group their situation can be characterized as an example of "selective optimization" (Baltes & Baltes, 1980). Individuals have a limited amount of time and energy. Based on an assessment of environmental demands and motivation, skills, and biological capacities, individuals select a pathway upon which to focus. Giving up a rewarding activity is difficult when there are no assurances that rewards will be available in the new activity.

Both for those youth who choose to drop out as well as for those who remain, it is reasonable to question whether their experience with sports has facilitated or impeded their competence. In other words, does skill mastery or lack of it transfer and generalize from one area to another? For those youth who have not felt competent in sports, do they begin their new pursuits with a lack of confidence about their ability to be successful? For those youth whose goals have changed, will they transfer and generalize what they have learned to their new activities? Finally, will those youth who persist in sport foreclose the opportunity to expand their identities and thus limit their competence?

Although mastery of skills in later adolescence is enhanced by mastery of related skills early in adolescence, what is not clear is how mastery in one area affects mastery in other areas. For example, Havighurst (1953) identifies developmental tasks related to intellectual development, social and interpersonal skills, and emotional development. What effect will competence in sport have on these various areas?

Auerbach (1986, p. 17), in writing about coping with stress, has raised some critical issues to answered. He asks:

How do we learn from positive experience? How does successful coping in stress situations affect future coping ability? Is there a buildup in generalized ego strength that produces a more competent individual capable of coping with a wider and wider range of situations, or is it simply a function of learning specific instrumental responses via trial and error which may then be applied to new situations? How important are the nature of the causal attributions one makes to himself regarding why he was able to manipulate a situation: that is, does success in dealing with stress automatically breed more and more success in such situations or are there significant moderator variables to be considered?

Observational data suggest that the relationship between success in dealing with crises and future ability in similar situations is complex and dependent on how an event was coped with, how the individual construed the way he coped with it to himself (i.e., the causal attributions he made regarding the reason for his success or failure), and whether coping behaviors used successfully in a given stress situation were appropriately generalized to a new situation.

It would appear then that, for competence to be generalized across the various domains and tasks identified by Harter and Havighurst, several factors must be present. First, the adolescent must understand what set of skills is required to be competent in each of the areas. Second, the adolescent must believe that he or she possesses these skills. Third, the adolescent must know how the skills were learned and how they can be transferred to a different domain or task. When an individual possesses the skills but cannot identify them, he or she is not likely to be able to apply them in another setting and may be unsuccessful in developing a generalized sense of competence.

For competence to be attained, or to have the skills related to competence transfer across domains and tasks and be maintained throughout development, the essential skills must be identified and taught. These skills called "life skills" include (a) learning to set and develop plans to reach goals; (b) acquiring the necessary knowledge to attain the goal; (c) developing sufficient skills (e.g., decision making, relaxation, imagery, positive self-talk, self-control) to attain the goal; (d) learning to assess the risks involved in goal attainment; and (e) identifying and obtaining the needed social support to reach the goal (Danish & D'Augelli, 1983). The Life Development Intervention Program developed by Danish and D'Augelli is designed to teach these skills. This program has been used in a number of contexts and has been described in considerable detail elsewhere (Danish & D'Augelli, 1980; Danish, D'Augelli, & Ginsberg, 1984; Danish & Hale, 1983; Danish, Smyer, & Nowak, 1980).

When taught to athletes, the general goal of the intervention is to assist them in gaining control over their lives by providing them

with skills to direct their future. As a result a sense of empowerment and efficacy develops. The teaching of these skills also enables the athlete to perform better athletically.

Two examples of life skills programs used with adolescents
will be described. The first, Athletes Coaching Teens, uses sport as
a vehicle to motivate high-risk, inner-city early adolescents to
reduce their health-compromising behaviors and increase their
health-enhancing behaviors (Jessor, 1984; Perry & Jessor, 1985).
The second, Success 101, is a one-credit course designed to ease
the transition from high school to college for freshmen student-
athletes.

(1) Athletes Coaching Teens (ACT) is a school-based program
implemented with selected high school students serving as peer
teachers for seventh-grade students in the Richmond City Public
Schools. ACT was developed as part of a three-year substance
abuse prevention demonstration project funded by the Office of
Substance Abuse Prevention. ACT is a comprehensive program
based on a life span developmental and critical life events model
(Danish, D'Augelli, & Ginsberg, 1984; Danish, Smyer, & Nowak,
1980). The focus of ACT is on developing the student's potential
and competence as a means to avoid health-compromising behaviors such as drug use, unsafe sexual activity, violent behavior, and
dropping out of school. The ACT program teaches students "what
to say yes to" as opposed to "just saying no."

The program is targeted at middle school students in the Richmond City Public Schools. These students are largely from minority and economically disadvantaged families who live in neighborhoods where the incidence of crime and drug use is high. In
1988 the ACT staff conducted a citywide study of seventh-grade
students in the school system ($N = 1,350$). The majority of these
students were black (87%), lived with the mother only (60%), and
qualified for the free or reduced school lunch program (60%).
Moreover, these seventh graders reported a high rate of health-
compromising behaviors including drug use, sexual activity, and
violence. Based on this survey, 30% of these students had smoked
cigarettes, 38% had used beer, 15% had used marijuana, 4% had
used cocaine/crack, 32% had shoplifted, 15% had threatened a
teacher, and 59% had sexual intercourse (mostly without ever
using contraception). More important, 11% of these students regu-

larly (i.e., at least once a month) used cigarettes, 13% regularly used beer, 7% regularly used marijuana, 2% regularly used cocaine/crack, 6% regularly shoplifted, 6% regularly threatened a teacher, and 36% regularly had sexual intercourse (Farrell et al., in press).

The ACT project is conducted by the Department of Psychology at Virginia Commonwealth University (VCU) in collaboration with the Office of Planning and Development of the Richmond City Public Schools. In addition to the VCU staff, professional, college, and high school athletes are involved in various stages of program implementation. Professional and college athletes present school assemblies where they discuss excellence through goal setting and attainment as well as the problems associated with drug involvement and other problem behaviors such as teen pregnancy and dropping out of school. The college athletes also assist in training the selected high school students to be ACT leaders. These students are chosen by their schools for their academic performance, leadership qualities, and athletic involvement. They receive special training provided by the ACT staff with the assistance of VCU college athletes. Because these high school students are regarded as positive role models and have grown up in Richmond, they are in a unique position to be effective teachers for middle school youth. Once high school athletes have completed the ACT training program, they implement a seven-session program within middle school health classes.

The purpose of the seven sessions is to teach five skills: (a) to learn to dream and set goals; (b) to learn to develop plans to attain the goals; (c) to identify and overcome roadblocks to reaching the goals; (d) to learn to problem-solve; and (e) to learn to rebound from temporary setbacks. It is our belief that, when students know what they want and how to attain it, they are more likely to feel a sense of personal control and confidence about the future. As a result they will make better decisions and ultimately become better citizens (Danish, Mash, & Howard, in press).

(2) Success 101 is a 10-week course designed to enhance the transition of student-athletes from high school to college. It also serves as a means of preventing the likely involvement of student-athletes with drugs. Research on drug use among adolescents suggests that two factors contribute to drug use among adoles-

cents: (a) needing to cope with the frustrations and stresses of life and (b) wanting to be involved in social activities with friends (Johnston & O'Malley, 1986).

When students arrive at college they experience new stresses and demands on their lives, whether or not they are athletes. Two of these stressors revolve around the increased work load and more difficult academic demands they encounter as well as the social pressures of making new friends and understanding new social norms. The first year, and especially the first semester or term, is a difficult one and more students drop out or decide not to return to school at this time than at any time afterward.

Student-athletes have additional demands. The demands involved in playing intercollegiate athletics are now almost year-round. Athletes must make an extensive time commitment. Athletes can spend as much as two to four hours per day or about 15 to 30 hours per week during the competitive season. Such a commitment is a drain on a student-athlete's time and energy. In addition to the time constraints, the pressures of travel and expectations of coaches, friends, family, fans, and the student him- or herself, as well as dealing with the media, increase the student-athlete's feelings of stress. These athletic-related demands, when added to the normal stresses a new student faces, place the student-athlete under considerable pressure and require the development of new coping strategies. Sometimes the coping is positive to the student-athlete's development; other times it is negative. The student-athlete may decide to focus on athletics rather than on academics. This may result in the student cutting corners in academic work, either taking easy courses and deciding to "major" only in staying academically eligible or doing poorly. The reverse may happen and the student-athlete may drop intercollegiate sports to concentrate on academics. This may leave the student-athlete feeling lost and purposeless if sports have been a major part of his or her life. This may also be financially difficult if the student-athlete is on scholarship.

It is more than likely that the student-athlete will try to cope with both demands. Effective coping requires goal setting, effective time management, good decision-making skills, and learning to relax. If successful in learning to cope, the student-athlete will achieve both academically and athletically. The result will be increased self-confidence. Ineffective coping, on the other hand, could lead to substance use, inappropriate control of emotions, lack of concentration, and other behaviors associated with a lack of academic and athletic success.

FROM COMPETENCE IN SPORTS TO COMPETENCE IN LIFE

When children begin to participate in sport, their physical prowess determines their athletic performance. With age the physical abilities of the adolescent athlete become less important and his or her level of mental preparation becomes increasingly more important. Thus by the time he or she reaches later adolescence, it is the quality and level of mental preparation that determines success as an athlete. Better athletes concentrate more, talk more positively to themselves, set clearer goals, develop more well-defined plans to reach their goals, and deal more effectively with the stress of competition. We believe that, for athletes to attain excellence in sport, they must not only possess these skills but know that they do. In other words, it is not enough for the athlete to be a good goal setter, or to concentrate well or to be able to relax under pressure; he or she must be able to recognize that he or she possesses these skills.

As life circumstances and developmental tasks change for young athletes, and they begin to focus on new domains to meet their needs, their efforts must be redirected. The skills necessary for effective mental preparation are not athletic in nature. These skills are *life* skills and they are what determines the level of excellence reached, regardless of whether they are applied to sport, business, politics, the arts, or the sciences. So for the skills to be transferred to the new setting, the athlete must recognize not only the existence of these skills but their transferability to other settings. Assuming that athletes will automatically recognize the existence and transferability of these skills is naive. Interventions must be designed to facilitate this understanding. The ACT program and Success 101 are examples of such interventions. As developmental psychologists, community psychologists, and sport psychologists gather more information about the relationship of sport and personal competence, more and better programs will be developed.

In 1983 the senior author of this chapter noted:

> Sport has taken on new meaning for many individuals as they discover new meaning in the experience of participation. Sport need not be a place where one continues to have to prove oneself, it can be a place where one begins to know oneself. When knowing becomes as important as proving, sport becomes an essential vehicle for developing personal competence. Sport can provide participants with immediate and specific feedback about their performance. There is a clear beginning and end and an opportunity to evaluate one's progress toward a goal. This opportunity is infrequent in our life experiences for we rarely have the criteria for evaluation. In sum, sport provides an environment which is more *personal, concrete, time-limited,* and *intense* than the rest of society. (Danish, 1983, pp. 237-238)

It is our belief that, although this statement is accurate, it is incomplete. The understanding it describes will not be developed without specific efforts designed to teach the athlete how to know him- or herself. Sport participation should not be seen as an end point but as a point of departure for developing personal competence across settings.

REFERENCES

Ambron, S. R., & Brodzinsky, D. (1979). *Lifespan human development.* New York: Holt, Rinehart & Winston.

Auerbach, S. (1986). Assumptions of crisis theory and a temporal model of crisis intervention. In S. M. Auerbach & A. L. Stolberg (Eds.), *Crisis intervention with children and families* (pp. 3-37). Washington, DC: Hemisphere/Harper & Row.

Baltes, P. B., & Baltes, M. M. (1980). Plasticity and variability in psychological aging: Methodological and theoretical issues. In G. Gurski (Ed.), *Determining the effects of aging on the central nervous system.* Berlin: Shering.

Browne, M. A., & Mahoney, M. J. (1984). Sport psychology. *Annual Review of Psychology, 35,* 605-625.

Burchard, J. D. (1977). *Competition and social competence.* Paper presented at the Canadian Psychomotor Learning and Sports Psychology Symposium, Banff, Canada.

Burchard, J. D. (1979). Competitive youth sports and social competence. In M. W. Kent & J. E. Rolf (Eds.), *The primary prevention of psychopathology: Vol. 3. Promoting social competence and coping in children.* Hanover, NH: University Press of New England.

Chalip, L., Csikszentmihalyi, M., Kleiber, D., & Larson, R. (1984). Variations of experience in formal and informal sport. *Research Quarterly for Exercise and Sport, 55,* 109-116.

Chartrand, J., & Lent, R. (1987). Sports counseling: Enhancing the development of the student-athlete. *Journal of Counseling and Development, 66,* 164-167.

Chickering, A. W. (1969). *Education and identity.* San Francisco: Jossey-Bass.

Coleman, J. S. (1961). *The adolescent society.* New York: Free Press.

Crandell, V., & Battle, E. (1970). The antecedents of adult correlates of academic and intellectual achievement efforts. In J. Hill (Ed.), *Minnesota Symposium on Child Psychology* (Vol. 4). Minneapolis: University of Minnesota Press.

Csikszentmihalyi, M. (1975). *Beyond boredom and anxiety.* San Francisco: Jossey-Bass.

Csikszentmihalyi, M., & Larson, R. (1984). *Being adolescent.* New York: Basic Books.

Danish, S. J. (1983). Musing about personal competence: The contributions of sport, health, and fitness. *American Journal of Community Psychology, 11*(3), 221-240.

Danish, S., & D'Augelli, A. R. (1980). Promoting competence and enhancing development through life development intervention. In L. A. Bond & J. C. Rosen (Eds.), *Competence and coping during adulthood* (pp. 105-129). Hanover, NH: University Press of New England.

Danish, S., & D'Augelli, A. R. (1983). *Helping skills II: Life development intervention.* New York: Human Sciences.

Danish, S., D'Augelli, A. R., & Ginsberg, M. (1984). Life development intervention: Promotion of mental health through the development of competence. In S. Brown & R. Lent (Eds.), *Handbook of counseling psychology* (pp. 520-544). New York: John Wiley.

Danish, S. J., D'Augelli, A. R., & Hauer, A. L. (1980). *Helping skills: A basic training program* (2nd ed.). New York: Human Sciences Press.

Danish, S. J., & Hale, B. D. (1983). Sport psychology: Teaching skills to athletes and coaches. *Journal of Physical Education, Recreation, and Dance, 11-13,* 80-81.

Danish, S., Kleiber, D., & Hall, H. (1987). Developmental intervention and motivation enhancement in the context of sport. In *Advances in motivation and achievement: Enhancing motivation* (Vol. 5, pp. 211-238). Greenwich, CT: JAI.

Danish, S., Mash, J. M., & Howard, C. W. (in press). "But will it play in Peoria?": The problem of technology transfer in alcohol and other drug use prevention programs. In J. Swisher & B. McColgan (Eds.), *Experiences in prevention with high risk youth.*

Danish, S., Smyer, M. A., & Nowak, C. A. (1980). Developmental intervention: Enhancing life-event processes. In P. B. Baltes & O. G. Brim, Jr. (Eds.), *Life-span development and behavior* (Vol. 3, pp. 339-366). New York: Academic Press.

Duke, M., Johnson, T. C., & Nowicki, S., Jr. (1977). Effects of sports fitness camp experience on locus of control orientation in children, ages 6 to 14. *Research Quarterly, 48,* 280-283.

Eitzen, D. S. (1975). Athletics in the status system of male adolescents: A replication of Coleman's The adolescent society. *Adolescence, 10,* 267-276.

Eitzen, D. S. (1984). *Sport in contemporary society.* New York: St. Martin's.

Erikson, E. H. (1950). *Childhood and society.* New York: Norton.

Erikson, E. H. (1959). Identity and the life cycle. *Psychological Issues, 1,* 1-171.

Farrell, A. D., Howard, C. W., Danish, S. J., Smith, A. F., Mash, J. M., & Stovall, K. L. (in press). Athletes coaching teens for substance abuse prevention: Substance use and risk factors in urban middle school students. In J. Swisher & B. McColgan (Eds.), *Experiences in prevention with high risk youth.*

Gould, D. (1987). Promoting positive sport experiences for children. In J. R. May & M. J. Asken (Eds.), *Sport psychology: The psychological health of the athlete.* New York: PMA.

Gould, D., & Horn, T. S. (1984). Participation motivation in young athletes. In J. M. Silva & R. S. Weinberg (Eds.), *Psychological foundations of sports.* Champaign, IL: Human Kinetics.

Harter, S. (1978). Effectance motivation reconsidered, toward a developmental model. *Human Development, 21,* 34-64.

Harter, S. (1981). The development of competence motivation in the mastery of cognitive and physical skills: Is there still a place for joy? *Psychology of Motor Behavior and Sport—1980,* 3-29.

Harter, S. (1983). The development of the self-system. In M. Hetherington (Ed.), *Handbook of child psychology: Social and personality development* (Vol. 4). New York: John Wiley.

Havighurst, R. (1953). *Developmental tasks and education.* New York: John Wiley.

Henry, M., & Renaud, H. (1972). Examined and unexamined lives. *Research Reporter, 7(1),* 5.

Institute for Social Research. (1985). *Time, goods & well-being.* Ann Arbor: University of Michigan.

Iso-Aloha, S., & Hatfield, B. (1986). *Psychology of sports: A social psychological approach.* Dubuque, IA: William C. Brown.

Jessor, R. (1984). Adolescent development and behavioral health. In J. D. Matarazzo et al. (Eds.), *Behavioral health: A handbook of health enhancement and disease prevention.* New York: John Wiley.

Johnston, L., & O'Malley, P. (1986). Why do the nation's students use drugs and alcohol: Self-reported reasons from nine national surveys. *Journal of Drug Issues, 16,* 29-66.

Kay, R. S., Felker, D. W., & Varoz, R. O. (1972). Sports interests and abilities as contributors to self-concept in junior high school boys. *Research Quarterly, 43,* 208-215.

Kleiber, D. A., & Kane, M. (1984). Sex differences and the use of leisure as adaptive potentiation. *Society and Leisure, 7,* 165-173.

Koocher, G. P. (1971). Swimming, competence, and personality change. *Journal of Personality and Social Psychology, 18,* 275-278.

Landers, D. M., & Landers, S. (1978). Socialization via interscholastic athletics: Its effects on educational attainment. *Research Quarterly, 47,* 75-83.

Lazarus, R. S., & Folkman, S. (1984). *Stress, appraisal and coping.* New York: Springer.

Magill, R. A., Ash, M. J., & Smoll, F. L. (Eds.). (1978). *Children in sports: A contemporary anthology.* Champaign, IL: Human Kinetics.

Marcia, J. E. (1966). Development and validation of ego-identity status. *Journal of Personality and Social Psychology, 3,* 551-558.

Martens, R. (Ed.). (1978). *Joy and sadness in children's sports.* Champaign, IL: Human Kinetics.

Martens, R. (1982). *The American coaching effectiveness program.* Champaign, IL: Human Kinetics.

Martens, R. (1983). Coaching to enhance self-worth. In T. Orlick, J. Partington, & J. Salmela (Eds.), *Mental training for coaches and athletes.* Ottawa: Coaching Association of Canada.

Michener, J. A. (1976). *Sports in America.* New York: Random House.

Morgan, W. P. (1980). The trait psychology controversy. *Research Quarterly Exercise Sports, 51,* 50-76.

Nelson, J. (1982, Winter). Sport in America: New directions and new potentials. In S. W. White (Ed.), *Sports in America* [Special issue]. *National Forum,* pp. 5-6.

Newman, B., & Newman, P. (1979). *Development through life.* Homewood, IL: Dorsey.

Ogilivie, R., & Tutko, T. (1971). Sport: If you want to build character, try something else. *Psychology Today, 5,* 61-63.

Orlick, T. D. (1972). *A socio-psychological analysis of early sports participation.* Unpublished doctoral dissertation, University of Alberta.

Orlick, T. D., & Botterill, C. (1975). *Every kid can win.* Chicago: Nelson-Hall.

Perry, C. L., & Jessor, R. (1985). The concept of health promotion and the prevention of adolescent drug abuse. *Health Education Quarterly, 12,* 169-184.

Petitpas, A. (1978). Identity foreclosure: A unique challenge. *Personnel and Guidance Journal, 56,* 558-561.

Petitpas, A. L., & Champagne, D. E. (1988). Developmental programming for intercollegiate athletes. *Journal of College Student Development, 29*(5), 454-460.

Piaget, J. (1954). *The construction of reality in the child.* New York: Basic Books.

Reppucci, N. D. (1987). Prevention and ecology: Teenage pregnancy, child sexual abuse and organized youth sports. *American Journal of Community Psychology, 15,* 1-22.

Seidel, R. W., & Reppucci, N. D. (1989). *The psychological development of nine year old males participating in youth sports.* Unpublished manuscript, University of Virginia.

Sherif, M., Harvey, O. J., White, B., Hood, W., & Sherif, C. (1961). *Inter-group conflict and cooperation: The Robbers Cave experiment.* Norman: University of Oklahoma Press.

Sherif, M., & Sherif, C. W. (1953). *Groups in harmony and tension.* New York: Harper & Row.

Sherif, M., White, B. J., & Harvey, O. J. (1955). Status in experimentally produced groups. *American Journal of Sociology, 60,* 370-379.

Singer, R. N. (1972). *Coaching, athletics, and psychology.* New York: McGraw-Hill.

Smith, R. E., Smoll, F. L., & Curtis, B. (1978). Coaching behaviors in Little League baseball. In F. L. Smoll & R. E. Smith (Eds.), *Psychological perspectives in youth sports.* New York: Hemisphere.

Smith, R. E., Smoll, F. L., & Curtis, B. (1979). Coach effectiveness training: A cognitive-behavioral approach to enhancing relationship skills in youth sport coaches. *Journal of Sport Psychology, 1,* 59-75.

Smoll, F. L., & Smith, R. E. (1984). Leadership research in youth sports. In J. M. Silva & R. S. Weinberg (Eds.), *Psychological foundations of sport.* Champaign, IL: Human Kinetics.

Sonestroem, R. J. (1982). Exercise and self esteem: Recommendations for expository research. *Quest, 33,* 124-139.

Stein, P. J., & Hoffman, S. (1978). Sports and male role strain. *Journal of Social Issues,* *34*(1), 136-150.

White, R. (1959). Motivation reconsidered: The concept of competence. *Psychological Review, 66,* 297-323.

White, R. (1963). Ego and reality in psychoanalytic theory: A proposal regarding independent ego energies. *Psychological Issues, 3*(3), Monograph 11. New York: International University.

White, R. W. (1974). Strategies of adaptation: An attempt at systematic description. In G. V. Coehlo, D. A. Hamburg, & J. E. Adams (Eds.), *Coping and adaptation.* New York: Basic Books.

7. Religion and Adolescent Social Competence

Darwin L. Thomas
Craig Carver
Brigham Young University

This chapter assesses the relative influence of religious variables on adolescent prosocial development. An attempt is made to situate the increasing interest in the study of religion and the social sciences with the renewed interest in charting the stages of religious growth and development along with adolescent growth and development. Although we do not agree with Hall (1904, Vol. 2, p. 301) that "religious conversion should occur in adolescence because it is a natural, normal, and universal process," we do propose that adolescence, in the Western world at least, does emerge as an important time of development for the adolescent, wherein religion emerges as a significant influence. The effect of religion in the life of the adolescent is developed by considering both theory and research as they contribute to our understanding of why and how the religion variables seem to lead to prosocial development of the adolescent in the areas of self-esteem, academic and occupational achievement, sexual attitudes and behavior, and substance addiction and abuse as well as in the various belief and behavioral dimensions of religiosity per se. Finally, the chapter attempts to derive central theoretical propositions by looking at the basic relationships that emerge in each of the above areas.

In this chapter we use the concept "social competence" in a general sense to refer to the degree that an adolescent develops the relevant attitudinal and behavioral repertoire that a given social order sees as good and desirable. Our general conceptualization sees social competence as consisting of a socially valued dimension defined by such characteristics as self-esteem, academic achievement, intellectual development, creativity, moral behavior, and/or an internal locus of control. The negative or socially devalued dimension is defined by such characteristics as deviance, aggression, substance abuse, teenage pregnancy, learning disabilities, or other attitudinal and/or behavioral problems (see Barber & Thomas, 1986a; Rollins & Thomas, 1979).

The theoretical formulation informing our discussion is a general social psychological one that assumes the human organism is equipped at birth to seek out those responsive elements in the environment that allow for maximal growth and development.

Although this can be seen as a position that emphasizes the biological base for human behavior, it should not be misread as merely a statement similar to Maslow's formulation that reduces ethics to biological competence. We agree with Smith (1974), who argues that any position that requires biology to carry ethics is deficient. We assume that the human organism is biologically equipped for prosocial behavior, but we see the environment as being at least partly responsible for the trajectory that growth and development take over the ensuing years of that organism's life. We also see the human being developing capacities so that at some point he or she becomes partly responsible for the trajectory that that development takes (see Rollins & Thomas, 1979, for a more in-depth discussion of these underlying assumptions). Following Etzioni (1989), the "judging self," not reducible solely to hedonistic motivation, mediates between social influence and the resultant socially competent or incompetent behavior and/or attitude.

A useful way of talking about environmental influences on social competence is to conceptualize any social order as varying on two fundamental axes: namely, the amount of emotional support and encouragement for individual growth and development and the amount of control or restriction placed upon individual development. This formulation has proved useful for analysis of the family's effect upon adolescent growth and development (see Barber & Thomas, 1986b; Rollins & Thomas, 1979, for exemplary discussions). D'Antonio (1983), Aldous and D'Antonio (1983), and Thomas and Cornwall (1990) have discussed the utility of using support and control dimensions in understanding some aspects of the religion and family interface. Our use of the concepts of support and control as important dimensions of the religious sphere allows us to call attention to the two important functions that religion performs: namely, being both a supportive and motivating force and a controlling and guiding force (Collins, 1982; Pescosolido & Georgianna, 1989; Thomas & Cornwall, 1990; Wellman, 1983). In this chapter we use the support and control constructs in the religious sphere to help assess religious influence upon social competence. We review the extant empirical research that links religiosity to various dimensions of social competence. We then attempt a theoretical discussion of some of the patterns emerging in the data on the religious environment's influence that help to identify lines of the profitable future research on social competence.

THE PLACE OF RELIGION IN
CONTEMPORARY ADOLESCENT RESEARCH

There is considerable agreement that since 1950 the social sciences have experienced an unusual resurgence of interest in the study of religion (Thomas, 1988; Thomas & Cornwall, 1990; Thomas & Henry, 1985). This new interest not only has generated more empirical studies of religion but has also manifested itself in an increasing number of social scientists organizing within various disciplines (sociology, psychology, economics, and so on) to encourage more research and theorizing about religion in contemporary society (D'Antonio & Aldous, 1983; Thomas & Henry, 1985; Thomas & Sommerfeldt, 1984). This in and of itself is an intriguing set of occurrences in the social sciences, given that from the early 1900s to 1950 the study of religion, at least in the United States, had dwindled significantly—to the point that the psychology of religion, for example, was pronounced dead (Beit-Hallahmi, 1974). In terms of the effect this new emphasis has had on this chapter, we should ask: Has the study of adolescence mirrored this increased interest in religion?

In attempting to answer this question, we consulted 60 textbooks published from 1960 to 1988 in the area of child and adolescent development and analyzed them in an attempt to see increasing or decreasing patterns of discussions of religion. We found no evidence of increasing interest in the study of religion as it relates to human growth and development, specifically in the substantive area of adolescence: 44 of the texts made no mention at all of religion, 9 of the texts briefly mentioned religion, and only 5 had what could be classified as an extended discussion within a chapter. Only 2 of the 60 books had a chapter that included the topic of religion in the title. Neither the word *religion* nor any of its derivatives were found in any of the 46 chapters in the fourth edition of the four-volume Mussen *Handbook of Child Psychology* (1983). In the index for the 3,819 pages, the two relevant entries are "religious conversion" and "religion and morality." Thus our conclusion is that the area of adolescence in the social sciences up to the present time has not reflected an increased interest in religion as have some other areas of study. Perhaps the presence of this chapter in a book on adolescent development as it relates to social competence may be indicative of the beginning of interest in religion.

RELIGION AND SOCIAL INCOMPETENCE

Our review of the extant empirical research leads us to conclude that, when empirical studies of religion and social competence have been carried out, they have more traditionally focused on low social competence; or, put another way, they have focused on those devalued adolescent attitudinal and behavioral variables. This is largely due to the fact that the topic of substance abuse concerning alcohol, drugs, and so on has been the major area in which religious influence has been analyzed.

Table 7.1 presents a summary of our review of that literature. Because the amount of published material in any of the four substantive areas is voluminous, we have selected only five studies with representative findings in each area. As can be seen from the table, it is clear that a consistent relationship emerges in the literature: The higher the involvement in the religious sphere, the lower the frequency, intensity, or duration of these various forms of antisocial behavior. Much of the available research merely measures religion as affiliation within a particular denomination. The denominations are seen as ones that have greater normative pressures against the use of particular substances or behavior. We then conclude that the denominations are influential in controlling and reducing this particular behavior.

The most convincing research, however, shows that, within any one denomination, the level of religious commitment that members of that denomination experience in their attendance patterns or belief patterns likewise predicts differential levels of acceptance of deviant behavior. Thus all of this research clearly shows that it is not just the denominational emphasis upon particular beliefs (Cornwall & Thomas, 1986) but the degree to which the adolescent has internalized those values related to the respective behavior.

Table 7.1 Relationship Between Religiosity and Various Dimensions of Social Incompetence

Author	Date	Age	N	Independent Variable	Dependent Variable	Results
Suicide						
K. D. Breault	1986		414	Church membership	Suicide	Beta = .31
Steven Stack	1985	15-29		Church attendance	Suicide	t significant at .05
D. Lester	1987		National data	Religious book production	Suicide	r = -.32
W. T. Martin	1984			Church attendance	Suicide	r = -.72
S. Stack	1985			Church affiliation/church membership	Suicide	B = .07
Delinquency (arrests, fighting, theft, vandalism, and so on)						
Albrecht, Chadwick & Alcorn	1977	14-25	326	Religious attitudes/ religious behavior	Delinquent acts: number of acts and severity	M. = r -.26* F. = r -.14* M. = r -.34* F. = -.43**
Peek et al.	1986	12-20	817	Religiosity across time 1986 1968	Deviance/police truancy Zero order correlation	R^2 .434 -.244 -.209
Rohrbaugh & Jessor	1976	14-18	575	Religiosity	Deviant behavior	M. r = -.16* F. r = -.22**
Jensen & Erickson	1979	14-18	3,268	Church affiliation	Delinquent acts 18-item scale (Catholic) (Protestant) (Mormon)	R^2 r = .45 .8% - 2.7% 1.0% - 4.8% 13.6% - 21.5%

Table 7.1 (continued)

Author	Date	Age	N	Independent Variable	Dependent Variable	Results
Elifson, Peterson, & Hadaway	1983		600	Importance of religion	Total delinquency measures	Gamma = -.31
Rhodes & Reiss	1970	14-18	9,235	Parents both attend church Parents don't attend church	Juvenile court records / truancy	-45 -21 53 11
Substance Abuse						
R. N. Wolfe	1985	14-20	408 M. 242 F.	Appropriateness / religiosity	Substance abuse	t = .902
Burkett	1987	14-19	264	Religious commitment	Substance abuse	r = -.44
Sorensen	1982		211	Mystical experiences	Substance abuse	r = .29
Marcos & Bahr	1986	17-18	17,000	Religiosity	Marijuana frequency Alcohol frequency	r = -.194 r = -.222
McLuckie et al.	1975	12-18	30,000	Religious attendance	Drug user, ex-user, nonuser	11% reg. attdr 26% never att
Sexual Activity						
Werebe	1983	12-20	386	Church attendance	Teenage pregnancy	Gamma = -.48
Studer and Thornton	1987	18	224	Personal religious commitment	Contraceptive use	Gamma = -.42
Hadaway	1984	Teens	600	Home family religiosity, personal belief in God	Number sex experiences	Chi Square = 15.51 Significant at .05

Table 7.1 (continued)

Author	Date	Age	N	Independent Variable	Dependent Variable	Results
Forste & Heaton	1988	15-19	7,969	Religious attendance	Female = premarital first intercourse by age	
					15 years: once year	.287
					2 month/weekly	.124
					17 years: once year	.644
					2 month/weekly	.337
					19 years: once year	.800
					2 month/weekly	.557
Ruppel	1970	17-21		Religiosity	Sexual permissiveness	Gamma M. = -.66 Gamma F. = -.64

The dominant theoretical orientation underlying virtually all of the extant research that sees religious involvement as inversely related to antisocial behavior is best described as social control theory. Religion is seen as an important institution of social control that discourages antisocial behavior by highlighting negative consequences not only in the here and now but likewise in the "world to come." Religion is seen as appealing to the adolescent who needs to have a social world in which divine providence will eventually be played out as rewards and punishments are meted out in a this-and-other-world scheme of things. The chief motivation for not engaging in antisocial behavior is the desire to avoid the hellfire consequences of one's behavior. The controlling and guiding influence of religious authority is emphasized. One searches almost in vain for analyses of the possible role of religion as socially supportive, motivational, or facilitative.

RELIGION AND SOCIAL COMPETENCE

Table 7.2 presents a review of extant literature that links religious involvement and commitment to various dimensions of social competence. First, when looking at the table, note that there are considerably fewer studies that link positive developmental aspects to religion. This is an important finding.

The most obvious pattern from the data is the consistency of results across these studies showing that involvement in and commitment to religion is positively correlated with social competence. This finding addresses a current controversy in the field: Is religion related to positive or negative outcomes (Batson & Ventis, 1982; Bergin, 1983; Judd, 1985; Thomas, 1988)? When the patterns of findings in Tables 7.1 and 7.2 are taken together, they show that, for the most part, religious involvement and commitment are consistently related to increasing the abilities and skills required for adequate functioning in society and to decreasing the tendency to develop attitudes and participate in activities that are devalued in society.

There are not enough studies in any one substantive area to make conclusive judgments about whether religion seems to be more effective at producing some positive outcomes rather than others. With fewer than five studies in any one substantive area,

Table 7.2 The Influence of Religiosity of the Positive Dimension of Social Competence

Author	Date	Age	N	Independent Variable	Dependent Variable	Results	
Smith, Weigert & Thomas	1979	14-18 adolescents 5 cultures	1,995	Religiosity-belief/ attendance	Self-esteem	Average r across 5 cultures = .22	
Greeley	1980	14-18	635	Religiosity	Social commitment	B = .09 Significance = < .03	
Zern	1987	18-20		Religiosity	Academic achievement	Strong positive relationship	
Cornwall	1985	18+	1,832	Religious integration/ number of active Latter-Day Saints friends	Educational attainment years of education	Eta = .21 Significant < .001	
Cornwall & Thomas	1986	NORC General Social Survey 1972-1985	14,967	Religious denomination	Average years of education	Baptist Sects like Protestant Lutheran Catholic Methodist Presbyterian Latter-Day Saints Episcopal Jews	10.77 11.27 11.90 11.97 12.14 12.90 13.12 13.65 14.12

Table 7.2 (continued)

Author	Date	Age	N	Independent Variable	Dependent Variable	Results
Albrecht & Heaton	1984	18+	7,446	Religious attendance	Education	r = .262 Significant < .05
Coleman	1987	14-18		Achievement/religion	Achievement test Public Private Vocabulary test Public Private	 = 1.46 = 2.39 = 1.75 = 2.10
Coleman	1987		18,062 1,703	Dropout rates/religion	Public Private	13.1% 2.6%
Coleman	1987		1,421 278	Dropout rates/religiosity	Often 1/week or more Rarely/never	2.7% 6.2%

a summary attempt such as this at best can present only tenuous suggestions. From the patterns that we think are suggested in the table, we tentatively conclude that religion has a greater influence on an individual's ability to function in another social setting such as the educational setting rather than in developing some ability that cuts across all social settings. Regarding religion's relationship to academic achievement, for example, it seems that, in this arena of interaction, what is learned in a religious setting is more directly transferable to how one operates and performs in an educational setting.

The data do not allow us to draw firm conclusions as to why this would be so. But we agree with basic Durkheimian formulations that integration into social orders is the critical element in preparing people to "live better." This theoretical explanation focuses on important social processes rather than pointing toward dimensions of personality or individual attitudes (see Cornwall, 1987; Pescosolido & Georgianna, 1989, for a similar formulation). We assume that, as the individual becomes integrated into the religious social sphere and accepts the set of values surrounding those social relationships, he or she becomes more sensitive to interpersonal expectations from significant others, finds it easier to develop goals, and more readily identifies personal abilities needed to achieve those goals. We see such interpersonal skills as being transferable to an educational setting, which assists the religious person in becoming a better student.

Further research will be needed to determine whether this interpretation holds, but we think the research reported by Zern (1987) is supportive of this line of reasoning. That research did not find religiosity to be predictive of grade point average (GPA) specifically but did find religiosity to be positively and strongly related to academic achievement based on ability, which combined GPA with SAT scores. When measures of ability (SAT scores) are included in the analysis along with academic achievement (grades), Zern concludes that religiously involved and committed adolescents are significantly better able to more consistently reach their potential.

The last finding from our comparison of Tables 7.1 and 7.2 leads us to what we think is the most important finding in our attempt to analyze extant research in which religion is linked to measures of social competence. The conclusion is a simple one, but the implications are far reaching. In essence, we think that because religion is linked to positive dimensions of social competence as well as negative dimensions, there is a need to reevaluate theoretically what religious involvement and commitment mean. The research literature used to further inform our theoretical speculations along these lines does not come specifically from research linking religion with adolescent growth and development, but we think the findings from that research can be used to interpret and give direction to future research in this area.

RELIGION AND ADOLESCENT PLANS FOR THE FUTURE

The most common pattern clearly shown in religion and adolescence research is to conceptualize religion as an effective control mechanism within society. Thus adolescents are seen as opting not to engage in antisocial behavior (delinquency and so on) because of the threat the religious institution holds over the thinking, feeling, and acting adolescent. A brief look at the deviance literature that studies religion will show this common interpretation of why religion is an effective social control mechanism. The various articles that focus on hellfire and other aspects of religion emphasize this point. As observers have noted, theorists are late in rethinking the controlling and supportive mechanisms of religion (Thomas & Cornwall, 1990).

Another area that has traditionally used a similar kind of explanation for one of the most recurring findings in the social sciences is the study of the relationship of religious involvement and commitment to marital satisfaction. In the marital satisfaction literature, one of the most consistent and oft-reported findings since the 1930s is the positive correlation between religious involvement and commitment and marital satisfaction. For years this finding tended to be ignored; that is, it was often just reported in the literature without theoretical discussion or attempts to understand it. Eventually attempts were made and a common interpretation was that the relationship between religious involvement and marital satisfaction was probably a spurious relationship and reflected the fact that religious people tended to be more tuned in to the normative expectations of appropriate behavior in a particular social setting. Thus because of their greater sensitivity to socially desirable answers, religious respondents would merely indicate that "yes, they were committed to religion and yes, things in their marriage were going along pretty well." This interpretation remained unchallenged in the literature until the late 1970s and early 1980s when a number of researchers began to question it.

Filsinger and Wilson (1984; Wilson & Filsinger, 1986), who looked seriously at the relationship and included measures of social desirability, showed that social desirability did not attenuate the relationship. In fact, controlling for social desirability increases the strength of the relationship between marital satisfaction and religious involvement. They suggest that social scientists are late in questioning what it is that religion contributes to the marital relationship other than simple mechanisms of social control (i.e., by stopping unhappy couples from divorcing). Other people (Schumm, Bollman, & Jurich, 1982) have also presented evidence that religious involvement and commitment may add some very important, positive elements to marital and family relationships.

The same rationale helps us understand the data on adolescent social competence and underscores the facilitative influence of religious involvement and commitment on the adolescent's social growth and development. Although we were unable to find a lot of research that addressed the question of how religion facilitates adolescent social competence, there is one line of recent research that allows more in-depth discussion. It is apparent from a number of kinds of research that socially competent adolescents are characterized by the ability to plan for the future. The socially competent adolescent does not live only in the present dimensions of life but anticipates coming stages of life and seems to make active plans for the future (Blinn, 1988; Dryfoos, 1988). Dryfoos presents a persuasive argument that adolescents who attain status in our contemporary society are clearly the ones who (for whatever reason) are able to make meaningful plans for the future (education, occupation, and so on). Blinn's research (1988) clearly shows that adolescents with low social competence, specifically those who find themselves in an early teen pregnancy, have very unrealistic and distorted views about what their lives will look like in the future. Not only do they lack specific plans for the future, the list of things they think life is going to provide to them is very unrealistic. Her research shows that, although some aspects of the adolescent's world change during the course of the pregnancy, their unrealistic views of future life for the most part remain unchanged. Additional research will have to determine when the pregnant adolescent begins to reorder her views of the future to more closely correspond with the hard reality that the future will probably bring.

Even more directly related research shows the impact of belief and involvement in the religious sphere on an adolescent's plan for the future (Ensign, 1984). Figures 7.1, 7.2, and 7.3 show LISREL models of basic findings from a sample of U.S. Mormon male adolescents between the ages of 12 and 18. This research shows that values and plans for the future (to get a college education, to get a good job, to go on a mission for the Mormon Church, to be married in a church ceremony, and so on) are significantly influenced by the level of personal religious commitment that the adolescent experiences in his or her life. Plans and values are also influenced by involvement in the religious, public sphere of church attendance and so on, but note that the influence of the public sphere is much less strong than that of the private religious sphere.

In addition to adolescent religiosity, there are two important sources of influence on the adolescent's future plans and values, namely, the family's home religious observance (scripture study, prayer, and so on) and the influence of the adolescent's adult religious adviser. Thus both the family and the church are important sources of influence in the life of the young person as he or she creates his or her own public and private approaches to religion and establishes values and plans for the future.

Figures 7.2 and 7.3 present the same LISREL models, but limited to the younger adolescents (those between the ages of 12 to 14) and the older adolescents (between the ages of 16 to 18). A comparison of those two age groups shows what changes occur in family influence and church influence during the life of the young person. Family influence is much stronger for the younger adolescent. Note that the influence of home religious observance on the private religious observance of the 12- to 14-year-old adolescent

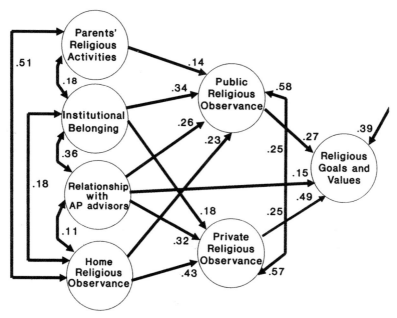

All subject (N = 766)

Figure 7.1 Family and Religion's Influence on Religious Goals and
Values

NOTE: Goodness of fit index is 0.996. Root mean square residual is 0.022.

is strong (.51 standardized coefficient) whereas the relationship
with the adviser and institutional belonging are weak (.16 and .19
standardized coefficients). However, when those values are compared with the values for the 16- to 18-year-old adolescent, home
religious observance drops to .31, whereas the relationship with
the "Aaronic Priesthood Advisor" increases to .47.

These data are consistent with the conclusion that, as adolescents move through these developmental years, the influence of
the home recedes in importance and other influences become more
important. In this data set the relationship that the young person
establishes with the significant other representing the church,
namely, the priesthood adviser, becomes much more important.

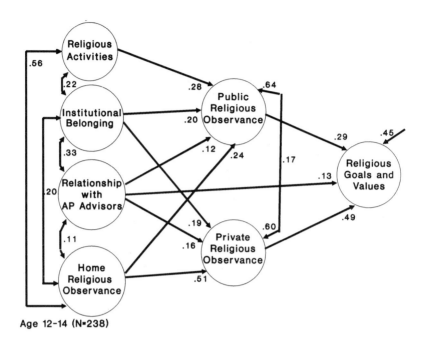

Age 12-14 (N=238)

Figure 7.2 Family and Religion's Influence on Religious Goals and
Values

NOTE: Goodness of fit index is 0.989. Root mean square residual is 0.043.

We interpret these findings to mean that the world of the adolescent is changing in focus from home to outside areas. In this case religion, symbolized through another adult figure, becomes important in establishing critical plans for the future. Instead of only showing religious involvement and commitment as social control mechanisms, we believe this research shows that religion assists and helps the adolescent create meaningful goals and internalize a set of values that lead to the enhancement of life and an increased ability to achieve those goals.

Research (Weed & Olsen, 1988), with a predominantly Mormon sample of 4,000 adolescents in schools throughout the State of Utah, shows the very important role of religion in combination with family as related to the peer, educational, and deviant worlds

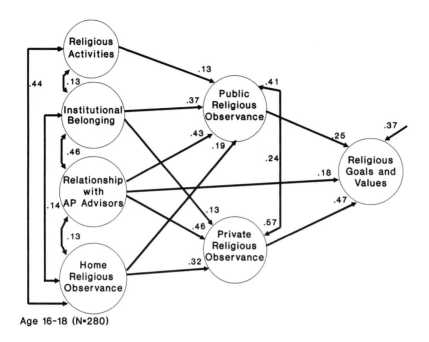

Figure 7.3 Family and Religion's Influence on Religious Goals and
          Values

NOTE: Goodness of fit index is 0.990. Root mean square residual is 0.025.

of the adolescent. Figure 7.4 shows the standardized path coefficients between a number of variables in that study.

In our interpretation, the significant relationship is the very
strong standardized beta coefficient between abstinent values and
sexual activity. Note that, in terms of predicting adolescent sexual
activity, these abstinence values are twice as good as other more
commonly found dimensions of the adolescent world, namely,
steady dating and alcohol and drug use. Note also that church
attendance is a very important predictor of this set of adolescent
abstinence values. This is further evidence of the impact of involvement in and commitment to religion as represented by church
attendance. This research clearly shows that agreement with parents on values, support one receives from peers for those values,

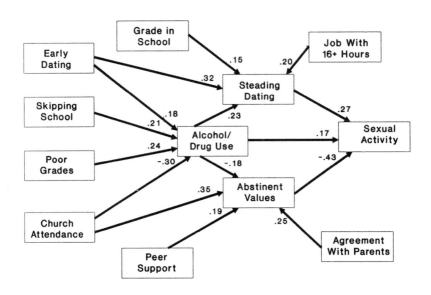

Figure 7.4 Standardized Regression Coefficients for Model of Sexual
        Activity
SOURCE: Adapted from Weed and Olsen (1988).

and adolescent involvement in the religious sphere are dominant
and important predictors of sexual attitudes and values, which in
turn affect actual sexual activity.

We think that, by combining these two sets of research, we can
make a persuasive argument for the supportive and facilitative
function that religion provides in forming a set of values around
which the adolescent is then able to create a set of specific goals
for the future. Having future goals provides motivation that
serves as a very significant buffer against some of those influences
in the adolescent world that lead to antisocial behavior. Religion
seems to facilitate the establishment of meaningful values along
with realistic goals for the future, thus enhancing the adolescent's
ability to reach his or her potential.

FUTURE RESEARCH

Given the above analysis, what are we to make of our assessment of the impact of religious involvement and commitment upon adolescent social competence? We suspect that the best research will conceptualize the influence of religion in terms not only of its social control ability but also of its positive life-sustaining and life-developing dimensions. Although we do not necessarily agree with Hall's observation that "religious conversion should occur in adolescence because it is a natural, normal, and universal process" (Hall, 1904, Vol. 2, p. 301), we do believe that the adolescent years can be defined as an important stage in the search for a meaningful worldview.

We see the significance of this stage as having essentially two dimensions. First, the adolescent comes to internalize a set of values that emphasizes the right of institutions in society to exercise social control. This is the restricting and guiding dimension required for normal social interaction that every society elicits from its members. We see this function as necessary and we see religion as contributing to it. The voluminous research on adolescence and deviant behavior also points to this interpretation. We see a critical need for further research to address how this function of religion is related to the second function of offering social support and motivation.

Future research should study how religion adds to the positive dimensions of adolescent growth and development. Here we think that religion and the family are the two central institutions within which adolescents attempt to work out their own views of life, focusing on aspects of life that require a positive commitment. Most crucial in defining this aspect of the adolescent's world is not the control and restriction dimension of the religious institution but the emotional support and encouragement that the adolescent receives through that religious institution. While the family recedes in importance as the institution begins to provide emotional support for the adolescent, we need to know who the religious significant others have become. The research reported in Figures 7.1 through 7.3 suggests the importance of these significant adults who represent the religious organization. We need to know how useful they are in assisting the adolescent in working through his or her plans for the future and internalizing social values.

We suspect that future research will show these adults in the religious sphere to be effective *not* because they emphasize the control and restriction dimension of religion but because they are people who provide significant social support and emotional sustenance in their relationships with adolescents. Here we think the religious functionary becomes very important in assisting the adolescent to come to know him- or herself and the social world so that plans for the future make sense, life in the present is basically a positive and rewarding experience, and the best life is lived with an eye to the future. In this sense we think that the universal nature of conversion that Hall was talking about is applicable in this broader social psychological arena within which we think these processes occur.

To the degree that control and restrictions are balanced with emotional support and encouragement, we think that both religion and family can be combined to effectively assist the adolescent to achieve maximal socially competent skills, attitudes, and behaviors.

Finally, let us represent through Figure 7.5 the basic dimensions of the adolescent's social world that have been studied and those which we think ought to be studied longitudinally to better appreciate the significance of social competence in the adolescent years. First, we assume that the religious, family, educational, and peer worlds are the most important spheres in the life of the adolescent. Second, we assume that social competence in the form of interpersonal skills, an interrelated set of values underscoring the positive dimensions of life, and a set of plans for the future are the critical outcomes in these years of growing up.

The importance of any of these institutional spheres (religion, family, education, peer) cannot be determined by studying them in isolation. The best research will be that which studies the adolescent's simultaneous involvement in and commitment to these multiple social institutions. Figure 7.5 represents some lines of influence that we think previous research and theory have supported. However, many relationships among the institutional, relational and individual variables have not been adequately studied.

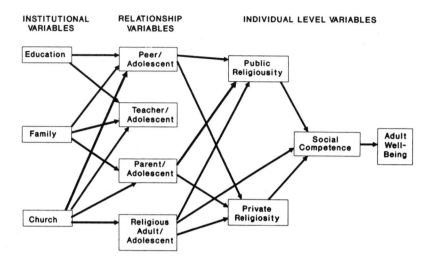

Figure 7.5 Model of Institutional, Relational, and Individual Variables
Effects on Young Adult Well-Being

NOTE: The arrows represent relationships that we judge to have been supported by empirical research

Longitudinal research on adolescent social competence in which the influence of multiple social institutions is analyzed will help social psychologists better understand the relationship of social competence to the normative order. For example, in the area of sexual activity, research shows that religiosity is negatively related to contraceptive use among adolescents. This highlights the normative order underlying the negative and positive dimensions of social competence. Currently, American society is ambivalent about whether it should define contraceptive use as prosocial or antisocial behavior (see Dryfoos, 1988; Moore, 1988; Olsen, 1988; Weed & Olsen, 1988, for exemplary discussions). The part of the social order that believes in abstinence for adolescents and opposes easy access to contraceptives sees the use of contraceptives as undesirable and, therefore, incompetent behavior. Another part of society that sees sexual activity as normal adolescent behavior and wants to encourage contraceptive use to prevent pregnancy will label contraceptive behavior as socially competent behavior.

Longitudinal research should be able to assess the relative influence on adolescents of the efforts of various social institutions. The attitudes and behavior developed in adolescence can then be linked to positive and negative outcomes in the young adult years to better see how social competence is developed and defined during times of rapid social change. When the social order (or parts of it) changes and defines attitudes/behavior as good that were previously seen as socially undesirable, which adolescents function most effectively in the new social order and why? How do religion, family, education, and peer worlds influence the adolescent during these changes?

We need to know to what extent religion, family, education, and peer worlds have independent effects over and above the effect that social competence has on young adult well-being. Research of this type will allow us not only to better understand social competence in adolescence but also to begin to see how experiences in the social psychological realm in the adolescent years are or are not related to the realities of the young adult world. To the degree that discussions of this type will lead to more carefully conceptualized and conducted longitudinal research, social psychology in general and adolescents in particular will benefit from that combined effort.

REFERENCES

Albrecht, S. L., Chadwick, B., & Alcorn, D. S. (1977). Religiosity and deviance: Application of an attitude-behavior contingent consistency model. *Journal for the Scientific Study of Religion, 16*(3), 263-274.

Albrecht, S. L., & Heaton, T. B. (1984). Secularization, higher education, and religiosity. *Review of Religious Research, 26,* 43-58.

Aldous, J., & D'Antonio, W. V. (1983). Introduction: Families and religions beset by friends and foes. In W. V. D'Antonio & J. Aldous (Eds.), *Families and religions: Conflict and change in modern society* (pp. 9-16). Beverly Hills, CA: Sage.

Bahr, S. J., & Marcos, A. C. (1986). Adolescent drug use. In T. K. Martin et al. (Eds.), *Utah Demographic Perspective.* Salt Lake City, UT: Signature.

Barber, B. K., & Thomas, D. L. (1986a). Dimensions of adolescent self-esteem and religious self-evaluations. *Family Perspective, 20*(2), 137-150.

Barber, B. K., & Thomas, D. L. (1986b). Dimensions of fathers' and mothers' supportive behavior: The case for physical affection. *Journal of Marriage and the Family, 48*(3), 783-794.

Batson, C. D., & Ventis, W. L. (1982). *The religious experience: A social-psychological perspective*. New York: Oxford University Press.

Beit-Hallahmi, B. (1974). Psychology of religion in 1880-1930: The rise and fall of a psychological movement. *Journal of the History of the Behavioral Sciences, 10,* 84-94.

Bergin, A. E. (1983). Religiosity and mental health: A critical re-evaluation and meta-analysis. *Professional Psychology: Research and Practice, 14*(2), 170-184.

Blinn, L. M. (1988). Stability and change in pregnant adolescents' perceptions of their future marriage and family life. *Family Perspective, 22*(3), 255-268.

Breault, K. D. (1986). Suicide in America: A test of Durkheim's theory of religious and family integration, 1933-1980. *American Sociological Society, 92*(3), 628-656.

Burkett, S. R. (1987). Religion, parental influence, and adolescent alcohol and marijuana use. *Journal of Drug Issues, 7*(3), 263-273.

Burkett, S. R., & White, M. (1975). Hellfire and delinquency: Another look. *Journal for the Scientific Study of Religion, 13,* 455-462.

Coleman, J., Hoffer, T., & Kilgan, S. (1982). High school achievement: Public, Catholic, and private schools compared. New York: Basic Books.

Collins, R. (1982). *Sociological insight*. New York: Oxford University Press.

Cornwall, M. (1985). *Personal communities: The social and normative bases of religion*. Unpublished doctoral dissertation, University of Minnesota, Department of Sociology.

Cornwall, M. (1987). The social bases of religion: A study of the factors influencing religious belief and commitment. *Review of Religious Research, 29,* 44-56.

Cornwall, M., & Thomas, D. L. (1986, May). *Religion and education in the secularization thesis: A look at the Mormons*. Paper presented at the Sunstone Symposium in Salt Lake City, UT.

D'Antonio, W. V. (1983). Family life, religion, and societal values and structures. In W. V. D'Antonio & J. Aldous (Eds.), *Families and religions: Conflict and change in modern society* (pp. 81-108). Beverly Hills, CA: Sage.

D'Antonio, W. V. & Aldous, J. (1983). Families and religions: Conflict and change in modern society. Beverly Hills, CA: Sage.

Dryfoos, J. G. (1988). Using existing research to develop a comprehensive pregnancy prevention program. *Family Perspective, 22*(3), 211-223.

Elifson, K. W., Peterson, D. M., & Hadaway, C. K. (1983). Religiosity and delinquency. *Criminology, 21*(4), 505-527.

Ensign. (1984, December). Aaronic Priesthood age boys' plans for the future, pp. 52-54.

Etzioni, A. (1989, February 1). The "me first" model in the social sciences is too narrow. *Chronicle of Higher Education*, p. A44.

Filsinger, E. E., & Wilson, M. R. (1984). Religiosity, socioeconomic rewards, and family development: Predictors of marital adjustment. *Journal of Marriage and the Family 46*(3), 663-670.

Forste, R. T., & Heaton, T. B. (1988). Initiation of sexual activity among female adolescents. *Youth and Society, 19*(3), 250-268.

Hadaway, C. K., Elifson, K. W., & Petersen, D. M. (1984). Religious involvement and drug use among urban adolescents. *Journal for the Scientific Study of Religion, 23*(2), 109-128.

Hall, G. S. (1904). *Adolescence: Its psychology and its relations to psysiology, anthropology, sociology, sex, crime, religion and education* (2 Vols.). New York: Appleton.

Jensen, G. F., & Erickson, M. L. (1979). The religious factor and delinquency. Another look at the hellfire hypotheses. *The religious dimension: New directions in quantitative research* (pp. 157-177). New York: Academic Press.

Judd, D. K. (1985). *Religiosity and mental health*. Unpublished master's thesis, Brigham Young University, Provo, UT.

Lester, D. (1987). Religiosity and personal violence: A regional analysis of suicide and homicide rates. *Journal of Social Psychology, 127*(6), 685-686.

Martin, W. T. (1984). Religiosity and United States suicide rates, 1972-1978. *Journal of Clinical Psychology, 40*(5), 1167-1169.

McLuckie, B. F., Zahn, M., & Wilson, R. A. (1975, Spring). Religious correlates of teenage drug abuse. *Journal of Drug Issues*, 129-139.

Moore, K. A. (1988). Teenage childbearing: Unresolved issues in the research/policy debate. *Family Perspective, 22*(3), 189-209.

Mussen, P. H. (Ed.). (1983). *Handbook of child psychology*. New York: John Wiley.

Olsen, J. A. (1988). The teenage pregnancy problem: Some alternate approaches to policy and research. *Family Perspective, 22*(3), 171-187.

Peek, Charles W., Curry, Even W., & Chalfant, Paul. (1985, March). Religiosity and delinquency over time. *Social Science Quarterly, 66*(1), 120-131.

Pescosolido, B. A., Georgianna, S. (1989). Durkheim, suicide, and religion: Toward a network theory of suicide. *American Sociological Review, 54*, 33-48.

Rhodes, A. L., & Reiss, A. J., Jr. (1970). The religious factor and delinquent behavior. *Journal of Research in Crime and Delinquency, 7*(2), 83-98.

Rohrbaugh, J., & Jessor, R. (1976). Religiosity in youth: A personal control against deviant behavior. *Journal for Scientific Study of Religion, 15*, 136-155.

Rollins, B. C., & Thomas, D. L. (1979). Parental support, power and control techniques in the socialization of children. In W. Burr et al. (Eds.), *Contemporary theories about the family* (pp. 317-364). New York: Free Press.

Ruppel, H. J., Jr. (1970). Religiosity and premarital sexual permissiveness: A response to the Reiss-Heltsley and Broderick debate. *Journal of Marriage and the Family, 47*, 647-655.

Schumm, W. R., Bollman, S. R., & Jurich, A. P. (1982). The "marital conventionalization" argument: Implications for the study of religiosity and marital satisfaction. *Journal of Psychology and Theology, 10*, 236-241.

Smith, C. B., Weigert, A. J., & Thomas, D. L. (1979). Self-esteem and religiosity: An analysis of Catholic adolescents from five cultures. *Journal for the Scientific Study of Religion, 18*, 51-60.

Smith, M. B. (1974). *Humanizing social psychology*. San Francisco: Jossey-Bass.

Sorensen, A. A., & Cutter, H. S. G. (1982). Mystical experience, drinking behavior and the reasons for drinking. *Journal of Studies on Alcohol, 43*(5), 588-592.

Stack, S. (1985). The effect of domestic/religious individualism on suicide, 1954-1978. *Journal of Marriage and the Family 47*, 431-447.

Studer, M., & Thornton, A. (1987). Adolescent religiosity and contraceptive usage. *Journal of Marriage and the Family, 49*, 117-128.

Thomas, D. L. (Ed.). (1988). *The religion and family connection: Social science perspectives*. Provo, UT: Brigham Young University, Religious Studies Center.

Thomas, D. L., & Cornwall, M. (1990). Religion and family in the eighties: Discovery and development. *Journal of Marriage and the Family, 52*(4).

Thomas, D. L., & Henry, G. C. (1985). The religion and family connection: Increasing dialogue in the social sciences. *Journal of Marriage and the Family, 47*(2), 369-379.

Thomas, D. L., & Sommerfeldt, V. (1984). Religion, family, and the social sciences: A time for dialogue. *Family Perspective, 18,* 117-125.

Weed, S. E., & Olsen, J. (1988). Policy and program considerations for teenage pregnancy prevention: A summary for policy makers. *Family Perspective, 22*(3), 235-252.

Wellman, B. (1983). Network analysis: Some basic principles. In R. Collins (Ed.), *Sociological theory, 1983* (pp. 155-200). San Francisco: Jossey-Bass.

Werebe, M. J. G. (with M. Reinhart). (1983). Attitudes of French adolescents toward sexuality. *Journal of Adolescence, 6,* 145-159.

Wilson, M. R., & Filsinger, E. E. (1986). Religiosity and marital adjustment: Multidimensional interrelationships. *Journal of Marriage and the Family, 48,* 147-151.

Wolfe, R. N., Welch, L. K., Lennox, R. D., & Cutler, B. L. (1985). Concern for appropriateness as a moderator variable in the statistical explanation of self-reported use of alcohol and marijuana. *Journal of Personality, 53*(1), 1-16.

Zern, D. S. (1987). The relationship of religious involvement to a variety of indicators of cognitive ability and achievement in college students. *Adolescence, 22,* 883-895.

8. Medical Interventions for the Enhancement of Adolescents' Physical Appearance: Implications for Social Competence

Thomas Pruzinsky
University of Virginia, Medical Center

Thomas F. Cash
Old Dominion University

With special focus on adolescence, this chapter reviews the various medical procedures for the correction or improvement of physical conditions that aesthetically
diminish physical appearance. These conditions range from minor physical anomalies and common conditions to extreme congenital or traumatic disfigurement.
The medical interventions involve a number of specialties—for example, plastic
and reconstructive surgery, orthodontics, and dermatology. The psychosocial effects of these appearance-altering treatments are examined in the contexts of the
available scientific evidence, clinical perspectives, and the particular developmental significance of physical appearance, self-consciousness, and body image during
the adolescent period.

A small and painfully shy boy of 14, Jack cannot remember ever
feeling anything but anger and hurt about his large, protruding
ears. Many of his classmates, who seem to take pleasure in teasing
Jack, only know him as "Dumbo," Walt Disney's animated elephant who flew with his ears.

Esther, an otherwise attractive, brown-eyed 18-year-old girl has
what she calls a "beak for a nose, just like Dad's." She tries to
avoid being in a position where others can see her profile. Her
parents think she will outgrow her "teenage vanity," but Esther
desperately wants cosmetic surgery to change the nose she so
despises.

AUTHORS' NOTE: *We would like to acknowledge the assistance of Jill Hangen in the
initial development of the chapter. Thomas Pruzinsky would like to acknowledge the
support of Milton Edgerton, M.D., and the Department of Plastic and Maxillofacial
Surgery at the University of Virginia Health Sciences Center.*

Beth, at age 13, has decided that she doesn't like boys and never wants to date one. Perhaps more to the point, she adds, "and they don't like me." Somewhat overweight, with thick glasses, badly aligned teeth, and an acned complexion, Beth has for several years had very prominent breasts. More than once she has left the school bus in tears while her classmates taunted her in song, "Beth Boobs put a bag on your head."

Each of these adolescents is struggling with the personal and social meaning and effects of his or her physical appearance. Such struggles are the focus of this chapter, which has two major goals: (a) to describe the psychological impact of self-perceived or actual physical deviations in appearance on the social competency of adolescents and (b) to describe the psychological motivation for and results of medical procedures designed to enhance physical appearance.

Therefore, the first part of this chapter elucidates some of the critical relationships between the social and self-perceptions of physical attractiveness and the development of social competency. A major focus is the genesis of physical self-consciousness and its influence on the development of problems in social competency. The second part of the chapter reviews the nature of requests for elective plastic surgery, orthodontic treatments, and dermatological interventions for relatively common aesthetic deviations. The psychological motivations for seeking these medical interventions and the medical, social, and psychological outcomes of these interventions are described. A major emphasis is on the need for combined medical-psychological assessment and treatment of adolescents requesting medical procedures to enhance physical appearance.

Regarding the scope of this chapter: Aesthetic deviations in appearance range from "minor" anomalies to major deformities and disfigurement, whether constitutional (e.g., short stature due to growth hormone deficiency), congenital (e.g., craniofacial malformations), or traumatic (e.g., burns). We have elected to focus on nontraumatic deviations that fall within a relatively "normal" aesthetic range. Such ideographic anomalies occur quite frequently. The reader is referred to other works for discussion of the less prevalent yet more profound appearance problems (see Bernstein, 1976; Pertschuk & Whitaker, 1987; Stabler & Underwood, 1986).

One would assume, given the voluminous literature on the psychology of physical appearance (Cash, 1981; Hatfield & Sprecher, 1986), that substantial scientific research would be available to document the psychosocial influences and outcomes of medical procedures to enhance appearance. However, the burgeoning medical subspecialty of adolescent medicine contains very little research focusing specifically on this topic. Thus the current review is based on extant empirical and clinical reports regarding medical treatment to improve adolescents' appearance. In the absence of direct scientific evidence, we must also extrapolate from our clinical experience and from research on the treatment of adults and children for anomalies in physical appearance.

PHYSICAL APPEARANCE AND THE DEVELOPMENT OF SELF-CONSCIOUSNESS IN ADOLESCENTS

Several crucial assumptions and empirical relationships set the stage for understanding the adolescent's request for medical intervention to change their appearance.

The relationship of physical appearance, self-esteem, and social competency. The relationship between physical appearance and the development of adolescent self-concept and social competency is covered in greater detail in a previous chapter of this volume. In short, our data-based assumption is that objectively and subjectively favorable attributes of physical appearance are often critical to the development of social competency and positive self-esteem (see Cash, 1985; Cash, Winstead, & Janda, 1986). The more we see ourselves as physically attractive and the more we are objectively (i.e., socially) viewed as physically attractive, the more positive our overall self-esteem and the more likely we are to develop higher levels of social competence. Conversely, physical unattractiveness elicits social attitudes and actions that may interfere with the development of social confidence and interpersonal skills (see Cash, 1985; Reis, Nezlak, & Wheeler, 1980; Snyder, Tanke, & Berscheid, 1977). Negative self-appraisal of one's appearance is even more strongly related to a poor self-concept, social anxiety, shyness, and social isolation (Archer & Cash, 1985; Cash, 1985; Cash, Winstead, & Janda, 1986).

We assume, in cases where such interventions are medically and psychologically indicated, that medical procedures designed to enhance physical appearance can *prevent* psychosocial dysfunction. That is, social competency can be enhanced through the positive changes in physical appearance that are possible using cosmetic surgery, orthognathic surgery, orthodontic procedures, and dermatological treatments (see Lefebvre & Arndt, 1988). The mechanisms of this preventive process are described later in the chapter.

Adolescent concern regarding physical appearance. Adolescence clearly entails many physical and biological changes. One might readily assume that these pubescent changes result in ubiquitous adolescent turmoil regarding body image. However, in his review of the development of and change in body image, Fisher (1986, p. 104) concluded that

> aside from the fact that there is a heightening of concern about the security of the body, little else has been empirically demonstrated. One is reminded that previous assumptions about adolescence being a time in which disturbance and turmoil flourish have not been ratified by objective inquiry.

Thus we assume that there is *no necessary* relationship between the developmental stage of adolescence and negative body-image experiences. Nevertheless, as clinicians and parents (and former teenagers), we are well aware of the degree to which adolescents can become preoccupied with their physical appearance. A study of over 20,000 adolescents (Offer, Ostrov, & Howard, 1981) found that, although the vast majority were satisfied with their overall appearance, over 60% of the females and 27% of the males desired some type of change in their appearance. The results of a recent national survey on body image (Cash, Winstead, & Janda, 1986) indicated that, especially for females, adolescence was the time of greatest body dissatisfaction. Clinical experience also suggests that teenagers become increasingly hypersensitive about their perceived deformities (M. T. Edgerton, personal communication, November 1988). Perhaps the most upsetting deviations for adolescents are those that relate to the gender-related norms—physical standards of masculinity, femininity, and sexual appropriateness (Ogundari, 1985).

For some this hypersensitivity is a passing phase. For others the preoccupation may indicate some other underlying psychological or social problem that is projected onto the screen of the major changes occurring in body experience during puberty. The feelings and perceptions of the adolescent must be understood within their social, physical, and psychological contexts. Adolescents are often hesitant to lower their defenses and talk about their perceptions of their appearance. Communication with parents on the subject of appearance (as well as on other personally significant topics) is likely to be poor. Very often it is not until the physician gives adolescents some indication that *real* improvement in physical appearance is medically possible that they are able to speak more openly about their concerns (M. T. Edgerton, personal communication, November 1988).

In an interesting Canadian survey of 730 adolescents (Hodgson, Feldman, Corber, & Quinn, 1986), although almost half reported worrying "a lot" or "some" about acne problems, only 39% of those adolescents who were worried had consulted a physician about these problems. Almost 26% of the total sample worried about being overweight, yet only one-fourth of these worried individuals sought medical consultation. Among the 8.8% of the sample who reported concerns about being short, only 19% sought consultation. The key point here is the discrepancy between the prevalence of adolescents with physical appearance concerns compared with the number who actually seek medical consultation. Significantly more adolescents would have liked to have had a medical consultation about their appearance problem but did not seek it. This discrepancy is particularly salient in view of the fact that medical care in Canada is socialized. Hodgson, Feldman, Corber, and Quinn (1986, p. 387) concluded that "many of the health concerns of adolescents are 'personal' as opposed to clinical" and "their impact on adolescent emotions and behavior must not be underestimated."

Some body-image concerns are more common in females than in males (Offer, Ostrov, & Howard, 1981). Females report more frequent and greater degrees of body-image dissatisfaction and more social pressure to be attractive (Freedman, 1984). The body-image survey by Cash, Winstead, and Janda (1986) indicated that, among 15- to 19-year-olds, 40% of females and 21% of males expressed generally negative evaluations of their appearance.

Although males may often feel it is a sign of "weakness" to acknowledge to others that they are disturbed by their appearance, once the topic is raised, they may be just as concerned as females with a similar deformity (Cash & Brown, 1989; Cash, Winstead, & Janda, 1986).

The relationship between degree of physical deviance and the psychological impact. An important corollary of the need to understand the subjective perception of a deformity is the observation that there is *not* necessarily a correlation between the degree of deformity and the degree of the psychological reaction to the deformity. As Cash (1985) observed regarding the psychology of physical appearance in general, there is a minimal relationship between the "outside view" of appearance (i.e., objective physical attractiveness) and the "inside view" (i.e., body image or self-perceptions of attractiveness). Clinically we have repeatedly learned that *very small* deformities (for example, very small deviations from the norm in breast growth) can result in very strong psychological reactions; conversely, large deformities do *not* always result in greater psychological maladjustment. The crucial point for physicians, teachers, and parents who have contact with adolescents is that the request for physical change must *not* be addressed in terms of the objective "external" perception of the physical problem.

THE GENESIS AND IMPACT OF PHYSICAL SELF-CONSCIOUSNESS

A salient factor that can interfere with the development of social competency is self-consciousness. When actual or perceived problems in physical appearance exist for the adolescent, the main psychological symptom present is self-consciousness. *Self-consciousness* refers to the experience of self-focused attention (Buss, 1980, 1985). The self-focused attention may be directed toward private inner events (e.g., thoughts and feelings), which is termed *private self-consciousness.* Attention may be focused on outer, observable aspects of the self (e.g., one's own behavior and physical appearance), which is termed *public self-consciousness* (Buss, 1980). At an extreme, there is an anxious preoccupation with others' perceptions of one's physical appearance or other overt personal attributes. Buss (1980, p. 244) has maintained that "adolescence is the peak period of private and public self-consciousness and of social anxiety," largely because of the novelty of the physical changes and sexual urges. Cash, Winstead, and Janda (1986) confirmed that, among all age groups and for both sexes, adolescents are the most appearance focused.

Induction and development of self-consciousness. Individuals who develop extreme, often debilitating, self-consciousness report remarkably similar experiences during its initial development. Harris (1982, p. 313) observed that "for patients with congenital malformations this was usually between five and six, and for patients with developmental disproportions [e.g., abnormally large breasts], during early adolescence." The development of self-consciousness for all individuals is most often engendered by the

> self-conceived realization that the abnormality existed or, more frequently, by another person commenting on its presence. After the realization of physical deviance (either actual or perceived), self-consciousness is perpetuated by self-criticism stemming from the individual's constant comparisons of him or herself with others. A similar abnormality in a parent seemed to heighten a subject's susceptibility to become self-conscious of his or her *own* abnormality. (Harris, 1982, p. 314)

Cash, Cash, and Butters (1983), for example, found that self-consciousness potentiates adolescents and young adults making social comparisons that diminish their own feelings of attractiveness. Self-consciousness can also be perpetuated by the critical attitudes of others. Social teasing about some childhood physical attribute is associated with subsequent and persistent concerns about one's appearance (Cash, Winstead, & Janda, 1986).

Development of self-consciousness in adolescence is strongly influenced by instances of developmental desynchrony, described in an earlier chapter of this volume. In terms of adolescent psychological development, "timing is everything." The adolescent does not want to be too tall, too short, too big breasted, or too small breasted in relation to peers. There are clear effects of the timing of physical development on the social status of the adolescent, and on the subsequent development of self-concept, with these differences being evident later in life (Northcraft & Hastorf, 1986).

Development of "defense mechanisms." Individuals experiencing self-consciousness invariably develop defense mechanisms to avoid or manage the discomfort of this state. Harris (1982, p. 315) describes *defense mechanisms* not in the traditional psychodynamic use of the term but as "the lengths to which subjects will go to hide their abnormalities from the sight of others and to disguise their self-consciousness of them."

These defense mechanisms include camouflage techniques and restrictions in life-style (Harris, 1982). *Camouflage techniques* include the development of postures and gestures to conceal defects. For example, individuals who are self-conscious about the appearance of their teeth may avoid smiling openly or may cover their mouths when laughing. Other techniques might include using clothes, hair styles, or cosmetics (Cash, 1987) or avoiding bright light to hide perceived or actual deformities. *Restrictions in life-style* entail an inhibition of behavior and avoidance of those situations in which the individual had experienced embarrassment. These avoidance behaviors include general withdrawal from social behaviors and avoidance of being photographed, of mirrors, of sunbathing, and so on. Who among us cannot recall avoiding some social event because of a bad haircut, a conspicuous facial blemish, or some other temporary physical dissatisfaction?

Difficulties in interpersonal relations. Individuals who experience self-consciousness report inhibition in relation to both intimate as well as general social interactions. These individuals are apt to be on guard constantly and to look for signs of rejection by others (Harris, 1982). More specifically, self-consciousness related to a negative body image is clearly linked to the experience of shyness, social anxiety, and poor self-esteem (see Cash, 1985; Cash, Winstead, & Janda, 1986).

Many self-conscious individuals have such an overwhelming preoccupation with their appearance that they are unable to adequately pay attention to others and, therefore, are unable to engage in effective reciprocal social interaction. This pattern can engender actual social rejection, thus promoting a downward spiral of preoccupation, fear of rejection, social isolation, and feelings of social inadequacy.

Diminution of self-concept. As a rule individuals experiencing a significant degree of physical self-consciousness also experience general lowering of their self-concept, feelings of inferiority, and mild to moderate depression (Cash, 1985; Cash, Winstead, & Janda, 1986; Harris, 1982; Noles, Cash, & Winstead, 1985). This self-imposed social isolation and personal preoccupation with self can further reinforce these negative self-perceptions (Archer & Cash, 1985).

The impact of self-consciousness on the developmental tasks of adolescence. In summarizing the developmental tasks of adolescence, Kelly and Hansen (1987) conclude that effective social interactions, such as dating, making friends, and becoming part of a peer group, are not to be considered a fortunate luxury. Rather attainment of these tasks is essential to the future overall functioning of the individual (see Hartup, 1983). Physical self-consciousness can lead to difficulties in successfully traversing these developmental tasks, leading the individual to be at risk for the development of a number of problems in social, emotional, and occupational functioning.

In sum, adolescents requesting medical intervention to change their physical appearance experience self-consciousness and a negative body image, which affects their behavior, self-concept, and their interpersonal relations. These feelings of physical self-consciousness are the core of the motivation for these individuals to seek medical consultation. Failure to understand the impact of self-consciousness and a flawed body image on the many facets of the adolescent's life can lead them to a further downward spiral of social dysfunction and the development of risk for the lifelong limiting effects of social incompetency.

MEDICAL-PSYCHOLOGICAL EVALUATION, TREATMENT, AND IMPACT

We turn now to the literature on the nature of requests for medical intervention to enhance physical appearance—requests for elective cosmetic surgery, orthodontic procedures, and treatment of skin disorders. We describe each physical problem, various perspectives (patient versus parental versus physician perception) on the problem, and physical and psychological outcomes of treatment. We conclude with recommendations regarding the decision-making process in considering adolescent patients as candidates for these treatments.

Elective Cosmetic Surgery in Adolescents: An Overview

Increasing numbers of adult and adolescent patients receive elective cosmetic surgery (American Society of Plastic and Reconstructive Surgery [ASPRS], 1986). For example, the number of individuals receiving cosmetic nasal surgery, or rhinoplasty (one of the more frequent procedures requested by adolescents), was 54,000 in 1981, over 70,000 in 1984, and over 82,000 in 1986 (ASPRS, 1986). Similarly, there were 72,000 breast augmentation patients treated in 1981 and well over 90,000 annually in 1984 and 1986.

Most information regarding the psychological impact of elective cosmetic surgery is based on adult patients (Pruzinsky, 1988). Differences exist between adults and adolescents in terms of the range of elective surgical procedures requested. For example, adults often request rhytidectomies (face-lifts), blepharoplasties (eyelid surgery), and liposuction as well as abdominoplasty ("tummy tuck"). Adolescents are not usually candidates for these procedures, which largely return portions of the body to a more "youthful" state. Both adolescents and adults are likely to seek rhinoplasty, breast reduction, and breast augmentation surgeries.

To our knowledge, only one report specifically focuses on the psychological aspects of cosmetic surgery in adolescence (Knorr, Hoopes, & Edgerton, 1968). Its authors are a team of two plastic surgeons and a psychiatrist who are among the most knowledgeable professionals regarding the psychological aspects of plastic surgery. Although their report is over 20 years old, current clinical experience with adolescent patients, plus contemporary research with adult populations, confirm that most of their conclusions are as valid today as when originally published.

Knorr, Hoopes, and Edgerton (1968) report the long-term psychological results of surgeries on 57 adolescents who underwent rhinoplasty (26), breast augmentation surgery (11), ear surgery (12), or scar-removal procedures (8). As their primary motivation for undertaking the surgery, most patients identified self-consciousness about the physical features that they wanted changed. Knorr, Hoopes, and Edgerton (1968, p. 248) make an interesting observation: "Patients with congenital deformities [e.g., "lop ears"], subjectively undesirable inherited traits [a nose with a significant "hump"], or inadequate or retarded physical development [e.g., breast development] feel the same need for reorganization of the body image."

In the majority of these patients there was no significant pre-operative psychopathology noted. However, there was some evidence of disruption (e.g., a large proportion of father absence) in the home-life of the rhinoplasty patients. Although there is no strong evidence for significant psychopathology in this patient population, Knorr, Hoopes, and Edgerton (1968, p. 252) warn that some "cosmetic surgery patients may focus on the presence of physical deformity as the basis for all of their emotional and social problems. Their expectations for surgery as a 'cure-all' are unrealistic." Thus when evaluating these patients, the nature of the motivations for the surgery and the expectations of the patients and families regarding the physical and psychological impact of the surgery must be carefully considered. Despite the existence of conflict and indications of other social and psychological problems in the lives of some adolescents seeking elective surgical procedures, the surgical and psychological outcomes for these procedures are generally quite positive. The one exception is in cases where patients seek scar removal for an acquired deformity (Knorr, Hoopes, & Edgerton, 1968). Often, adolescents and adults with acquired deviations in physical appearance (i.e., through injury or disease) adjust less positively to their deviation and to subsequent reconstructive surgeries than do individuals with congenital deformities (see Bernstein, 1976). In terms of the overall adaptation of adolescents to elective surgery procedures, Knorr, Hoopes, and Edgerton (1968) concluded that adolescents are able to integrate the surgical changes into their body image much more easily than most adults, in addition to experiencing fewer and less severe postoperative emotional problems in reaction to surgery.

Rhinoplasty

The nose is a very prominent feature of the face and is often the focus of requests for surgical change. Goldwyn (1981, p. 77) has noted that most rhinoplasty patients are adolescent girls who desire to "blend with their peers and not stand out because of an unattractive feature." These patients do not usually desire a perfect or a beautiful nose, "rather, they wish to get rid of an 'ugly' nose" (Goldwyn, 1981, p. 77). Goldwyn (1981) recommends, for both physical and psychological reasons, that the patient wait until at least the age of 14 to have rhinoplasty. Physically, the development of the facial growth may not be complete. Perhaps as important, the patient may not have had adequate time to adjust to the ongoing changes in facial form during this early stage of adolescence.

Adolescent rhinoplasty patients typically "describe the nose as not fitting the rest of the face" (Knorr, Hoopes, & Edgerton, 1968, p. 248). In some instances this is an accurate perception (from a surgeon's or others' perspectives), whereas in other cases the patient has well-proportioned facial features, thus making it difficult for the family, peers, or surgeon to understand the nature of the patient's request for surgical change.

We must keep in mind that the patient's subjective perception of the nose (or other body part) is the most important perspective. As we argued earlier, the surgical request reflects the desire for reduced self-consciousness and a more satisfying body image. However, the surgeon must also assess to what degree the request for surgical change can be realized and must understand, in great detail, the motivation for surgery (Edgerton & Langman, 1982; Pruzinsky, 1988).

Goldwyn (1981) warns that in some atypical instances the request for rhinoplasty is initiated by one of the parents, usually the mother of an adolescent. The mother may have undergone the procedure herself and received benefit or may have wanted the surgery for herself but had never done it (Goldwyn, 1981). If the surgical request is an attempt to please or to acquiesce to someone else, then any surgical change is much less likely to be accepted and successfully integrated into the patient's body image (Edgerton & Langman, 1982). Indeed, self-consciousness could increase as a result. Moreover, as Cash and Horton (1983) have observed, rhinoplasty may alter appearance without necessarily enhancing the person's objective physical attractiveness. Negative social reactions to changed appearance can precipitate patient dissatisfaction, particularly if the patient's motivation was to please others rather than to improve his or her self-image (Cash & Horton, 1983; Goin & Goin, 1981).

In terms of patient perception of the results of rhinoplasty: "Almost every adolescent girl will be happy with the result" (Goldwyn, 1981, p. 83). This conclusion holds even in the event of the surgeon's or parent's dissatisfaction with some aspect of the surgical outcome (Goldwyn, 1981). McKinney and Cook (1981) reported an 85% satisfaction among adolescents. Knorr, Hoopes, and Edgerton's (1968) long-term follow-up of female patients revealed that these patients would again choose to have the surgery if they had to do it over. Perhaps more important, the patients reported that after surgery they felt less psychologically inhibited and more socially confident.

Although the authors' evaluation of male patients' outcomes was precluded by too few cases, they maintained that in general "higher degrees of psychopathology seem to exist in males requesting plastic surgery" (Knorr, Hoopes, & Edgerton, 1968, p. 249). This is a common observation in the literature on the psychological aspects of elective cosmetic surgery (e.g., Edgerton & Langman, 1982; Goin & Goin, 1981; Pruzinsky, 1988) although some researchers have questioned this conclusion (Cash, 1986; McKinney & Cook, 1981); in addition, whether it applies to the adolescent population is not known. Nevertheless, the clinical literature suggests greater caution in considering males' requests for surgery. In general, partly due to societal gender norms and perceptions of gender role appropriateness, males may require a higher threshold of psychological distress before pursuing appearance-altering surgeries.

Breast Surgeries in Adolescence

Among the many physical changes experienced by adolescents, one particularly salient change for adolescent girls is breast development. Girls (and boys) focus on this aspect of female development with great interest, paying attention to the size, shape, and rate (or lack) of development as well as to cultural and peer group norms of attractiveness (Benedeck, Poznanski, & Mason, 1979).

Breast reduction surgery. The breast tissue characteristic of individual females appears early and is maintained throughout maturation, although obesity can cause significant changes

(Benedeck, Poznanski, & Mason, 1979). Generally, large-breasted girls tend to develop breast tissue early in addition to developing other secondary sexual characteristics earlier than their peers. As adults these women recall being ashamed of their rapid breast development during adolescence (Harris, 1983). Their unfolding self-consciousness follows the progression outlined earlier. Women seeking breast reduction surgery report recalling feelings of self-consciousness at the age of 10 or 11 that led to difficulties in their male and female relationships. Patients report being envied by other girls and a tendency of males to make suggestive remarks (Goin, 1982), events that can foster anxiety related to feminine identity development.

Additionally, females with hypertrophic breast development experience problems with lower back pain, inability to perform some sporting activities, and great difficulty finding clothes that fit properly. Albeit unconsciously, some may even gain weight to camouflage breast development (Goin & Goin, 1981). Inhibition of sexual pleasure obtained from the breasts is reported by these females as well as more anxiety and depression than for normal controls (Goin & Goin, 1981).

Breast reduction surgery is typically conducted after the age of 18. As a rule, these women typically report both physical and psychological relief (Goin, 1982; Goin & Goin, 1981; Hollyman, Lacey, Whitfield, & Wilson, 1986; Stevens, 1987). Despite their almost invariable reports of being satisfied with the surgery, however, patients in one study (Goin, Goin, & Gianini, 1977) revealed "a surprisingly high incidence of postoperative psychological disturbances" (Goin & Goin, 1981, p. 209). These emotional reactions are transient and include body-image disturbances, grief over the loss of breast size, and sexual disturbances. Although such reactions are not likely to be expressed to the surgeon, if detected, they can be addressed with sincere reassurance as a "way of defusing the often frightening and confusing emotional sequelae of the operation" (Goin & Goin, 1981, p. 209).

Surgical treatment of gynecomastia. Gynecomastia is a condition occurring most frequently in male adolescents wherein there is enlargement of breast tissue. Although the majority of these individuals are otherwise entirely normal in their sexual development, this medical condition is especially problematic in that "the development of visible, and especially of pendulous, breast hypertrophy can be distorting and in some cases catastrophic to the male adolescent's self esteem" (Simon, 1985, p. 241).

Schonfeld (1962) investigated the psychological impact of gynecomastia among 284 individuals with this diagnosis. Males with adolescent-onset gynecomastia reported a general withdrawal from many activities, development of ambiguous sexual orientation, and inadequate perceptions of their ability to fulfill the masculine role. Given the social developmental tasks of adolescence outlined earlier, these feelings could easily interfere with accomplishment of these tasks. Medical treatment of gynecomastia is typically a straightforward surgical procedure (Simon, 1985) with positive surgical and psychological results. However, Schonfeld (1962) argues strongly for pre- and postoperative psychotherapy to optimize adjustment to and integration of the physical changes that have occurred through surgery.

Breast augmentation. Breast development in the average female is completed between the ages of 13 and 18 (Tanner, 1974). Because most females have attained their maximum breast development by the age of 18, breast augmentation surgery is seldom conducted prior to this age. In fact, the typical augmentation mammaplasty patient is approximately 30 years old (Goin & Goin, 1981). Whether adolescent or adult, these patients report the usual patterns of physical self-consciousness and social inhibition, especially in the context of intimate sexual relationships, and fully 81% of patients in one study reported feeling "conspicuously unfeminine" (Beale, Lisper, & Palm, 1980).

A significant number of surgical complications can occur in breast augmentation surgery, primarily capsular contracture, resulting in unusual hardening of the breasts. However, patients are typically very pleased with the surgical outcome and would have the procedure again, many times in spite of experiencing some significant surgical complication (Goin & Goin, 1981; Hetter, 1979; Sihm, Jagd, & Pers, 1978). Knorr, Hoopes, and Edgerton (1968, p. 250) found that "all patients felt the procedure had helped them to achieve maturity and femininity. Inhibitions such as the reluctance to swim or wear low-cut dresses, are quickly dissipated following surgery." A more recent scientific study (Beale, Hambert, Lisper, Ohlsen, & Palm, 1984) similarly confirmed positive changes in feelings of femininity and a variety of social behaviors indicating reduced self-consciousness.

Summary

Thus the adolescent's motivations for and the outcomes of elective cosmetic surgical procedures are very similar to those of the adult population. The motivations for the surgery are to reduce the amount of negative physical self-consciousness experienced in relation to perceived physical deviance. The adolescent experience of the psychological outcome of elective surgical procedures may be even more positive than the quite satisfying outcomes reported by adults (Pruzinsky, 1988; Wengle, 1986a, 1986b). This may be due in part to the "adaptability" of the adolescent body image to change (Knorr, Hoopes, & Edgerton, 1968). Reduction in self-consciousness is often reported to directly lead to a noticeable, and sometimes dramatic, improvement in self-esteem and social interaction.

Dental Procedures for Aesthetic Improvement

In this section we review orthodontic and surgical (orthognathic) treatment of adolescents for dental and jaw deformities. Orthodontic treatment focuses on repositioning teeth through the use of braces. "Malocclusion is impairment of the anatomical relations and functioning of the teeth and adjacent craniofacial structures" (Albino, 1984, p. 918). Surgical treatment of malocclusions refers to the surgical repositioning of the jaws so that teeth are in better alignment. Orthodontic procedures and malocclusion surgery are often conducted in combination.

Psychological Impact of Dental Deviations

Empirical research has documented the negative social perception of dental deviations (Albino, 1984). That is, "there is probably some negative social feedback associated with highly visible and less attractive forms of dental-facial malocclusions" (Albino, 1984,

p. 921). For some individuals these negative social perceptions adversely affect their social interactions and self-concepts (Albino, 1984). Moreover, as noted in other contexts, the objective amount of aesthetic impairment is not directly related to subjective self-perceptions of malocclusion (Albino, 1984).

Treatment of Dental Deviance

Treatment for dental deviance is usually begun in early adolescence. These patients are often physician referred for treatment of functional problems (e.g., pain, swallowing difficulties, increased risk of periodontal disease). However, frequently, "the most salient effects of the condition are esthetics [with] . . . about 80% of those seeking treatment . . . for cosmetic reasons" (Albino, 1984, p. 918).

It is interesting that requests for orthodontic treatment are most often initiated by parents (Graber, 1980). This observation leads to important points regarding the selection of patients for treatment, especially with respect to the patient's motivation for the surgery and compliance with the treatment process. In fact, "some dentists are rightfully hesitant about providing long-term, difficult and expensive orthodontic treatment (the aim of which is primarily cosmetic) for young people who may simply adjust to the minor aesthetics impairments involved" (Albino, Tedesco, & Conney, 1984, p. 10). Problems can develop in those adolescent patients who have not incorporated, at least in part, the functional and aesthetic goals of the treatment as their own (Graber, 1980). Furthermore, even though the ultimate result is one of emotional improvement, both orthognathic surgery and conventional orthodontics produce considerable stress that exceeds most patients' expectations (Kiyak, McNeill, & West, 1985; Oulette, 1978).

When compared with patients with major craniofacial abnormalities (e.g., cleft lip and palate), "malocclusions are the easiest deformities to correct surgically and patients with prognathasism or retrognathism show the most dramatic postoperative improvement in appearance and self-esteem" (Lefebvre & Arndt, 1988, p. 455). Overall the objective and subjective evaluations of the physical changes are positive, with change being noted in self-concept, mood, and social functioning (Graber, 1980). Moreover, controlled experimentation has confirmed that adolescents' orthodontic treatment outcomes include enhanced physical and interpersonal attractiveness (Korabik, 1981).

Acne and Dermatological Interventions

Perhaps because the human face is the source and focus of much social communication, prominent dermatologist A. M. Kligman (1985, p. 7) has asserted: "In a psychological sense, there are no minor blemishes, especially on the young face." Chronic inflammatory diseases of the skin afflict about 15% of the population (Kligman, 1985), with acne being quite prevalent among adolescents.

A variety of studies have examined associations between acne, its severity, and psychosocial functioning. Though designed to examine the hypothesis that dysphoric emotions are dermopathogenic, such correlational data may also reflect the opposite causal connections—namely, that acne affects emotional well-being. In either case, acne sufferers do seem to score higher on various measures of state and trait anxiety, with more anxiety among more severe acne patients (Cassileth, Lusk, & Tenaglia, 1982; Medansky, Handler, & Medansky, 1981; Wu, Kinder, Trunnell, & Fulton, 1988). The more severe one regards one's acne condition to be, the lower one's self-esteem (Wu, Kinder, Trunnell, & Fulton, 1988). If psychological stress indeed exacerbates acne (e.g., Lorenz, Gizham, & Wolf, 1953) and acne engenders psychological distress, then we can understand the frustrating self-perpetuating nature of this condition within the social world of adolescence where physical appearance can be so important.

To our knowledge, there are no systematic studies of the psychosocial effects of dermatological treatments of acne (e.g., topical medicines and regimens of diet and hygiene) or surgical treatments of acne scars (e.g., dermabrasion). In the Knorr, Hoopes, and Edgerton (1968) report cited earlier, adolescents undergoing scar-removal procedures were small in number. However, the basic conclusion regarding treatment in the acne-scarring cases is that there is a less positive response than in other procedures. As a general rule patients undergoing plastic surgery procedures for acquired deformities are less satisfied with the outcome of surgery than those individuals undergoing surgery for congenital deformities (Bernstein, 1978).

One investigation has examined the efficacy of a program of basic skin care and the use of facial cosmetics (for camouflaging) among young college women with facial blemishes. Although the study unfortunately did not include a control group, the treated women did report enhanced emotional well-being from pretreatment to three months after the program. These data suggest that interventions to facilitate appearance management among persons with appearance concerns may be helpful in providing concrete coping-compensatory strategies for managing self-consciousness.

CONCLUSION

Substantial research supports the conclusion that the subjective experience and objective perception of physical attractiveness are important variables in the development of social competency. The adolescent's request for medical intervention to enhance physical appearance should be responded to and respected rather than dismissed as a "passing phase" of adolescent turmoil or as a symptom of vanity. Ideally the parent or teacher, when hearing of the adolescent's appearance-related concerns, should attempt to empathically understand the adolescent's perspective on the problem—this is the *only* perspective that really matters. If possible the adolescent should be allowed to consult with a physician (e.g., plastic surgeon, orthodontist) to obtain an opinion regarding the adolescent's concerns and whether there is a medical indication for treatment. The request for medical intervention must be considered in the context of the overall psychosocial functioning of the individual. Clinical and empirical data have consistently demonstrated that medical interventions to enhance physical appearance often lead to positive experiential changes—the most important of which are reductions in physical self-consciousness, improvements in body image, marked increases in self-esteem, and increased social confidence and competence.

REFERENCES

Albino, J. E. (1984). Psychosocial aspects of malocclusion. In J. D. Matarazzo, S. M. Weiss, J. A. Herd, N. E. Miller, & S. M. Weiss (Eds.), *Behavioral health: A handbook of health enhancement and disease prevention* (pp. 918-929). New York: John Wiley.

Albino, J. E., Tedesco, L. A., & Conny, D. J. (1984). Patient perceptions of dental-facial esthetics: Shared concerns in orthodontics and prosthodontics. *Journal of Prosthetic Dentistry, 52,* 9-13.

American Society for Plastic and Reconstructive Surgery (ASPRS). (1986). *Report of surgical procedures conducted by board certified plastic and reconstructive surgeons.* Chicago: ASPRS, Director of Communications Executive Office.

Archer, R., & Cash, T. F. (1985). Physical attractiveness and maladjustment among psychiatric inpatients. *Journal of Social and Clinical Psychology, 3,* 170-180.

Beale, S., Hambert, G., Lipser, H., Ohlsen, L., & Palm, B. (1984). Augmentation mammaplasty: The surgical and psychological effects of the operation and prediction of the result. *Annals of Plastic Surgery, 13,* 279-297.

Beale, S., Lipser, H., & Palm, B. (1980). A psychological study of patients seeking augmentation mammaplasty. *British Journal of Psychiatry, 136,* 133-138.

Benedeck, E. P., Poznanski, E., & Mason, S. (1979). A note on the female adolescent's psychological reaction to breast development. *Journal of the American Academy of Child Psychiatry, 18,* 537-545.

Bernstein, N. R. (1976). *Emotional care of the facially burned and disfigured.* Boston: Little, Brown.

Buss, A. H. (1980). *Self-consciousness and social anxiety.* San Francisco: Freeman.

Buss, A. H. (1985). Self-consciousness and appearance. In J. A. Graham & A. M. Kligman (Eds.), *The psychology of cosmetic treatments* (pp. 125-132). New York: Praeger Scientific.

Cash, T. F. (1981). Physical attractiveness: An annotated bibliography of theory and research in the behavioral sciences. *Social and Behavioral Sciences Documents, 11* (Ms. 2370).

Cash, T. F. (1985). Physical appearance and mental health. In J. A. Graham & A. M. Kligman (Eds.), *The psychology of cosmetic treatments* (pp. 196-216). New York: Praeger Scientific.

Cash, T. F. (1986). Rhinoplasty results revisited. *Annals of Plastic Surgery, 16,* 84-85.

Cash, T. F. (1987). The psychology of cosmetics: A review of the scientific literature. *Social and Behavioral Sciences Documents, 17* (Ms. 2800).

Cash, T. F., & Brown, T. A. (1989). *Gender and body images: Stereotypes and realities.* Manuscript submitted for publication.

Cash, T. F., Cash, D. W., & Butters, J. (1983). "Mirror, mirror, on the wall . . .": Contrast effects and self-evaluations of physical attractiveness. *Personality and Social Psychology Bulletin, 9,* 351-358.

Cash, T. F., & Horton, C. E. (1983). Aesthetic surgery: Effects of rhinoplasty on the social perception of patients by others. *Plastic and Reconstructive Surgery, 72,* 543-548.

Cash, T. F., Winstead, B., & Janda, L. H. (1986). The great American shape-up: Body image survey report. *Psychology Today, 126,* 305-316.

Cassileth, B. R., Lusk, E. J., & Tenaglia, A. M. (1982). A psychological comparison of patients with malignant melanoma and other dermatologic disorders. *Journal of the American Academy of Dermatology, 7,* 742-751.

Edgerton, M. T., & Langman, M. W. (1982). Psychiatric considerations. In E. H. Courtiss (Ed.), *Male aesthetic surgery* (pp. 17-38), St. Louis: C. V. Mosby.

Fisher, S. (1986). *Development and structure of the body image* (Vol. 1). Hillsdale, NJ: Lawrence Erlbaum.

Freedman, R. J. (1984). Reflections of beauty as it relates to health in adolescent females. *Women and Health, 9,* 29-45.

Goin, M. K. (1982). Psychological reactions to surgery of the breast. *Clinics in Plastic Surgery, 9,* 347-354.

Goin, J. M., & Goin, M. K. (1981). *Changing the body: Psychological effects of plastic surgery.* Baltimore: Williams & Wilkens.

Goin, M. K., Goin, J. M., & Gianini, M. H. (1977). The psychic consequences of a reduction mammaplasty. *Plastic and Reconstructive Surgery, 59,* 530-534.

Goldwyn, R. M. (1981). *The patient and the plastic surgeon.* Boston: Little, Brown.

Graber, L. W. (1980). Psychological considerations of orthodontic treatment. In G. W. Lucker, K. A. Ribbons, & J. A. McNamara (Eds.), *Psychological aspects of facial form* (pp. 81-117). Ann Arbor: University of Michigan Press.

Harris, D. L. (1982). The symptomatology of abnormal appearance: An anecdotal survey. *British Journal of Plastic Surgery, 35,* 281.

Harris, D. L. (1983). Self-consciousness of disproportionate breast size: A primary psychological reaction to abnormal appearance. *British Journal of Plastic Surgery, 36,* 191-195.

Hartup, W. W. (1983). Peer interaction and the behavioral development of the individual child. In W. Damon (Ed.), *Social and personality development: Essays on the growth of the child* (pp. 220-233). New York: Norton.

Hatfield, E., & Sprecher, S. (1986). *Mirror, mirror . . .: The importance of looks in everyday life.* Albany: SUNY Press.

Hetter, G. P. (1979). Satisfactions and dissatisfactions of patients with augmentation mammaplasty. *Plastic and Reconstructive Surgery, 64,* 151.

Hodgson, C., Feldman, W., Corber, S., & Quinn, A. (1986). Adolescent health needs II: Utilization of health care by adolescents. *Adolescence, 21,* 383-390.

Hollyman, J. A., Lacey, J. H., Whitfield, P. J., & Wilson, J. S. P. (1986). Surgery for the psyche: A longitudinal study of women undergoing reduction mammaplasty. *British Journal of Plastic Surgery, 39,* 222-224.

Jensen, S. H. (1978). The psychosocial dimensions of oral and maxillofacial surgery: A critical review of the literature. *Journal of Oral Surgery, 36,* 447-453.

Kelly, J. A., & Hansen, D. J. (1987). Social interactions and adjustment. In V. B. Van Hasselt & M. Hersen (Eds.), *Handbook of adolescent psychology* (pp. 131-146). New York: Pergamon.

Kiyak, H. A., McNeill, R. W., & West, R. A. (1985). The emotional impact of orthognathic surgery and conventional orthodontics. *American Journal of Orthodontics, 88,* 224-234.

Kligman, A. M. (1985). Medical aspects of skin and its appearance. In J. A. Graham & A. M. Kligman (Eds.), *The psychology of cosmetic treatments* (pp. 3-25). New York: Praeger Scientific.

Knorr, N. J., Hoopes, J. E., & Edgerton, M. T. (1968). Psychiatric-surgical approach to adolescent disturbance in self-image. *Plastic and Reconstructive Surgery, 41,* 248-253.

Korabik, K. (1981). Changes in physical attractiveness and interpersonal attraction. *Basic and Applied Social Psychology, 2,* 59-65.

Lefebvre, A. M., & Arndt, E. M. (1988). Working with facially disfigured children: A challenge in prevention. *Canadian Journal of Psychiatry, 33,* 453-458.

Lorenz, T. H., Gizham, D. T., & Wolf, S. (1953). The relation of life stress and emotions to human sebum secretion and the mechanism of acne vulgaris. *Journal of Laboratories in Clinical Medicine, 41,* 11-28.

McKinney, P., & Cook, J. Q. (1981). A critical evaluation of 200 rhinoplasties. *Annals of Plastic Surgery, 7,* 357-361.

Medansky, R. S., Handler, R. M., & Medansky, D. L. (1981). Self-evaluation of acne and emotion: A pilot study. *Psychosomatics, 22,* 379-382.

Noles, S. W., Cash, T. F., & Winstead, B. A. (1985). Body-image, physical attractiveness, and depression. *Journal of Consulting and Clinical Psychology, 53,* 88-94.

Northcraft, G., & Hastorf, A. (1986). Maturation and social behavior: A framework for the analysis of deviance. In C. P. Herman, M. P. Zanna, & E. T. Higgins (Eds.), *Physical appearance, stigma and social behavior: The Ontario Symposium* (pp. 221-243). Hillsdale, NJ: Lawrence Erlbaum.

Offer, D., Ostrov, E., & Howard, K. (1981). *The adolescent: A psychological self-portrait.* New York: Basic Books.

Ogundari, J. T. (1985). Somatic deviations in adolescence: Reactions and adjustments. *Adolescence, 20,* 179-183.

Oulette, P. L. (1978). Psychological ramifications of facial change in relation to orthodontic treatment and orthognathic surgery. *Journal of Oral Surgery, 36,* 787-790.

Pertschuk, M. J., & Whitaker, L. A. (1987). Psychosocial considerations in craniofacial deformity. *Clinics in Plastic Surgery, 14,* 163-168.

Pruzinsky, T. (1988). Collaboration of plastic surgeon and medical psychotherapist: Elective cosmetic surgery. *Medical Psychotherapy: An International Journal, 1,* 1-13.

Reis, H. T., Nezlak, J., & Wheeler, L. (1980). Physical attractiveness in social interaction. *Journal of Personality and Social Psychology, 38,* 604-617.

Schonfeld, W. A. (1962). Gynecomastia in adolescence: Effect on body image and personality adaptation. *Psychosomatic Medicine, 24,* 379-389.

Sihm, F., Jagd, M., & Pers, M. (1978). Psychological assessment before and after augmentation mammaplasty. *Scandinavian Journal of Plastic and Reconstructive Surgery, 12,* 295-298.

Simon, B. E. (1985). Body image and plastic surgery: In J. A. Graham & A. M. Kligman (Eds.), *The psychology of cosmetic treatments* (pp. 238-246). New York: Praeger Scientific.

Snyder, M., Tanke, E. D., & Berscheid, E. (1977). Social perception and interpersonal behavior: On the self-fulfilling nature of social stereotypes. *Journal of Personality and Social Psychology, 35,* 656-666.

Stabler, B., & Underwood, L. E. (Eds.). (1986). *Slow grows the child: Psychosocial aspects of growth delay.* Hillsdale, NJ: Lawrence Erlbaum.

Stevens, L. A. (1987). The psychological aspects of breast surgery. In R. S. Blacher (Ed.), *The psychosocial experience of surgery* (pp. 87-98). New York: John Wiley.

Tanner, J. M. (1974). Sequence and tempo in the somatic changes in puberty. In M. M. Grumbach, G. D. Grave, & F. E. Mayer (Eds.), *Control of the onset of puberty.* New York: John Wiley.

Wengle, H. P. (1986a). The psychology of cosmetic surgery: A critical overview of the literature 1960-1982—Part 1. *Annals of Plastic Surgery, 16,* 435-443.

Wengle, H. P. (1986b). The psychology of cosmetic surgery: Old problems in patient selection seen in a new way—Part 2. *Annals of Plastic Surgery, 16,* 487-493.

Wu, S. F., Kinder, B. N., Trunnell, T. N., & Fulton, J. E. (1988). Role of anxiety and anger in acne patients: A relationship with the severity of the disorder. *Journal of the American Academy of Dermatology, 18,* 325-333.

PART III

CONCLUDING REMARKS

9. Social Competence and the Language of Adequacy as a Subject Matter for Psychology: A Quadripartite Trilevel Framework

Robert D. Felner
A. Michele Lease
Ruby S. C. Phillips
University of Illinois, Urbana-Champaign

This chapter provides an integration of the contributions of the previous chapters into developmental perspectives on adolescence. Of particular concern will be the ways in which a better understanding of the adaptive tasks and ecological contexts that shape the lives of adolescents can help us to better articulate the nature of social competence during this period as well as the factors that facilitate its development and/or hinder its emergence.

> In applying clinical ways of thinking formulated out of experience with broken adults, we were slow to see how the *language of adequacy* to solve life's challenges could become the subject matter of psychological science. Thus there are thousands of studies of maladjustment for each one that deals directly with the ways of managing life's problems with personal strength and adequacy. The language of problems, difficulties, inadequacies, of antisocial or delinquent conduct, or of ambivalence and anxiety is familiar. We know that there are devices for correcting, bypassing, or overcoming threats, but for the most part these have not been studied. (Murphy, 1962)

Since the time that Lois Murphy wrote these words, the study of "positive mental health" has come into vogue in psychology and related disciplines. Resilience, coping, life skills, social skills, mastery, hardiness, empowerment, self-esteem, and social competence are all constructs that have moved into the forefront of attention and study. Indeed that ubiquitous and "traditional" bastion of psychopathology and the illness model of disorder, the *Diagnostic and Statistical Manual of the Mental Disorders (DSM-III-R*; American Psychiatric Association [APA], 1987) now devotes an entire diagnostic axis to the consideration of the highest level of functioning of the person on positive mental health. Explicit in this addition is the recognition that "ratings of highest level of functioning during the past year will frequently have prognostic significance" and that "ratings of current functioning will generally reflect the current need for treatment or care," even given the presence of other dysfunction (*DSM-III-R*, APA, 1987, p. 20).

In terms of attention to and recognition of their potential significance, the focus on positive mental health characteristics has come far during the past two decades. Less clear is the extent to which we have successfully developed a language for furthering our cumulative understanding of these aspects of human functioning. A careful reading of the chapters in this volume, and elsewhere, that deal with the construct of "social competence" reveals an almost bewildering array of definitions and inclusive elements. A careful reading of this work also reveals that we have learned much about the conditions, in a variety of contexts and developmental circumstances, that contribute to relatively better or poorer mental health outcomes. Less successful are our efforts to think systematically about the interrelationships among the elements of positive mental health characteristics that are of interest.

A consideration of our differential facility in considering conditions of disorder versus health illustrates this point. We have a number of well-developed approaches for making relatively clear distinctions among different "pathological" conditions. Achenbach's (e.g., Achenbach & Edelbrock, 1981) now-classic work on topologies of behavioral problems, and more recent studies of *DSM-III-R* that indicate the relative reliability with which clinicians can distinguish at least among the superordinate categories of dysfunction (*DSM-III-R*, APA, 1987), nicely demonstrate our sophistication in this area. Lengthy debates during the past century about intrapsychic versus behavioral or cognitive substrates for the disorders with which we are concerned have helped to make the figure and ground of what questions to ask, if not their answers, very well defined. This definition enables researchers to examine the relative contributions of each process to etiological pathways—critical issues that must be addressed to allow for adequate intervention. For positive mental health these distinctions and processes are far less clear.

Work by Cowen and his colleagues (e.g., Gesten, 1976; Weissberg, Cowen, Lotyczewski, Boike, Orara, Stalonas, Sterling, & Gesten, 1987) provides a good example of the difficulties in this area. This work has focused on the development of a scale for obtaining teacher/classroom behavioral ratings of positive mental health. These authors have found that the independence of factor analytically derived scores of "adaptive behaviors" in classrooms has been far less than among the ratings of behavioral problems provided. It appears that when teachers tell you a kid is "good," they can give him or her high ratings in multiple spheres of adaptive functioning. But when they identify a child who is showing behavioral problems, they may be far more able to be specific about the focal nature of the problems: Now, for example, they may be able to specify that problems are of an "acting-out" type rather than a learning condition related, or due to "anxiety."

As any graduate student knows a basic principle in psychology is that, before a construct can be adequately investigated, it must be carefully defined and delineated. Further, if this is done well, a testable hypothesis about its function and form can and should be formulated. The precision with which social competence has been defined leaves much to be desired when viewed against these criteria. A key objective of the remainder of this chapter is to move us closer to a level of precision that will enable us to develop the cumulative knowledge base necessary in this area to advance our understanding of social competence, its function, and the creation of intervention and prevention programs that may be built upon it. Given the many excellent scientists who have already attempted to provide the definition of *social competence,* we will not have the temerity to pursue this path. Rather what we will attempt is to offer what we feel are some useful organizational frameworks and some key distinctions that may facilitate the pursuit of an adequate multidimensional conceptualization of social competence.

One caveat before we continue: Much of what follows is based on the work in the preceding chapters and the work referenced therein. We will avoid the cumbersome construction of "as noted above" or "in the preceding chapters and elsewhere" unless we are making reference to specific points in one or the other sources rather than presenting an overall synthesis based on that material.

Abilities, Transactional Processes, Markers, and Outcomes

In pursuing a definitional structure or framework for understanding social competence, a good starting point may be to attempt to categorize those ways in which it has previously been used. The *Random House College Dictionary* (1982) definition of *competent* includes "having suitable or sufficient skill, knowledge, experience, etc., for some purpose; properly qualified." From this one could extrapolate that *social competence* would include having sufficient skills, knowledge, and experience to engage in successful social interactions. Further analysis of this definition reveals that it contains three interrelated elements that may capture much of what we have seen subsumed in more empirically and theoretically driven perspectives of social competence. First, social competence is defined by the presence of a set of skills and abilities in a person that allow for success in the social arena. Second, it is implicit that the transactional processes that are engaged when using these abilities are well suited to the characteristics of the social environment in which success is sought. That is, to judge their adequacy requires an understanding of and sensitivity to the cultural and ecological regularities of the behavioral context. Third, there is an outcome-specific nature to social competence or at least to determining its presence in an individual.

Elsewhere (Felner & Felner, 1989) we have proposed a transactional-ecological model that may be useful here for understanding the development of competence and disorder. Without going into the full model a key element provides for distinguishing between person-focused prevention programs and transactionally focused programs. "Person-focused interventions" are defined as those that seek to reverse or forestall the development of deficits whose locus is in the person. These deficits are seen as being brought by the person to all situations, and the degree to which risk is associated with their presence depends on the demand level of the environment. In a transactionally focused (or transactionally centered) definition of risk or competence, the "locus of risk" and the assessment of the presence of competence is seen as residing in some very specific combination of person and environmental conditions. Such definitions for social competence, despite often including many of the same features of the person-centered definitions of social competence, make explicit the need to consider the utility and appropriateness of the behavior in the social context. An excellent example of such a definition is provided by Zigler and Trickett (1978). They suggest that one major criteria for social competence is the success of a person in meeting social expectations. Clearly, in different contexts these expectations may be quite different, and the success of the person in meeting them, and thus his or her "competence," may vary accordingly.

The final level for defining social competence consists of what one may think of as more positive mental health diagnostic assessment criteria. Here characteristics of the person are again the focus. However, in contrast to the person-focused (or perhaps better labeled here as "person-centered") definitions above, these outcome-focused definitions do not pertain to features of the person that shape the degree of adaptation that is attained. Rather, now the characteristics of the person that are of interest are the result of, or maintaining factors in, the adequacy of these adaptive efforts.

What should be becoming clear by now is that each of these elements of social competence is built on the next, and they are intertwined. That is, abilities and skills at the person-centered level are necessary, if not sufficient, for transactional competence to be attained. Similarly, the levels of skills, abilities, and transactional competence the person attains will help to shape the "outcome" levels. Although this trilevel scheme may seem to provide a "blinding glimpse of the obvious," it is one we feel has not generally been fully articulated in the past that, as we hope to show below, has important implications for future research and interventions focused on social competence. Indeed, as we have seen in the studies reviewed above, empirical explorations have generally failed to attend to these distinctions in providing a context for understanding their results. More typically they have only focused on sub-elements of one or the other of these levels as the full operationalization of social competence in their work. In the discussion that follows, we will illustrate this point further. In this discussion our first step will be to explore the features of social competence that define the key processes and elements at each level; it is to this exploration that we now turn.

PERSON-CENTERED SOCIAL COMPETENCE: SKILLS, CAPACITIES, AND ABILITIES

Person-centered definitions of social competence generally start with the view that there are certain essential skills, abilities, capacities, and knowledge bases that all individuals need to have to successfully negotiate the demands of the social world. A vast array of person-centered competencies have been identified. Many of these, however, are specific to quite narrow tasks. Peterson and Leigh (Chapter 4) refer to social skills definitions that pursue this strategy as taking an "atomistic" approach and underscore that such an approach may preclude our ability to see the "whole elephant." We agree that any definitional strategy that tries to provide a laundry list of all of the skills, abilities, and competencies that a person "should" have to meet the demands of all social interactions is simply not fruitful. Although the assessment of the presence of a set of predetermined specific skills and abilities may be useful for inferring the presence of a superordinate set of competencies, we should not lose sight of the fact that it is these superordinate competencies that are our focus, especially as they may be manifested cross-situationally. As Cowen (1985, p. 39) notes in discussing programs that target the development of these skills: "Acquiring (having) such skills and/or having such experiences (that develop these skills) is presumed to radiate positively to adjustment." *Adjustment* here is used in the general sense, independent of a particular circumstance or setting.

A Quadripartite Framework

What are these categories of superordinate or "bedrock" competencies that are required for effective social interaction? Based on an analysis of the work presented in the preceding chapters, which we have reviewed elsewhere (see Felner & Felner, 1989), and based on the essential elements of all human development, we propose a "quadripartite" framework. This four-pronged definition includes (a) cognitive processing, decision-making, and/or judgment skills and abilities, including both the ability to learn and the acquisition of necessary information; (b) emotion-focused self-regulation and coping capacities; (c) behavioral skills; and (d) motivational sets and expectancies.

In examining the person-centered definitions of *social competence* that have been employed as they relate to either the presence of disorder or the focus of interventions (see Felner & Felner, 1989; Kent & Rolf, 1979; Rathjen & Foreyt, 1980), we often find that one or the other of these elements is emphasized to the general exclusion of the others. To illustrate, the now-classic work by Spivak and Shure (e.g., Shure & Spivak, 1982) on the nature and development of interpersonal-cognitive problem-solving skills in children and adolescents has received extensive attention as a basis for enhancing social competence in these groups. But, this work has focused almost exclusively on the enhancement of cognitive decision-making skills as a means of changing behaviors. As Kennedy and Felner (1988) have shown, without a thorough understanding of the motivational or "moral" development levels of the target groups, the extent to which changes in or levels of decision-making skills actually affect behavior may be underestimated or misunderstood. The key issue here is that each of these underlying sets of competencies may encompass a necessary but not sufficient domain of competence to attain positive adaptive outcomes.

How does this relate to our concerns? In the past research demonstrating that deficits in one set of skills and abilities are related to the presence of disorder or dysfunction often served as the basis of preventive programming. This preventive programming has had the dual function, at least when done well, of attempting to reduce disorder and serving as an experimental test of the etiological significance of the focal competency (Felner & Felner, 1989). If the necessary but not sufficient nature of the competency is not recognized, as it often is not, then the etiological significance of the capacity, as well as the potential that the particular intervention holds for prevention, may both be underestimated. Thus if we take Spivak and Shure's approach to enhancing interpersonal-cognitive decisional skills, and note that changes in these skill levels are not associated with changes in adaptive outcomes, we may conclude that such interventions and the skills they enhance actually have little importance. However, if we examine the extent to which changes in a skill influence adaptive outcomes in the presence of adequate behavioral skills to carry out the decision, and the necessary motivational and emotional sets that would make the person actually want to exhibit the behavior, then we might better understand the significance of the intervention and the deficits in decision-making skills.

To pursue this issue further let us "unpack" a typical social behavior. Before a person will exhibit a behavior, he or she must first perceive it as something that he or she would like to do. This element requires (a) knowledge of the situation, (b) the cognitive ability to identify the behaviors and differentiate it from others (i.e., identify it as a viable alternative in the situation), and (c) the presence of a motivational set that makes the individual want to attempt the behavior. Once the person has identified the behavior as one he or she would like to engage in, successful adaptation to the situation still requires that the person have the behavioral skills and abilities to carry out the strategy he or she has elected to employ. But even if these skills are present, we know that under affective arousal skills may be blocked and decision making impaired. So if the situation is one that is emotionally demanding, and the person cannot adequately regulate or "handle" the affective arousal that accompanies it, he or she may still either fail to make a good decision about the strategy to employ or not be able to successfully execute the desired behavior.

An example is a case in which a youth knows well what the socially appropriate response would be, and has the skills in his behavioral repertoire, but, either because of failing to see the socially desirable response as one he cares about (e.g., he does not care about getting in "trouble"), or because he is unable to self-regulate successfully in the emotionally laden, "hot" situation, he does not respond appropriately. Thus he may still hit another student or go along with peer pressure to engage in problematic behaviors even when many of the other basic competencies are present. What then falls into each of our quadripartite categories? Let us briefly examine each of the elements.

Cognitive skills and abilities. Cognitive skills and abilities have been fairly well mapped by the social competence literature and by enhancement efforts. At the most basic level, the skills include simply having the information necessary to function in society. Much of this information, as Johnson, Jason, and Betts (Chapter 5) remind us, is transmitted and acquired through academic channels. Indeed, a major focus of public education in the United States has been and remains the provision of the fund of cultural and social knowledge necessary to be an effective citizen. In addition, many academic skills and abilities are required for adolescents to become productive members of society who can hold jobs and handle the demands of such basic daily transactions as buying goods or filling out forms. In addition, there is a wealth of additional information in such domains as health (e.g., knowledge of sexuality, contraception, AIDS, factors that place one at risk for heart disease or cancer) and the rules of society that must be acquired both through academic channels and other socializing agents (parents, peers, coworkers, and so on).

To be socially competent in any culture requires recognition of the need to acquire the information that makes one culturally literate and the ability to acquire such information. Individuals must also actually acquire the developmentally appropriate fund of information. Despite this transactional or situation-specific component, having the ability to gain and process such information across all contexts in at least an "adequate" fashion is the person-centered characteristic that is salient here.

A second major element to cognitive skills, as we have seen in this volume and elsewhere (e.g., Felner & Felner, 1989), is sound decision-making ability. This includes both interpersonal decision-making skills and impersonal ones. The former have received widespread attention in preventive programs aimed at helping people develop protective social competencies (e.g., Elias et al, 1986; Shure & Spivak, 1982; Weissberg, 1989). The generation of alternative problem solutions, the development of viable plans for attaining desired ends, and the ability to predict the consequences of behaviors selected for implementation are, among others, all key elements of what has come to be called interpersonal cognitive problem solving (ICPS).

Impersonal problem-solving skills may be focused on similar processes but those that relate less directly to interpersonal decision making. Still it must be clear that decisions individuals make and skills they have in such "impersonal" arenas as financial planning will have great significance for their functioning in society. Hence they must be considered part of social competence more generally, even if they are at times carried out in momentary isolation. Sound decision-making skills (if not decision content) are clearly ones that generalize to competence across situations.

Behavioral skills.   When deciding which behavior to attempt when more than one path to a desired end exists, a person must consider whether or not a possible behavior is one that is available to him or her. As we will see in our discussion of transactional issues, although there are a variety of situational and cultural conditions that may limit these choices, at the most person-centered level, the absolute number of behaviors in which the person is skilled or that he or she is capable of acquiring will be critical factors cross-situationally. As is clear from the literature on problem- or action-focused coping, the greater the degree of behavioral freedom an individual has, when all other elements are held constant, the more likely it is that he or she will cope effectively with any situational demands (Felner & Rowlison, 1986).

Although there are literally thousands of specific behavioral skills one could delineate that might be useful, in defining social competence there are several overarching sets that we have seen identified in this volume that subsume large numbers of these specific skills. The further identification and mapping of these cross-situational skills will be a challenge for social competence researchers. Among those skill sets already identified are negotiation, role or social perspective taking, adaptive assertiveness, and support and/or information acquisition (Durlak, 1983).

Emotional competencies.   A third group of basic competencies consists of the individual's affective capacities and coping abilities. Management of stress-, anxiety-, and anger-generating situations is required for an individual to function effectively in society. To effectively problem-solve in situations that give rise to any of these emotions, a person may be required to regulate and moderate his or her affective responses. If not, even if he or she has decisional abilities or behavioral skills that in emotionally "cold" circumstances would be effectively engaged, he or she may act impulsively and/or show other substantial impairment in adaptive performance.

In addition to the ability to deal with negative affect, a second set of important emotional competencies involves positive relationships with others. The ability to form positive bonds, to develop trusting and mutually supportive relationships, to affectively role-take and be empathic are all requirements for fulfilling relationships. Children and youth raised in harsh situations—for example, abusive family relationships—may have significant impairments in these areas that impede the development of social competencies. A second element of the definition of social competence offered by Zigler and Trickett (1978) is that a competent person will be capable of self-actualization and development. Clearly, relationship deficits resulting from a lack of competence in these domains would preclude such outcomes.

Motivational and expectancy sets. One element of social competency that often has been overlooked involves the "performance" aspect of social competence. That is, it may well be within the range of the person's competency to make the correct decision, show the appropriate behavior, and/or regulate his or her emotional outbursts. But if the person fails to see these acts as desirable or ones that will result in valued outcomes, he or she may fail to execute one or all of them. For researchers attempting to assess the presence of the three other elements of person-centered social competence, this element is a particularly critical one for determining whether any apparent deficit is the result of an actual deficit in the focal area or simply a lack of motivation to perform.

Motivational elements that have been articulated as potentially salient for socially competent behavior fall into at least three quite different domains. The first set is the one given the most attention. Included here is the basic value structure of the individual. Such factors as a motivation to achieve academically, to be accepted socially, to develop positive relationships, or to attain particular vocational outcomes all require attention in any full consideration of competence. The two additional sets are special cases of the person's overall value structure. One pertains to the moral development level of the person and the other emphasizes his or her sense of personal efficacy and control.

Failure to perform in a socially competent fashion may thus arise from three quite different motivational circumstances. (1) The particular behavior may not have a result that the person values highly. (2) The moral reasoning the person engages in may lead him or her to select a solution that may not be the one defined as the "appropriate one" by the researchers. This issue is especially relevant for developmental researchers or those working with individuals from cultures that do not fully reflect the same values held in the context in which the behavior is examined. Now, for example, because of quite normal developmental variation, individuals within the same age cohort may range across several moral development levels. If such variation is not considered, then deficits in other areas of competence (e.g., decision making) might be inferred that may not actually be present. (3) Finally, the adolescent may value the most socially competent behavior and have all the skills and abilities necessary to carry it out successfully but, if lacking a sufficient sense of self-efficacy or internal control, he or she may still fail to emit the behavior because of an incorrect sense that the effort might be unsuccessful.

For those of us concerned with the development of a more complete understanding of social competence, one major task that confronts us is the delineation of the characteristics that constitute the four superordinate person-centered competence domains we have proposed. A second major challenge to researchers in this area is to develop a more complete understanding of the adaptive significance of each element and the subelements of each. To do so, the implications of specific adaptive difficulties or deficits in any area must be examined only in a context in which the ability levels present on other relevant domains of social competence are fully considered.

Much of the research cited in this volume illustrates the often contradictory, inconclusive, and indeed counterintuitive results that may be obtained if only parts of our "elephant" are attended to or if they are dealt with as if they were interchangeable elements of some global construct. The use of the quadripartite model we have proposed here may help us to more systematically identify, separately or in various combinations, any differential or interactive effects that may be associated with deficiencies in each area. That is, it may be helpful to explore the adaptive significance of various "profiles" from the proposed competence dimensions to fully understand the direct and interactive adaptive significance of each. The accomplishment of these tasks will in turn greatly enhance our ability to delineate the situational features of social competence-relevant transactions that are key to differential adaptive success. It is to some of these issues that we now turn.

Transactional Issues in Defining the
Domain of Social Competence

In pursuing transactional perspectives on social competence, the central criterion that must be addressed is that adaptation or socially competent functioning is seen to be a function of some specifiable characteristics that are person centered as well as some specifiable characteristics of the environment for which these characteristics will provide a good "match." That is, at this level one can no longer define an individual as competent merely by assessing whether or not he or she shows some "absolute" level of our quadripartite elements of competence. Now the judgment or research criteria is whether the person is able to adapt appropriately to some task within a focal context. Here one would also need to be careful to define both the task and the context in which the task is carried out in specifying whether competence is present. To illustrate, one now would not say that a youth is competent in peer interactions. Instead one would have to make a statement more closely approximating the following form: "Youth X is highly competent in peer interaction with both same and opposite gender peers in both informal and formal settings when these peers are from the same socioeconomic class. However, when placed in a context with peers from different cultural or economic backgrounds, she has Y difficulties."

Why might this occur and how can what we have discussed thus far be helpful in developing a research strategy to identify primary sources of difficulty for youth who show this or other patterns? Using our quadripartite elements we can see a number of issues of concern or points for intervention but nonetheless ones to which we are immediately directed. To illustrate, at the cognitive level we may ask whether the person either lacks the necessary information or holds assumptions about possible alternatives, routes to action, or consequences for decisions that may have been viable in one context but that may not have the same functional pattern in the other. Alternatively, the means for coping with emotion or displaying it may be quite different affectively across contexts even though the actual underlying competence is the same. Thus youths from an ethnic or socioeconomic group in which displays of emotion are acceptable who begins to interact with those from another context may need to redefine or relearn the ways they demonstrate the same affect. But the underlying processes of regulation will be similar. Motivationally, they may not perceive the new peers as sufficiently like themselves to "bother" with engaging them using their considerable social skills. Finally, the repertoire of behavior that may have been more than sufficient with one group may be completely inappropriate to the norms and expectations of the new group.

From this illustration we can see how a transactional level of analysis of competence and its definition can easily be added to the most basic person-centered one. Now researchers' assessments would focus on the degree to which the skills, information, abilities, and capacities are suitable to the particular situations of concern. The initial research question remains the degree to which a person demonstrates the presence of the particular skills or abilities in some absolute sense (including the method used to determine this). Now, however, a next step would have the researcher define what the appropriate demonstration or nature of the competence would be for the particular context. A final step in the process would be to engage in efforts to understand whether adaptive pattern(s) of concern result from absolute capacity levels or if instead variation in the degree to which the match of the content or form of the person's skills and abilities with contextual demands provides a better explanation of the results.

This last step is key to tailoring interventions to particular target groups. For example, if we wish to reduce substance abuse-related behaviors in two different groups using this strategy, we might find that one group has clear deficits in their ability to generate sound problem solutions. By contrast, we might find that in the second group there is no such "absolute" person-centered deficit. Rather it may be that the range of choices they see as available to them for actual utilization is truncated by environmental circumstance or modeling. Indeed, we might find that what looks like poor problem solving is actually highly adaptive problem solving once we understand the motivational context and assumptions of the adolescent. A youth who sees little in the way of high-paying job opportunities, or few jobs in which he could at least maintain a modicum of dignity, may see becoming involved in distributing drugs as simply the "smart" alternative to working in a minimum wage job. Thus our intervention for the former group might be ICPS training, although, for the latter, information about the availability of funds to attend college or developing well-paying "blue-collar" jobs in the community might be far more effective.

It is critical to recognize that, from a transactional perspective, behavior that may appear incompetent in one context may be quite competent in another. Thus in placing "blame" or making personological attributions about the locus of dysfunction or when using this criterion for assessment, we must be very careful not to always see the youth as the primary seat of such dysfunction or differential competence or as the appropriate target of intervention. Nonetheless, it is still the case that whether difficulties in coping with the demands of life arise from some basic person-centered competence deficit, or from a poor match between the abilities of the person and the context in which he or she is acting, such difficulties may result in significant psychological difficulties and vulnerability. It is to this final criterion for assessing the presence of competence that we turn next.

SOCIAL COMPETENCE AS AN OUTCOME

In the preceding chapters this element has been the one that has perhaps been most often used to evaluate the linkage between such diverse factors as biological conditions, physical appearance, religion, and athletics to social competence. The key indicator used has generally been self-esteem although there is a wide array of associated conditions (e.g., anxiety levels and internal locus of control). A danger in this use of social competence is that it runs the risk of becoming almost synonymous with the presence of positive mental health. A prime illustration of this ever-widening domain of the definition of social competence, when used in this fashion, is provided by Peterson and Leigh (Chapter 4, this volume) when they state that "researchers have linked these declines in the quality of parenting to such aspects of adolescent social competence as problems with interpersonal associations, heterosexual relationships, the independence process, self-esteem, achievement, greater noncompliance, more aggression, and increases in emotional turmoil, anxiety, and psychopathology." Such a nonspecific and all-encompassing use of social competence clearly makes the construct both not very useful and extremely difficult from which to carry out systematic research.

Perhaps the central issue to "unpack" here is the relationship of social competence to positive mental health in general. As Zigler and Trickett (1978) note in their discussion of social competence, any definition of it is arbitrary, and the key issue in any definition is its usefulness. To move toward the goal of utility we make the following distinctions between the concepts of social competence and positive mental health. Social competence, as we have pursued its development in this chapter, is a necessary component of, but is not equivalent to, positive mental health. The former is subsumed under the latter when used in this fashion but does not fully overlap with it. That is, for positive mental health outcomes to be obtained, it seems necessary that an individual possess a level of competence adequate to deal appropriately and effectively with the demands of his or her environment. It is also possible, however, to conceive of the case where a person possesses requisite social competencies but for other reasons still fails to obtain positive mental health outcomes (e.g., severe early childhood experience, social and economic disadvantage).

An associated issue concerns the mechanisms whereby some of the elements that would be included in a more general positive mental health assessment may in fact facilitate or be part of social competence. For this issue we return to self-esteem as an exemplar. From the extant literature it is clear that a lack of competence in dealing effectively with the social world may result in a poor self-image. Conversely, success in these endeavors is a predictor of more positive outcomes. Self-esteem outcomes, however, may also act reciprocally to shape the level of social competence performance. That is, if we return to our quadripartite model, we see that the level of self-esteem a person has at a particular time fits well with the motivational elements of our model. Thus in this way self-esteem can be seen as both resulting from the level of prior competence as well as being a shaper of competence in future interactions and thus self-esteem. The reciprocal nature of our model is essential to keep in mind to understand the suggestions for research below.

SUMMARY

In considering the quadripartite elements of social competence, and the three quite different levels of analysis of the presence of such elements, it becomes somewhat less confusing as to why apparently powerful predictors of adjustment in other domains of adaptation have yielded such disappointing or inconsistent associations with social competence. If one moves between these levels and domains without attention to the quite different areas and types of functioning to which they pertain, it may be the case that predictor variables will have the "real" and quite different associations they may have with each domain "masked" when thrown together into one amorphous stew. One can, for example, develop clear and well-defined hypotheses about why physical appearance should relate to self-esteem but have more difficulty in developing similarly powerful reasoning for why it should directly affect problem-solving skills. Further, suppressor effects may also be present. Thus if one fails to attend to whether there is equivalence among experimental subjects on other domains of social competence or exposure to contextual conditions that influence relative competence, then it may appear that the domain of social competence on which we do choose to focus has far less salience than it would if the variance associated with these conditions were controlled.

To build upon our model to develop a further understanding of the nature of social competence, there are several clear research questions and strategies that may be of use. The first set of questions for resolution quite naturally flows from the model presented above. If one understands that the influence of the domains of competence at each of these levels is both reciprocal across domains and stages, and that, across levels, prior stages provide the foundations upon which functioning and outcomes at later stages are built, then we must further understand the interrelationships of these elements and how the presence of each shapes the development and functioning of the others. To accomplish an accurate representational model of these processes, because of their reciprocal nature, we will require longitudinal models and data. Only then will we be able to understand more clearly the extent to which, for example, person-centered abilities generalize to competency in new environments and the degree to which cultural and situational circumstances may also shape such success.

By moving from a global model of social competence to one that articulates the basic process and elements that are necessary across situations and life stages, without being atomistic, we can begin such an exploration. Such a model should more adequately allow us to attend to questions such as the stability of elements of competence, across situations and developmental levels, independent of the particular content required.

Of course, in the development of any understanding of the adaptive implications of elements of social competence, correlational models may be helpful but are nonetheless insufficient. Experimental tests are required for hypotheses derived from correlational and theoretical work to be adequately tested. For social competence there are rich opportunities to do so. Preventively focused experimental field trials are well suited to the concerns of social competence researchers and afford such an opportunity for more rigorous experimental scrutiny. In testing hypotheses about etiological pathways to disorder or adaptation, there are only two alternatives. One is to attempt an experimental manipulation that induces disorder. This alternative is clearly unacceptable on moral and ethical grounds. On the other hand we may develop clear hypotheses about conditions that lead to dysfunction or serve as protective agents and, through the modification of these conditions, either reduce risk or enhance resilience and thus demonstrate a reduction in the incidence of the target disorder(s).

Intervention programs that seek to enhance social competence to reduce disorder clearly fit well within this paradigm. Further, the degree to which the success of such efforts may be appropriately evaluated, and the specificity of our hypotheses about how the particular competence or competencies being developed should link to specific outcomes or to differential ones for target groups in differing social conditions or with differing associated competencies, will be greatly enhanced by data from those studies in which these associations are the focal research questions.

We have come far from where we were several decades ago when we failed to attend to positive mental health. But in developing the level of sophistication necessary to more fully understand the origins and functions of the component elements of positive mental health, we have been hampered by a lack of conceptual precision and definitional clarity. We hope that this volume, and the framework and issues discussed above, will move us closer to the next level of clarity in our pursuit of the more systematic study of a "language of adequacy" called for by Murphy nearly three decades ago.

REFERENCES

Achenbach, T. M., & Edelbroch, C. S. (1981). Behavior problems and competencies reported by parents of normal and disturbed children aged four through sixteen. *Monographs of the Society for Research and Development, 46,* 1(No. 188).

American Psychiatric Association (APA). (1987). *Diagnostic and statistical manual of the mental disorders* (rev. ed.). Washington, DC: Author.

Cowen, E. L. (1985). Person-centered approaches to primary prevention in mental health: Situation-focused and competence-enhancement. *American Journal of Community Psychology, 13,* 31-48.

Durlak, J. A. (1983). Social problem-solving as a primary prevention strategy. In R. D. Felner, L. A. Jason, J. N. Moritsugu, & S. S. Farber (Eds.), *Preventive psychology: Theory, research and practice.* New York: Pergamon.

Elias, M. J., Gara, M., Ubriaco, M., Rothbaum, P. A., Clabby, J. F., & Schuyler, T. (1986). Impact of a preventive social problem-solving intervention on children's coping with middle-school stressors. *American Journal of Community Psychology, 14,* 259-275.

Gesten, E. L. (1976). A health resources inventory: The development of a measure of the personal and social competence of primary grade children. *Journal of Consulting and Clinical Psychology, 44,* 775-786.

Kennedy, M. G., Felner, R. D., Cauce, A. M., & Primavera, J. (1988). Social problem-solving and adjustment in adolescence: The influence of moral-reasoning level, scoring alternatives, and family climate. *Journal of Clinical Child Psychology, 17*(1), 73-83.

Kent, M. W., & Rolf, J. E. (Eds.). (1979). *Primary prevention of psychopathology: Vol. 3. Social competence in children.* Hanover, NH: University Press of New England.

Murphy, L. (1982). *Paths toward mastery.*

Random House College Dictionary. (1982). New York: Random House.

Rathjen, D. P., & Foreyt, J. P. (Eds.). (1980). *Social competence: Interventions for children and adolescents.* New York: Pergamon.

Rowlison, R. T., & Felner, R. D. (1988). Major life events, hassles and adaptation in adolescence: The conceptualization and measurement of life stress and adjustment revisited. *Journal of Personality and Social Psychology, 55,* 432-444.

Shure, M. B., & Spivak, G. (1982). Interpersonal problem-solving in young children: A cognitive approach to prevention. *American Journal of Community Psychology, 10,* 341-356.

Weissberg, R. P., Caplan, M. Z., & Sivo, P. J. (1989). A new conceptual framework for establishing school-based social competence promotion programs. In L. A. Bond & B. E. Compas (Eds.), *Primary prevention and promotion in schools.* Newbury Park, CA: Sage.

Weissberg, R. P., Cowen, E. L., Lotyczewski, B. S., Boike, M. F., Orara, A., Stalonas, P., Sterling, S., & Gesten, E. L. (1987). Teacher ratings of children's problems and competence behaviors: Normative and parametric characteristics. *American Journal of Community Psychology, 15,* 387-402.

Zigler, E., & Trickett, P. K. (1978). I.Q., social competence, and evaluation of early childhood intervention programs. *American Psychologist, 33,* 789-796.

Index

About the Editors

Gerald R. Adams (Ph.D.) is Professor and Chair of the Department of Family Studies at the University of Guelph in Ontario, Canada. He is a fellow of the American Psychological Association and has been awarded the James D. Moran Research Award from the American Home Economics Association. He is associate editor of the *Journal of Adolescence* and the *Journal of Primary Prevention.* He has authored or coauthored numerous articles, chapters, and books. Some of his current publications include *Today's Marriages and Families* (1986), *Adolescent Life Experiences* (2nd ed., 1989), and *Understanding Research Methods* (2nd ed., 1991).

Thomas P. Gullotta (M.S.W.) is CEO of the Child and Family Agency of Southeastern Connecticut, in New London. He is the Editor of the *Journal of Primary Prevention,* serves on the editorial boards of the *Journal of Early Adolescence* and *Adolescence,* and is a consultant for state and federal agencies. He is a visiting instructor at several state colleges throughout Connecticut. He is coauthor of *Adolescent Life Experiences* (1983, 1989) and of *Today's Marriages and Families* (1986). His research interests include human sexuality, adolescent social problems, prevention and intervention program effectiveness, and social policy formulation.

Raymond Montemayor (Ph.D.) is Assistant Professor of Psychology at the Ohio State University. He has taught at the City University of New York, the University of Utah, and has held visiting appointments at Harvard University and the Oregon Social Learning Center. He has published widely in journals, such as *Child Development, Developmental Psychology,* and *Journal of Early Adolescence,* has coedited two special journal issues on adolescence, and is coauthor, with David Ausubel, of a book on adolescence. He is Associate Editor of the *Journal of Adolescent Research* and the *Journal of Early Adolescence.* His research interests include parent-adolescent conflict, transformations of family relations as children enter adolescence, the impact of parents and peers on adolescent drug use and sexuality, and the effects of divorce on adolescents.

About the Contributors

David M. Betts received his master's degree in social service administration from the University of Chicago in 1986. He is currently directing an NIMH research grant designed to study preventive interventions with high-risk elementary school transfer students. He has previously worked with elderly services programs, public school districts, and institutionalized children and adults.

Martin Bloom (Ph.D., Social Psychology, University of Michigan; Diploma in Social Study, University of Edinburgh, Scotland) currently teaches at the School of Social Work, Virginia Commonwealth University. His writings in human development and primary prevention include *Primary Prevention: The Possible Science* (1981); *Configurations of Human Behavior: Live Span Development in Social Environments* (1984); and *Life Span Development: Bases for Preventive and Interventive Helping* (2nd ed., 1985—an anthology).

Gilbert J. Botvin (Ph.D.) is Associate Professor in the Department of Public Health and Psychiatry and is the Director of the Laboratory of Health Behavior Research at Cornell University Medical College. He is also Visiting Associate Professor in the Department of Health Education of Columbia University Teacher's College and serves as a consultant to the School of Social Work at Columbia University. After completing graduate work at Columbia University, he was with the American Health Foundation until taking his current position. Botvin's research on the Life Skills Training approach to problem behavior prevention and health promotion among adolescents represents the forefront of theory and empirical knowledge on interventions for American youth.

Craig Carver is a doctoral candidate in family studies at Brigham Young University in the Department of Family Sciences with emphasis in the area of Human Development. His current work focuses on adolescence. He has fourteen years experience in religious instruction with the Church of Jesus Christ of Latter-day Saints education system.

Thomas F. Cash is Professor of Psychology at Old Dominion University in Norfolk, Virginia. He received his Ph.D. in clinical psychology from George Peabody College of Vanderbilt University in 1974. His principal program of research concerns the psychology of physical appearance and includes over 60 publications on physical attractiveness, body image, grooming behaviors, and aesthetic surgeries as well as other articles on psychopathology and cognitive-behavioral therapies. With Dr. Pruzinsky, he is coeditor of the forthcoming volume *Body Images: Development, Deviance, and Change.*

Steven J. Danish is Professor and Chair of the Department of Psychology and Professor of Preventive Medicine at Virginia Commonwealth University. He has also held academic positions at Pennsylvania State University and Southern Illinois University. He received his Ph.D. in counseling psychology from Michigan State University in 1969. He is an active member of the American Psychological Association, having been elected a Fellow of the Association and President of the Division of Community Psychology. He is also a member of AAASP, the current Chair of the Intervention/Performance Enhancement Section, and a member of the executive committee. He is the author of over 40 articles and eight books in the areas of counseling, community, industrial, and life span developmental psychology; health, fitness, and nutrition; and sport psychology.

A. Chris Downs received his B.A. in psychology in 1973 from Indiana University at South Bend and his Ph.D. in developmental psychology in 1978 from the University of Texas at Austin. After one year (1978-1979) at the Department of Psychology at Moorhead State University, in Minnesota, he joined the Program in Human Sciences at the University of Houston-Clear Lake, Houston, Texas. After being promoted to Associate Professor (1985), he served as the Program Coordinator of the five departments in Human Sciences from 1986 to 1988. His research has focused on three primary areas: physical attractiveness, sex-typed roles/socialization, and men/masculinity issues. He has written numerous journal articles in these areas and among these are two of his published scales: The Attitudes Toward Men Scale and The Attitudes Toward Physical Attractiveness Scale. His teaching has earned him three university-level citations for excellence. He has served as the Charter and ongoing Faculty Advisor for the Psychology Club and Psi Chi Chapter at the University of Houston-Clear Lake.

Robert D. Felner (Ph.D.) is currently Professor of Psychology and Education at Teachers College of Columbia University. He is on leave from the University of Illinois in Urbana-Champaign, where he was Professor of Psychology and Director of the clinical/community psychology program. He has published extensively in the areas of primary prevention and risk, and vulnerability and resilience among socially and economically disadvantaged youth.

Bruce D. Hale obtained an M.S. in 1973 and a Ph.D. in 1981 in physical education from Pennsylvania State University. He is currently employed as an instructor in exercise and sport science and an academic-athletic counselor by Pennsylvania State University. He is also currently registered as an educational sport psychologist with the U.S. Olympic Sports Medicine Committee and has consulted with numerous college and elite athletes in performance enhancement strategies. He is a member of the American Psychological Association, the North American Society for Psychology of Sport and Physical Activity, and other professional organizations. He has presented numerous lectures at professional meetings and published a variety of sport psychology articles.

Leonard A. Jason is Professor of Psychology at DePaul University and specializes in community and preventive psychology. He has published over 150 articles and chapters and coauthored or edited four books: *Behavioral Community Psychology: Progress and Prospects, Preventive Psychology: Theory, Research, and Action, Prevention: Toward a Multidisciplinary Perspective,* and *Preventing Drug Abuse Among Children and Adolescents.* He has received three National Media Awards from the American Psychological Association.

Joseph H. Johnson is a doctoral candidate in clinical child psychology at DePaul University. He is currently working with Dr. Leonard Jason on an NIMH research grant designed to study preventive social and academic interventions with high-risk elementary school transfer students. He has previously taught in a public elementary school.

A. Michele Lease is in the graduate program in clinical/community psychology at the University of Illinois. Her primary research interests are in mapping the nature of social competence from an ecological fit perspective, and the development of primary prevention programs for children.

Geoffry K. Leigh is Associate Professor of Family Relations and Human Development at Ohio State University. His areas of scholarly interest are parent-adolescent relationships, marital and family therapy, and adolescent sexuality. Specific research topics have included the timing of the transition to sexual intercourse and contraceptive use by adolescents and the analysis of the determinants of a delayed marriage. He is coeditor of *Adolescents in Families* and editor of the *Family Science Review.*

Alfred L. McAlister (Ph.D.) is Associate Director of the Center for Health Promotion Research and Development at the University of Texas. He is currently based at the center's field office in Austin. After graduate training at Stanford University, he took a faculty position at Harvard University. He has considerable experience in research and demonstration projects in community health promotion, which covers such projects as the Stanford Three Community and Five City Projects in California, the North Karelia Project in Finland, and a new study of risk reduction and health promotion behavior change among Hispanic Americans.

Mario A. Orlandi (M.P.H., Ph.D.) was trained in neurobiology, psychology, and public health at Duke University and Harvard University. He is Chief of the Division of Health Promotion Research at the American Health Foundation and Senior Research Associate at the Columbia University School of Social Work. He also holds appointments at the Bowman-Gray School of Medicine in Chapel Hill, North Carolina, and at the World Health Organization in Geneva, Switzerland. He has scientific expertise in skills development intervention research with youth at risk for health behavior problems.

Gary W. Peterson is Professor and Chair of Family Resources and Human Development at Arizona State University. His research and scholarly interests have focused on parent-adolescent relations, adolescent socialization, and family theory. Specific research topics have included parental power and behavior as predictors of adolescent autonomy and conformity, the development of adolescent social competence, and the socialization of low-income rural youth. He is coeditor of *Adolescents in Families*.

Albert J. Petitpas is Associate Professor in the Psychology Department at Springfield College, where he directs the graduate training program in athletic counseling and coordinates the Advisory Resource Center for Athletics. He received his Ed.D. in counseling psychology from Boston University and is a licensed psychologist. He is also a registered sport psychologist for the Sports Medicine Division of the U.S. Olympic Committee, a member of the American Psychological Association, the Association for the Advancement of Applied Sports Psychology, the National Association of Academic Advisors for Athletics, and a clinical member of the American Association for Marriage and Family Therapists.

Ruby S. C. Phillips is a graduate student in the clinical/community psychology program at the University of Illinois and is involved in the infancy leadership program there. Her primary research interests are factors that influence the expectations and aspirations of high risk children and youth, and the fashion in which these variables impact developmental trajectories to adaptation.

Thomas Pruzinsky (Ph.D.) is Assistant Professor of Plastic and Maxillofacial Surgery and of Behavioral Medicine and Psychiatry at the University of Virginia School of Medicine in Charlottesville. He received his Ph.D. in clinical psychology from Pennsylvania State University in 1986. His research interests concern persons with craniofacial anomalies, especially individual and family adjustment to these deformities and their treatments. He is coordinator of psychosocial services at the University of Virginia Burn Center and is involved in the assessment and treatment of children, adolescents, and adults seeking elective cosmetic surgery or surgical reconstruction after disease or trauma.

Steven P. Schinke (Ph.D.) received graduate training in research methodology at the University of Wisconsin and served on the faculty of the University of Washington. He is now a Professor at the Columbia University School of Social Work. At Columbia, he is part of a research group comprising investigators from the American Health Foundation, Cornell University Medical College, and the University of Texas who are engaged in studies of health promotion and preventive interventions for American adolescents.

Darwin L. Thomas is Professor of Sociology and former Director of the Family and Demographic Research Institute at Brigham Young University. He has written and/or edited four books and published numerous journal articles. His research interests have focused on the social psychological dimensions of family socialization, with his latest work attempting to unravel the independent and combined effects of religion and family variables on attitudes and behavior. He received his B.A. and M.A. from Brigham Young University and his Ph.D. from the University of Minnesota. He has taught at the University of Minnesota, Washington State University, the University of Wisconsin, and Brigham Young University.